Albert-Reiner Glaap
Gerhard Haefner
Friedhold Schmidt
T. Lothar Wullen

Spotlights on Literature

Textband

Max Hueber Verlag

3. 2. 1.	Die letzten Ziffern
1997 96 95 94 93	bezeichnen Zahl und Jahr des Druckes.

Alle Drucke dieser Auflage können, da unverändert, nebeneinander benutzt werden.
1. Auflage

Verlagsredaktion: Gaby Bauer-Negenborn, München
Layout und Umschlag: Erentraut Waldau, Ismaning
Satz: FoCoTex Klaus Nowak, Berg / Starnberger See
Druck: Allgäuer Zeitungsverlag, Kempten
Printed in Germany
ISBN 3-19-002375-1

Inhalt

Vorwort

Zielsetzung

Spotlights on Literature orientiert sich an den in neueren Richtlinien formulierten Rahmenzielen für die Sekundarstufe II zur Analyse literarischer Texte. Im einzelnen sind folgende Ziele bestimmend:

- Hinführung zur Literaturbetrachtung: Grundbegriffe, Methoden, Besprechungsvokabular
- Analyse fiktionaler sowie zugeordneter literaturkritischer Texte
- Einführung in die literarischen Gattungen und deren typische Elemente
- Begegnung mit repräsentativen Beispielen zeitgenössischer Literatur und deren Themen
- Anreiz zur Eigenlektüre englischer und amerikanischer Ganzschriften.

Aufbau und Methode

Die vier Gattungen *poetry, short story, novel, drama* werden in eigenständigen Kapiteln vorgestellt, wobei jeweils primären Texten/Textauszügen sekundäre Texte wie z.B. *book review, essay, blurb, interview with the author, literary criticism* zugeordnet sind. Die Eigenständigkeit der jeweiligen Gattung bestimmt den unterschiedlichen Aufbau und das unterschiedliche methodische Vorgehen der einzelnen Kapitel. Alle vier Teile enthalten Fragestellungen zu den Primärtexten bzw. zur Verknüpfung von Primär- und Sekundärtexten sowie unter der Rubrik *project work* übergreifende Fragen und umfangreichere Aufgabenstellungen.

Auswahlproblematik

Aus Gründen der Wirtschaftlichkeit und der Handlichkeit wurde der Umfang des Buches von vornherein eingeschränkt und das Problem der Auswahl verschärft. Bei der Wahl der Texte waren folgende Gesichtspunkte entscheidend:

- Präsentation von weniger bekannten literarischen Texten
- Präsentation von repräsentativen modernen/zeitgenössischen Texten
- Präsentation von geeigneten literaturkritischen Texten
- Einsetzbarkeit des jeweiligen Werkes als Ganzschrift im Unterricht (bei *drama* und *novel*).

In allen vier Teilen wurde darauf geachtet, daß weniger bekannte, aber im Ursprungsland angesehene Autorinnen und Autoren vertreten sind, während von namhaften Literaten ein weniger bekanntes, aber geeignetes Werk ausgewählt wurde.

Einsatzmöglichkeiten

Spotlights on Literature soll die Thematisierung von Literatur und „Literaturbetrieb“ ermöglichen. Die Konzentration auf literarische Gattungen kann dabei als Gegenpol bzw. als Ergänzung zu Unterrichtsreihen mit vornehmlich nicht-fiktionalen Texten verstanden werden. Das Werk eignet sich außerdem zur selbständigen Erarbeitung oder Wiederholung literarischer Grundbegriffe und Fragestellungen. Schließlich ist aber auch die Herauslösung und Gruppierung von thematischen Aspekten quer durch die Gattungen und die Ergänzung durch anderweitige Texte denkbar.

Friedhold Schmidt
T. Lothar Wullen

Poetry

Contents

1 What is Poetry? – Approach

Approaches to Poetry

There are, broadly speaking, two main ways of thinking about poetry. One approach is to concentrate on the poet himself. Underlying this approach very often is the idea that poetry is primarily an expression of the poet's emotions. The clearest statement of this viewpoint is a comment by Wordsworth that 'poetry is the spontaneous overflow of powerful feelings'. The focus of our attention as critics in this approach is on what the poem can tell us about the poet's innermost being as revealed in the work: we read the poem in order to learn about the figure behind it. Although this is a popular approach to poetry, it is not a very practical one for the reader who is simply baffled by a poem or who cannot see what the 'feelings' are that the poet is expressing and therefore cannot appreciate them. The other shortcoming of this way of looking at poetry is that it is more concerned with the mind and personality behind the poem than with the text itself. It is, then, an unsatisfactory approach, not least because it bypasses the real problem we all experience: reading the poem and trying to understand it.

The second approach, and the one we shall be following throughout this section, concentrates on discussing the poem itself. The focus of our attention here is on the words on the page. Such an approach involves a very different conception of poetry from that outlined above: there the poet is regarded as an elusive, mysterious figure behind the text; here the emphasis is on the poet as 'a maker', a maker of meanings with word. The moment we stress this element of craftsmanship it becomes possible to talk about both the content and form of poetry in much more tangible terms.

Content is what a poem says, what it is about, its subject matter. Form is the way in which it says it, how it is written, the language it uses, the patterns it employs. If we are to come to grips with poetry it does seem essential that we try to account for its most obvious feature, its use of patterned language. Most poems are written in lines of the same length; usually these lines are arranged into the symmetrical groups we call stanzas; often the poem has a repeated rhyme pattern running through each stanza which is usually fairly conspicuous. One reason why we find poetry difficult is that all these patterns serve to concentrate and compress the words into much more meaningful relationships with each other than in prose. This does not mean, however, that the poet is therefore dealing with much more complicated issues than we find in prose. The most common misunderstanding of poetry is the assumption that it is concerned with esoteric, abstract matters remote from everyday experience.

This is not the case. While poetry itself is a complicated way of writing about experience, its basic subject matter is usually far from complicated.
In theory a poem can be about anything. There are, however, certain topics that concern us all and these are the recurrent themes of poetry. Love is a central experience in life, and it is not surprising that love poems outnumber all others. Death is also a major concern to us all, and this can be linked with religion: most people at some time wonder whether life ends with death or if they are part of some greater pattern. Poets need not, however, concern themselves with such weighty topics: they might wish to write about nature, or their families or some other domestic matter. Poetry becomes less frightening if we realise that it is always concerned with ordinary human concerns, with the daily matters of everybody's life.

J. Peck/M. Coyle, *Literary Terms and Criticism,* Macmillan, London 1984, pp. 11–12.

Inside a Poem

EVE MERRIAM

It doesn't always have to rhyme,
but there's the repeat of beat, somewhere
an inner chime that makes you want to
tap your feet or swerve in a curve;
a lilt, a leap, a lightning-split: –
thunderstruck the consonants jut,
while the vowels open wide as waves in the non-blue sea.

You hear with your heels, your eyes feel
what they never touched before:
fins on a bird, feathers on a deer;
taste all colors, inhale
memory and tomorrow and always the tang is today.

Repr. from: M. Cranmore/V. Olsen, *The World of Language,*
Follett, Chicago n.d., p. 284.

Vocabulary

lilt regular pattern of rising and falling sound, pleasant sound – *to jut* to stand out (from the rest) – *tang* strong taste or smell

Assignments

1. Explain Eve Merriam's view of poetry.
2. Discuss the presentation of her view.

2 *Sound and Pattern*

The Language of Poetry

The popular misconceptions about poetry arise, in part at least, from the fact that poetry is written in a different form from that with which people are most familiar – prose. The form, with its dependency upon figurative language and rhythmic regularity – resulting in a visually unfamiliar structure – tends to inhibit the beginning reader, discouraging him from pursuing the study of poetry to any significant end. But is it not foolish to be intimidated by an unfamiliar form of expression and therefore deprived of some very pleasurable aesthetic moments? The wise individual learns all about the form so that he may use it to achieve the experience the poem is offering him. After all, it is primarily through the form that the poet makes *concrete* the idea, the emotion, the experience (all abstractions) that he is trying to communicate. In fact, the reader has a *responsibility*, both to himself and to the poet, to familiarize himself with the characteristics of the genre before passing judgment on its communicative value. When he has satisfied that responsibility, he is likely to discover that poetry is a very sensitive, very precise, and often a very complete expression of the world in which he lives. If he continues to examine poetry in all its various aspects, he will eventually achieve that ideal state in which he will become so familiar with the techniques or devices of poetry that he no longer consciously considers them when he is responding to the poem; they will have become a part of his nature, wherein they operate almost intuitively whenever he is considering a poem. At this point, his response to and understanding of poetry will be as effortless as the poem itself appears to be. One might say that learning to read poetry is like learning to understand and thereby more fully appreciate a piano concerto. One who knows nothing about music is necessarily limited in his understanding and appreciation of the performance of a work. But one who has practiced the piano until technique has become ingrained in him will apply his experience in achieving a greater understanding and appreciation of the performance he is witnessing. Though most of us may never achieve this ideal state, either as pianists or poets, any attempt to do so will bring us closer to the complete artistic experience than if we did nothing at all.

A. Carli/T. Kilman, *The Now Voices,* Ch. Scribner's, New York 1971, pp. 3–4.

Metre and Rhythm

When people talk about rhythm in a poem, they often mean metre, but the two are not the same.

Everyone knows that in music there are a certain number of beats in a bar and that some beats are stronger than others. In a waltz, for example, there are three beats in a bar, the first being stronger than the other two. When you are learning to dance a waltz you will probably repeat the rhythm under your breath: **strong** weak weak, **strong** weak weak, **strong** weak weak, and so on.

Similarly, nearly all verse has a basic, underlying rhythm, which is called its metre, and, as in music, it can be reduced to small regular units. In verse the units are called feet, and not bars, and we say there are so many syllables in a foot, and not so many beats in a bar. In music some beats are stronger than others: in verse some syllables are stronger than others.

And his cohorts were gleaming with silver and gold.

If you say this line aloud, you will find that the natural stresses in your voice go as follows:

weak weak **strong**, weak weak **strong**, weak weak **strong**, weak weak **strong**.

This can be written out in a shorthand form as:

u u / | u u / | u u / | u u / |

Each metre has a name of its own, and the following can be found in English verse:

1. The Iambus (Iambic metre):

u/|u/|u/|u/|

O Brignall banks are wild and fair,
And Greta woods are green,
And you may gather garlands there
Would grace a summer-queen.

(*Brignall Banks:*
Sir Walter Scott, 1771–1832.)

2. The Trochee (Trochaic metre):

/u|/u|/u|/u|

Willows whiten, aspens quiver,
Little breezes dusk and shiver.

(*The Lady of Shalott:*
Alfred Lord Tennyson, 1809–92.)

3. The Anapaest (Anapaestic metre):

/ u u / | u u / | u u / | u u / |

And no voice but was praising this Roland of mine,
As I poured down his throat our last measure of wine.

(*How We Brought the Good News:*
Robert Browning, 1812–89.)

4. The Dactyl (Dactylic metre):

uu|/uu|/uu|/uu|

Cannon to right of them,
Cannon to left of them,
Cannon in front of them.

(*The Charge of the Light Brigade:*
Tennyson.)

If you are asked to scan a poem, you divide each line into feet, and then put over each syllable the appropriate mark for stressed (/) or unstressed (u). Usually the stresses go over the syllables which are stressed in normal speech.

u / u / u /
And now | there came | both mist |
u /
and snow, |
u / u / u /
And it | grew won | drous cold: |
u / u / u /
And ice, | mast-high, | came float |
u /
ing by, |
u / u / u /
As green | as em | erald. |

(*The Ancient Mariner:*
Samuel Taylor Coleridge, 1772–1834.)

So we can say that *The Ancient Mariner* has an iambic metre. That is not to say that every single foot is iambic. In verse, unlike most music, it is quite usual to find irregularities, especially at the beginnings and ends of lines. But all the same, in spite of the exceptional feet, it is true to say that the basic metre of every one of *The Ancient Mariner's* 625 lines is iambic. But having decided this, we have not said anything of much value. What is important is the way in which the poet uses his metre; the way he speeds it up, or slows it down; the way he changes it to good effect by introducing variations; the way in which he builds up the metre from line to line and from verse to verse. This, and not just the succession of stressed or unstressed syllables, makes the rhythm of a poem. And this leads us into the heart of the matter.

L.E.W. Smith, *A Short Course on Poetry,* Methuen, London 1964, pp. 20–22.

Rhythm and Meaning

Rhythm in poetry need by no means be perfectly smooth and regular and, indeed, it seldom is. A perfectly regular beat, i.e. without any variation, sounds mechanical and monotonous, which is certainly not a merit, unless monotony is an intended effect that strengthens the meaning of a poem as such.

It is true that in each poem a basic metre is employed, but it is less this basic metre than any deviation from it that is important for effect and, hence, for interpretation. Deviation from the basic metre, i.e. any irregularity or variation of the rhythm, becomes significant for the support or reinforcement of meaning.

As a matter of fact, good poetry comes to life from the tension between a basic metre, say iambic pentameter, which leads the reader or listener to expect a certain regularity and the unexpected actual or audible rhythm of the words, i.e. the poet's or speaker's individual variation that does not always coincide with expectation. In this way, audible rhythm and expected rhythm are counterpointed, thus enhancing the overall effect.

If there is no variation at all, the result is dullness. If the variation is too great, the metre, i.e. the expected basic rhythm, is destroyed and the result is free verse or prose.

Sound Patterns

The patterning of poetry includes sound patterns, i.e. the more or less regular recurrence of sounds, which, in addition to rhythm, confers on poetry its musical character. Thus, any unit of sound – whole lines or even stanzas, phrases, words, syllables or individual consonants and vowels – may be repeated for special effects. In good poetry repetition of any kind is not gratuitous, but used for the purpose of expressiveness, emphasis, or structure. Sound repetition may also be used simply to make a poem, or any text for that matter, more pleasant to the ear, more melodious, more musical.

If only the initial consonant or consonants of a syllable are repeated, this is called *alliteration*, as in

s*w*iftly *w*alk over the *w*estern *w*ave,

whereas the repetition of consonants in syllable-final position, as in

a stro*k*e of lu*ck* or

the whizzing of larger bir*ds* overhea*d* in a woo*d*, such as crows, puddocks, buzzar*ds*

is known as *conconance*. The repetition of vowels, as in

All burns! The reddest r*o*se is a gh*o*st;
Sparks whirl up, to exp*i*re in the m*i*st:
  the w*i*ld
F*i*ngers of fire are making corruption
  clean.

is *assonance*, and the combination of assonance and consonance is *rhyme*. More precisely, rhyme is the repetition of a stressed vowel with all the sounds that follow it.

Several types of rhyme are usually distinguished:

1. *masculine* ['mæskjulɪn], when the rhyme is limited to one syllable;
2. *feminine* ['femɪnɪn], when the rhyme comprises two or more syllables;
3. *internal or medial,* when one or both rhyme words are within a line;
4. *end rhyme,* when the rhyme words are at the ends of lines;
5. *half-rhyme,* when in a feminine rhyme only the stressed syllables rhyme;
6. *eye-rhyme,* when the words only look as if they form a rhyme but their sounds are not identical: *bough* [baʊ] – *trough* [trɔf] or *food* [fu:d] – *blood* [blʌd].

If rhyme recurs at regular intervals, it forms a *rhyme pattern* or *rhyme scheme* and in this way may establish a particular *stanza form* as e.g. the Spenserian stanza (ababbcbcc) or the Shakespeare sonnet (ababcdcdefefgg).

Basically, the above patterns are forms of repetition just like *metre*, repetition, in the broadest sense, being, besides imagery, the most essential element of all poetry.

Another common type of repetition is the recurrence of an expression (one word or several words) at the beginning of consecutive lines, clauses or sentences. It is known as *anaphora*.

Internal and External Pattern

The total effect of a well-constructed poem relies on the interplay and interdependence of all its component elements. Not a single line, word or rhythmic element could be changed without altering the poem as a whole. Apart from its internal structure, i.e. the logical order or arrangement of thoughts and images, a poem is determined through its outward pattern, its more or less symmetrical form.

With regard to outward form, Laurence Perrine (*Literature,* Harcourt Brace, New York 1983) roughly distinguishes between three kinds: *continuous* form, *stanzaic* form, and *fixed* form.

With *continuous form,* regular formal patterning is slight and dictated solely by the units of meaning, so that no recurrent pattern is recognizable.

Stanzaic form shows a clear subdivision into recurrent line patterns, often with a regular metric pattern and a recognizable rhyme scheme. There are traditional stanza patterns such as, for instance, *terza rima* (three-line stanzas with the rhyme scheme aba bcb cdc ded etc., an Italian verse form used by Dante in the *Devine Comedy* but also used by many English poets), the *Ballad stanza* (with the rhyme scheme ab cb and four stressed syllables in the first and third lines, and three in the second and fourth lines), or the *Spenserian stanza* (a nine-line stanza with the rhyme scheme ab ab bc bc c, with the first eight lines being iambic pentameters and the ninth line an Alexandrine). However, poets may also use stanza patterns of their own invention.

Fixed form means that a whole poem is constructed on a traditional pattern which cannot be altered by the poet. Thus, the subliterary form of the *limerick*, exclusively used for humorous verse, always uses the same pattern. Another fixed form with a long tradition and widely used by English poets is the *sonnet*, which consists of fourteen lines, usually in iambic pentameter. Sonnets are of two major types: a) the Italian or Petrarcan sonnet and b) the English or Shakespearean sonnet. The Petrarcan sonnet consists of an eight-line octave with the rhyme scheme abba abba and a six-line sestet rhyming cde cde or cdc dcd, with the octave presenting a problem or posing a question and the sestet suggesting the solution or answer. The Shakespearean sonnet consists of three four-line units or quatrains plus one two-line unit or couplet, with the quatrains developing an idea and the couplet summing up the poet's conclusion or message. The most common rhyme scheme of the Shakespearean sonnet is abab cdcd efef gg.

“maggie and milly and molly and may”

E.E. Cummings

maggie and milly and molly and may
went down to the beach (to play one day)

and maggie discovered a shell that sang
so sweetly she couldn’t remember her troubles, and

milly befriended a stranded star
whose rays five languid fingers were;

and molly was chased by a horrible thing
which raced sideways while blowing bubbles: and

may came home with a smooth round stone
as small as a world and as large as alone.

For whatever we lose (like a you or a me)
it’s always ourselves we find in the sea

Repr. from: M. Harrison (ed.), *New Dragon Book of Verse,* OUP, London 1977, p. 53.

Assignments

1. Say what happens in the text.
2. Why does the text have to be considered as poetry?
3. Point out and name the poetical elements used in the text and describe them and their effect as precisely as you can (you may refer to the preceding theoretical texts).
4. The device of carrying on the grammatical structure of a line into the next without a pause is known as *enjambement* [ɪn'dʒæmmənt] or *run-on line*. It contrasts with so-called *end-stopped lines*, in which the end of the line coincides with the end of a syntactic unit and a pause. Point out to what extent enjambement is used in the above poem and try to explain its effect.

Roman Wall Blues

W.H. AUDEN

Over the heather the wet wind blows,
I've lice in my tunic and a cold in my nose.

The rain comes pattering out of the sky,
I'm a Wall soldier, I don't know why.

The mist creeps over the hard grey stone,
My girl's in Tungria; I sleep alone.

Aulus goes hanging around her place,
I don't like his manners, I don't like his face.

Piso's a Christian, he worships a fish;
There'd be no kissing if he had his wish.

She gave me a ring but I diced it away;
I want my girl and I want my pay.

When I'm a veteran with only one eye
I shall do nothing but look at the sky.

Repr. from: M. Harrison (ed.), *New Dragon Book of Verse,* OUP, London 1977, p. 144.

Vocabulary

languid weak, lacking strength – *to patter* to make a number of light, quickly repeated noises – *Tungria* the area around Tongern (Belg.) – *to dice* here: to lose by playing dice (= Würfel)

Assignments

1. Scan the poem, marking the stressed and unstressed syllables (cf. text *Metre and Rhythm*, p. 13). Then discuss to what extent the poet makes use of metric regularity.
2. Besides rhythm, what other regularities help to shape the poem?
3. Explain the title of the poem.

I Am

JOHN CLARE

I am – yet what I am, none cares or knows;
My friends forsake me like a memory lost:
I am the self-consumer of my woes –
They rise and vanish in oblivious host,
Like shadows in love frenzied stifled throes
And yet I am, and live – like vapours tost

Into the nothingness of scorn and noise,
Into the living sea of waking dreams,
Where there is neither sense of life or joys,
But the vast shipwreck of my life's esteems;
Even the dearest that I love the best
Are strange – nay, rather, stranger than the rest.

I long for scenes where man hath never trod
A place where woman never smiled or wept
There to abide with my Creator God,
And sleep as I in childhood sweetly slept,
Untroubling and untroubled where I lie
The grass below, above, the vaulted sky.

Repr. from: M. Harrison (ed.), *New Dragon Book of Verse*, OUP, London 1977, p. 233.

Vocabulary

woe great sorrow – *throes* (esp. lit.) violent pains – *hath* (old use or biblical) has

Assignments

1. What does the speaker of the poem say about himself? What are his problems and what is he longing for?
2. What is the pattern of the poem and how is it brought about?
3. According to its form and meaning, the poem falls into two units. Explain the use of enjambement (run-on line) in this context.
4. In more conventional poetry the language is often characterized by archaisms and literary/formal lexical choices. Point out to what extent this is the case in the above poem.

Wind

TED HUGHES

This house has been far out at sea all night,
The woods crashing through darkness, the booming hills,
Winds stampeding the fields under the window
Floundering black astride and blinding wet

Till day rose; then under an orange sky
The hills had new places, and wind wielded
Blade-like, luminous black and emerald,
Flexing like the lens of a mad eye.

At noon I scaled along the house-side as far as
The coal-house door. I dared once to look up –
Through the brunt wind that dented the balls of my eyes
The tent of the hills drummed and strained its guyrope,

The fields quivering, the skyline a grimace,
At any second to bang and vanish with a flap:
The wind flung a magpie away and a black-
Back gull bent like an iron bar slowly. The house

Rang like some fine green goblet in the note
That any second would shatter it. Now deep
In chairs, in front of the great fire, we grip
Our hearts and cannot entertain book, thought,

Or each other. We watch the fire blazing,
And feel the roots of the house move, but sit on,
Seeing the window tremble to come in,
Hearing the stones cry out under the horizons.

Repr. from:
L. Perrine, *Literature,*
Harcourt Brace,
New York 1983, p. 711.

Vocabulary

brunt the heaviest part of (an attack) – *guyrope* rope used to hold a tent in place – *goblet* drinking vessel with a stem and base but no handle

Assignments

1. What is the experience presented in the poem?
2. Point out all the sound effects (including rhythm and metre) in the poem and discuss their contribution to its meaning.

3 *Imagery and Figurative Language*

Imagery

We have seen how rhythm can make us feel what the poet is describing. Another way in which the poet can make us 'see' (and so feel) what he is describing, is by giving us word 'pictures' which our senses can appreciate. These word pictures are the imagery of the poem, and through the images he uses, the poet can make us respond to what is being described.

The word 'pictures' is really misleading, as the impression the poet can give us affects not only sight, but also touch, smell, hearing, and taste. For example, when Keats writes of *globed peonies*, the word *globed* makes us not only 'see' the roundness of the peony flower, but also makes us feel the smooth roundness in our finger-tips, as if our hands were cupped round the silky outer-petals.

Of course we do not in reality 'see' or 'feel' the thing being described: it is only in our imagination that sensatory processes are stimulated: but it is here, in the stimulation of imagination, that poetry can have its most powerful effect on us – if we let it.

It is often said that the imagery of a poem is its figurative language, but this is not necessarily so. Most figures of speech do contain images, but not all images are figures of speech.

Have you seen but a bright lily grow
Before rude hands have touched it?
Ha' you marked but the fall o' the snow
Before the soil hath smutched it?
Ha' you felt the wool of beaver
Or swan's down ever?

Or have smelt o' the bud o' the briar?
Or the nard in the fire?
Or have tasted the bag of the bee?
O so white! O so soft! O so sweet is she!
(*Her Triumph:* Ben Jonson, 1573–1637.)

Just by asking a series of questions Ben Jonson gives us a complete sense-impression of purity, beauty, softness and sweetness of scent and taste. The *bright lily* touched by the *rude hands* is both a visual and tactile image: in our imagination it is our own hands that touch the lily. In the image of the falling snow, not only sight is involved, but also hearing: Jonson wants an image which will convey how quiet and gentle his lady is, as well as saying how pure and unblemished are both her skin and character. (We must remember that the sun-tanned beauties of our own age would have been scorned in Jonson's time. The fashion then was to have a pure white skin.) The *wool of the beaver* and the *swan's down* are tactile images; the *bud of the briar* (rose) and the *nard* (sweet smelling wood) *in the fire* are images of scent; and the *bag of the bee* (honey) an image of taste. And so all five of our senses have been involved in one stanza.

L.E.W. Smith, *A Short Course on Poetry,* Methuen, London 1964, pp. 54–55.

Figurative Language and Figures of Speech

Figurative Language: Intentional departure from the normal order, construction, or meaning of words in order to gain strength and freshness of expression, to create a pictorial effect, to describe by ANALOGY, or to discover and illustrate similarities in otherwise dissimilar things. *Figurative language* is writing that embodies one or more of the various FIGURES OF SPEECH, the most common of which are: ANTITHESIS, APOSTROPHE, CLIMAX, HYPERBOLE, IRONY, METAPHOR, METONYMY, PERSONIFICATION, REPETITION, SIMILE, SYNECDOCHE. These figures are often divided into two classes: TROPES, literally meaning "turns", in which the words in the figure undergo a decided change in meaning, and RHETORICAL FIGURES in which the words retain their literal meaning but their rhetorical pattern is changed.

Figures of Speech: The various uses of language which depart from customary construction, order, or significance in order to achieve special effects or meanings. *Figures of speech* are of two major kinds: RHETORICAL FIGURES, which are departures from customary or standard uses of language to achieve special effects without a change in the radical meaning of the words; and TROPES, in which basic change in the meaning of words occur. *"Figures of speech"* is a term sometimes used as synonymous with RHETORICAL FIGURES, and "figures of thought" as synonymous with TROPES; but "figures of speech" and "figures of thought" in this distinction have undergone so many changes and direct reversals of meaning from the classical rhetoricians to the present that their use in this way almost always results in confusion. It is, therefore, best to use *figures of speech* as the generic term and to use RHETORICAL FIGURES and TROPES as the subgenera.

C. Hugh Holman, *A Handbook to Literature,* The Odyssey Press, Indianapolis 1975, pp. 223–224.

Denotation and Connotation

To write so clearly that they might bring "all things as near the mathematical plainness" as possible – that was the goal of scientists according to Bishop Thomas Sprat, who lived in the seventeenth century. Such an effort would seem bound to fail, because words, unlike numbers, are ambiguous indicators. Although it may have troubled Bishop Sprat, the tendency of a word to have multiplicity of meaning rather than mathematical plainness opens broad avenues to poetry.

Every word has at least one **denotation**: a meaning as defined in a dictionary. But the English language has many a common word with so many denotations that a reader may need to think twice to see what it means in a specific context. The noun *field*, for instance, can denote a piece of ground, a sports arena, the scene of a battle, part of a flag, a profession, and a number system in mathematics. Further, the word can be used as a verb ("he fielded a grounder") or an adjective ("field trip", "field glasses").

A word also has **connotations**: overtones or suggestions of additional meaning that it gains from all the contexts in which we have met it in the past. The word *skeleton*, according to a dictionary, denotes "the bony framework of a human being or other vertebrate animal, which supports the flesh and protects the organs." But by its associations, the word can rouse thoughts of war, of disease and death, or (possibly) of one's plans to go to medical school. Think, too, of the difference between "Old Doc Jones" and "Abner P. Jones, M.D." In the mind's eye, the former appears in his shirtsleeves; the latter has a gold nameplate on his door. That some words denote the same thing but have sharply different connotations is pointed out in this anonymous Victorian jingle:

Here's a little ditty that you really ought to know:
Horses "sweat" and men "perspire", but ladies only "glow".

The terms *druggist, pharmacist,* and *apothecary* all denote the same occupation, but apothecaries lay claim to special distinction.

Few people care more about the connotations of language than do advertisers, who know that connotations make money. Recently a Boston automobile dealer advertised his secondhand cars not as "used" but as "pre-owned", as if fearing that "used car" would connote an old heap with soiled upholstery and mysterious engine troubles that somebody couldn't put up with. "Pre-owned", however, suggests that the previous owner has taken the trouble of breaking in the car for you. Not long ago prune-packers, alarmed by a slump in sales, sponsored a survey to determine the connotations of prunes in the public consciousness. Asked, "What do you think of when you hear the word *prunes*?" most people replied, "dried up", "wrinkled", or "constipated". Dismayed, the packers hired an advertising agency to create a new image for prunes, in hopes of inducing new connotations. Soon, advertisements began to show prunes in gay, brightly colored settings, in the company of bikinied bathing queens.

In imaginative writing, connotations are as crucial as they are in advertising. Consider this sentence: "A new brand of journalism is being born, or spawned" (Dwight Macdonald writing in *The New York Review of Books*). The last word, by its associations with fish and crustaceans, suggests that this new journalism is scarcely the product of human beings. And what do we make of Romeo's assertion that Juliet "is the sun"? Surely even a lovesick boy cannot mean that his sweetheart is "the incandescent body of gases about which the earth and other planets revolve" (a dictionary definition). He means, of course, that he thrives in her sight, that he feels warm in her presence or even at the thought of her, that she illumines his world and is the center of his universe. Because in the mind of the hearer these and other suggestions are brought into play, Romeo's statement, literally absurd, makes excellent sense.

X.J. Kennedy, *Literature,* Little Brown, Boston 1976, pp. 512–513.

The Forge

SEAMUS HEANEY

All I know is a door into the dark.
Outside, old axles and iron hoops rusting;
Inside, the hammered anvil's short-pitched ring,
The unpredictable fantail of sparks
Or hiss when a new shoe toughens in water.
The anvil must be somewhere in the centre,
Horned as a unicorn, at one end square,
Set there immovable: an altar
Where he expends himself in shape and music.
Sometimes, leather-aproned, hairs in his nose,
He leans out on the jamb, recalls a clatter
Of hoofs where traffic is flashing in rows;
Then grunts and goes in, with a slam and flick
To beat real iron out, to work the bellows.

Repr. from: L. Perrine, *Sound and Sense,*
Harcourt Brace, New York 1973, p. 56.

Vocabulary

anvil iron block on which metal is hammered into shape – *unicorn* imaginary horse-like animal with one horn growing from its forehead

Assignments

1. Point out the images in the poem, classify them and state their function. How is the work done in the forge characterized by the images used in lines 6–9?
2. In what way are past and present (old and new) contrasted and evaluated in the poem?

Digging

EDWARD THOMAS

To-day I think
Only with scents – scents dead leaves yield,
And bracken, and wild carrot's seed,
And the square mustard field;

Odours that rise
When the spade wounds the root of tree,
Rose, currant, raspberry, or goutweed,
Rhubarb or celery;

The smoke's smell, too,
Flowing from where a bonfire burns
The dead, the waste, the dangerous,
And all to sweetness turns.

It is enough
To smell, to crumble the dark earth,
While the robin sings over again
Sad songs of Autumn mirth.

Repr. from: B. Kellow/J. Krisak (eds.), *Poetry and Language*, McGraw Hill, Toronto/Montreal 1983, p. 77.

Vocabulary

bracken kind of fern – *goutweed* (bot. = Giersch) – *robin* (= Rotkehlchen) – *mirth* merriness and gaiety

Assignments

1. How does the speaker experience the day and the season and what are his feelings? By what different types of images are his sensations and feelings suggested?
2. What are the connotations of *scent, odour, smell*? Find other words to denote "smell" and explain their connotations.
3. What are the sound features of the poem?

Hope Is the Thing with Feathers

EMILY DICKINSON

Hope is the thing with feathers
That perches in the soul,
And sings the tune without the words,
And never stops at all,

And sweetest in the gale is heard;
And sore must be the storm
That could abash the little bird
That kept so many warm.

I've heard it in the chillest land,
And on the strangest sea;
Yet, never, in extremity,
It asked a crumb of me.

Repr. from: D. Bergmann/D.M. Epstein (eds.), *The Heath Guide to Poetry,* D. Heath & Co., Lexington/Toronto 1983, p. 127.

Vocabulary

to perch to come to rest on a branch, rod, etc. – *to abash* to upset or ruffle

Assignments

1. *Hope* is metaphorically presented as a "little bird". How is the metaphor developed in the poem (extended metaphor)?
2. By what contrasting images are the strength and perseverance of hope emphasized?

Because I Never Learned

(For my brother John)
Patrick Lane

Because I never learned how
to be gentle and the country
I lived in was hard with dead
animals and men, I didn't question
my father when he told me
to step on the kitten's head
after the bus had run over
its hind quarters.

Now, twenty years later,
I remember only:
the silence of the dying
when the fragile skull collapsed
under my hard bare heel,
the curved tongue in the dust
that would never cry again
and the small of my father's back
as he walked tall away.

Repr. from: B. Kellow/J. Krisak (eds.), *Poetry and Language*, McGraw Hill, Toronto/Montreal 1983, p. 76.

Assignments

1. What event does the speaker remember and what is his attitude towards it twenty years later? Does he see his father differently now?
2. Point out and evaluate the images used in the poem.

The Premonition

Theodore Roethke

Walking this field I remember
Days of another summer.
Oh that was long ago! I kept
Close to the heels of my father,
Matching his stride with half-steps
Until we came to a river.
He dipped his hand in the shallow:
Water ran over and under
Hair on a narrow wrist bone;
His image kept following after, –
Flashed with the sun in the ripple.
But when he stood up, that face
Was lost in a maze of water.

Repr. from: J. Poulin (ed.), *Contemporary American Poetry,* Houghton Mifflin, New York 1980, p. 403.

Assignments

1. In what way is the speaker's remembrance presented through images?
2. Explain the title of the poem.
3. Discuss similarities and differences between this poem and *Because I Never Learned.*

To Spring

WILLIAM BLAKE

O Thou with dewy locks, who lookest down
Through the clear windows of the morning, turn
Thine angel eyes upon our western isle,
Which in full choir hails thy approach, O Spring!

The hills tell each other, and the listening
Valleys hear; all our longing eyes are turned
Up to thy bright pavilions; issue forth,
And let thy holy feet visit our clime.

Come o'er the eastern hills, and let our winds
Kiss thy perfumed garments; let us taste
Thy morn and evening breath; scatter thy pearls
Upon our love-sick land that mourns for thee.

O deck her forth with thy fair fingers; pour
Thy soft kisses on her bosom; and put
Thy golden crown upon her languished head,
Whose modest tresses were bound up for thee!

Repr. from: L. Perrine (ed.), *Sound and Sense*,
Harcourt Brace, New York 1973, p. 80.

Vocabulary

thy (old use) your – *clime* (poet.) climate – *thee* (old use) you

Assignments

1. The principal figure of speech employed in this poem is *personification*. Gather all the examples from the poem which illustrate this stylistic device. What is the picture of spring created in this way?
2. What images are used to present people and nature waiting for spring? How is the speaker's position reflected in the language of the poem?
3. The language of the poem differs a great deal from everyday modern English. Point out such differences with regard to lexis and grammar. Then state the effect produced.

Mushrooms

SYLVIA PLATH

Overnight, very
Whitely, discreetly,
Very quietly

Our toes, our noses
Take hold on the loam,
Acquire the air.

Nobody sees us,
Stops us, betrays us;
The small grains make room.

Soft fists insist on
Heaving the needles,
The leafy bedding,

Even the paving.
Our hammers, our rams,
Earless and eyeless,

Perfectly voiceless,
Widen the crannies,
Shoulder through holes. We

Diet on water,
On crumbs of shadow,
Bland-mannered, asking

Little or nothing.
So many of us!
So many of us!

We are shelves, we are
Tables, we are meek,
We are edible,

Nudgers and shovers
In spite of ourselves.
Our kind multiplies:

We shall by morning
Inherit the earth.
Our foot's in the door.

Repr. from: A.J. Porter/H.L. Terrie (eds.), *American Literature,* Ginn/Lexington, Mass. 1981, p. 700.

Assignments

1. How do rhythm and sound contribute to the presentation of the subject?
2. Point out the use of personification and its effect.
3. Find and explain images that are particularly vivid in portraying the mushrooms.
4. What symbolic interpretation does the poem suggest?

4 *Tone and Meaning*

Tone

Tone is the writer's or speaker's attitude towards a topic, a character, his listeners or readers or towards himself. It significantly contributes to the total meaning of what is written or said in that it provides an emotional colouring without which the message would be one of bare fact.

In the spoken language, tone is easily achieved and recognized by means of tone of voice, i.e. voice inflection, intonation, degree of loudness, and stress. Thus, one and the same statement, say "I'm going to be married tomorrow" may be uttered with a variety of tones expressing enthusiasm, irony, resignation, satisfaction, self-pity, bitterness, despair, etc. Ignoring the specific tone would mean missing an important part of the message, with misinterpretation possibly leading to an inappropriate reaction.

In a written text, as for instance in a poem, tone is equally essential but not as easily recognizable as with spoken language. How can we sense that the attitude expressed in a poem is playful or solemn, deferential or contemptuous, calm or excited, ironic or even sarcastic? To determine tone in a poem, all the elements of poetry – lexical choice, connotation, collocation, imagery, irony, syntax, rhythm and pattern – must be carefully scrutinized and judged. Tone is, as it were, the sum total of all the elements of a poem.

Last Lesson of the Afternoon

D.H. Lawrence

When will the bell ring, and end this weariness?
How long have they tugged the leash, and strained apart,

My pack of unruly hounds! I cannot start
Them again on a quarry of knowledge they hate to hunt,
I can haul them and urge them no more.

No longer now can I endure the brunt
Of the books that lie out on the desks; a full threescore
Of several insults of blotted pages, and scrawl

Of slovenly work that they have offered me.
I am sick, and what on earth is the good of it all?
What good to them or me, I cannot see!

So, shall I take
My last dear fuel of life to heap on my soul
And kindle my will to a flame that shall consume
Their dross of indifference; and take the toll
Of their insults in punishment? – I will not! –

I will not waste my soul and my strength for this.
What do I care for all that they do amiss!
What is the point of this teaching of mine, and of this
Learning of theirs? It all goes down the same abyss.

What does it matter to me, if they can write
A description of a dog, or if they can't?
What is the point? To us both, it is all my aunt!
And yet I'm supposed to care, with all my might.

I do not, and will not; they won't and they don't; and that's all!
I shall keep my strength for myself; they can keep theirs as well.
Why should we beat our heads against the wall
Of each other? I shall sit and wait for the bell.

Repr. from: B. Kellow/J. Krisak (eds.), *Poetry and Language,*
McGraw Hill, Toronto/Montreal 1983, p. 155.

Vocabulary

to tug to pull hard – *leash* (= Leine) – *abyss* a great hole which seems to have no bottom – *it is all my aunt* (coll.) it's all rubbish

Assignments

1. Explain in your own words what the poem is about.
2. What is the tone of the poem and by what means is it brought about? How does it reflect the speaker's attitude?

Elegy for Alfred Hubbard

TONY CONNOR

Hubbard is dead, the old plumber;
who will mend our burst pipes now,
the tap that has dripped all the summer,
testing the sink's overflow?

No other like him. Young men with knowledge
of new techniques, theories from books,
may better his work straight from college,
but who will challenge his squint-eyed looks

in kitchen, bathroom, under floorboards,
rules of thumb which were often wrong;
seek as erringly stopcocks in cupboards,
or make a job last half as long?

He was a man who knew the ginnels,
alleyways, streets – the whole district,
family secrets, minor annals,
time-honored fictions fused to fact.

Seventy years of gossip muttered
under his cap, his tufty thatch,
so that his talk was slow and clotted,
hard to follow, and too much.

As though nothing fell, none vanished,
and time were the maze of Cheetham Hill,
in which the dead – with jobs unfinished –
waited to hear him ring the bell.

For much he never got round to doing,
but meant to, when weather bucked up,
or worsened, or when his pipe was drawing,
or when he'd finished this cup.

I thought time, he forgot so often,
had forgotten him but here's Death's pomp
over his house, and by the coffin
the son who will inherit his blowlamp,

tools, workshop, cart, and cornet
(pride of Cheetham Prize Brass Band),
and there's his mourning widow, Janet,
stood at the gate he'd promised to mend.

Soon he will make his final journey;
shaved and silent, strangely trim,
with never a pause to talk to any-
body: how arrow-like, for him!

In St. Mark's church, whose dismal tower
he pointed and painted when a lad,
they will sing his praises amidst flowers
while, somewhere, a cellar starts to flood,

and the housewife banging his front-door knocker
is not surprised to find him gone,
and runs for Thwaite, who's a better worker,
and sticks at a job until it's done.

Repr. from: L. Perrine, *Literature,* Harcourt Brace, New York 1983, p. 659.

Vocabulary

stopcock (= Absperrhahn) – *ginnel* = gennel (dial.) long narrow passage between houses – *tufty thatch* here: mass of thick, untidy hair – *blowlamp* (= Lötlampe)

Assignments

1. How is A. Hubbard characterized?
2. What is the speaker's attitude towards the deceased and how is it mirrored in the poem?
3. Look up the term *elegy* and discuss what features of an elegy the poem has.
4. What may be the intended message of the poem?

The Weather

DAVID IGNATOW

Live for myself
said the wind
Live for myself
said the rain
Live for myself
said the night
I bent my head
turned up my collar

Repr. from: B. Kellow/J. Krisak (eds.), *Poetry and Language,* McGraw Hill, Toronto/Montreal 1983, p. 128.

Assignments

1. Describe the situation and the speaker's reaction to it.
2. What is revealed about the speaker's attitude?
3. Discuss the pattern of the poem and its effect.

Epitaph on a Tyrant

W.H. AUDEN

Perfection, of a kind, was what he was after,
And the poetry he invented was easy to understand;
He knew human folly like the back of his hand,
And was greatly interested in armies and fleets;
When he laughed, respectable senators burst with laughter,
And when he cried the little children died in the streets.

Repr. from: B. Kellow/J. Krisak (eds.), *Poetry and Language,* McGraw Hill, Toronto/Montreal 1983, p. 173.

Assignments

1. Why is the poem called an *epitaph*?
2. How is the tyrant characterized? – Explain each line of the poem.
3. Why may the poem be called ironic?

5 Types

Types of Poetry

Though many poems defy a neat classification, handbooks usually distinguish three basic types: *dramatic, narrative*, and *lyric*. These types, however, can only be considered as very broad divisions between which overlapping is not infrequent.

Dramatic poetry is characterized by the fact that one or more characters speak either to the reader or to each other in a situation of conflict. As this kind of poetry is restricted to poetic drama (e.g. Shakespeare's plays) and to what is known as dramatic monologue, some manuals reduce poetry to only two main types, namely, *narrative* and *lyric*. Indeed, almost all poems fall into one of these two categories.

Narrative poetry tells the story of some action or occurrence. This category includes the *epic*, a narrative poem of great length dealing with the exploits of a national hero (Homer, the *Iliad*, the *Odyssey*; Virgil, the *Aeneid*; Dante, the *Divine Comedy*; John Milton, *Paradise Lost,* etc.), and the *ballad*, a relatively short narrative poem with set characteristics, such as a fixed stanza form, incremental repetition (i.e. repetition of a stanza with variations and additions that advance the story) and a refrain.

Most poems, however, can be described as *lyric*, so called because they were originally accompanied by a musical instrument called the *lyre*. They are often, but not always, short and song-like. The form, mood and subject matter of lyrical poems may vary enormously, and there are numerous sub-categories (hymn, sonnet, song, ode, elegy, etc.), but they all have two things in common: they are neither narrative nor dramatic and they convey a direct response to experience – they are an expression of personal emotion or subjective meditation.

Ballad of the Bread Man

CHARLES CAUSLEY

Mary stood in the kitchen
Baking a loaf of bread.
An angel flew in through the window.
We've a job for you, he said.

God in his big gold heaven,
Sitting in his big blue chair,
Wanted a mother for his little son.
Suddenly saw you there.

Mary shook and trembled,
It isn't true what you say.
Don't say that, said the angel.
The baby's on its way.

Joseph was in the workshop
Planing a piece of wood.
The old man's past it, the neighbours said.
That girl's been up to no good.

And who was that elegant feller,
They said, in the shiny gear?
The things they said about Gabriel
Were hardly fit to hear.

Mary never answered,
Mary never replied.
She kept the information,
Like the baby, safe inside.

It was election winter.
They went to vote in town.
When Mary found her time had come
The hotels let her down.

The baby was born in an annex
Next to the local pub.
At midnight, a delegation
Turned up from the Farmer's Club.

They talked about an explosion
That cracked a hole in the sky,
Said they'd been sent to the Lamb & Flag
To see god come down from on high.

A few days later a bishop
And a five-star general were seen
With the head of an African country
In a bullet-proof limousine.

We've come, they said, with tokens
For the little boy to choose.
Told the tale about war and peace
In the television news.

After them came the soldiers
With rifle and bomb and gun,
Looking for enemies of the state.
The family had packed and gone.

When they got back to the village
The neighbours said to a man,
That boy will never be one of us,
Though he does what he blessed well can.

He went round to all the people
A paper crown on his head.
Here is some bread from my father.
Take, eat, he said.

Nobody seemed very hungry,
Nobody seemed to care.
Nobody saw the god in himself
Quietly standing there.

He finished up in the papers.
He came to a very bad end.
He was charged with bringing the living to life.
No man was that prisoner's friend.

There's only one kind of punishment
To fit that kind of a crime.
They rigged a trial and shot him dead.
They were only just in time.

They lifted the young man by the leg,
They lifted him by the arm,
They locked him in a cathedral
In case he came to harm.

They stored him safe as water
Under seven rocks.
One Sunday morning he burst out
Like a jack-in-the-box.

Through the town he went walking.
He showed them the holes in his head.
Now do you want any loaves? he cried.
Not today, they said.

Repr. from: *Voices, The Third Book,*
Penguin Education, London 1968, p. 55.

Assignments

1. Retell the story narrated in the poem.
2. In what phases is the story developed? To what extent has it been changed and modernised and what effect does this have?
3. Gather information on the *Ballad* and point out its typical elements in the poem.

Silver

Walter de la Mare

Slowly, silently, now the moon
Walks the night in her silver shoon;
This way, and that, she peers, and sees
Silver fruit upon silver trees;
One by one the casements catch
Her beams beneath the silvery thatch;

Couched in his kennel, like a log,
With paws of silver sleeps the dog;
From their shadowy cote the white breasts peep
Of doves in a silver-feathered sleep;
A harvest mouse goes scampering by,
With silver claws and a silver eye;
And moveless fish in the water gleam,
By silver reeds in a silver stream.

Repr. from: R. Smith/M.F. Schulz (eds.), *Journeys, Delta,* Harcourt Brace, New York 1982, p. 333.

Vocabulary

shoon (old use/poet.) shoes – *casement* here: frame of a window

Assignments

1. State why the poem is purely descriptive. Then explain how the description is developed.
2. What is the poem about? Why is its title appropriate?
3. What formal elements does the effect of the poem rely on?

Poem

WILLIAM CARLOS WILLIAMS

As the cat
climbed over
the top of

the jamcloset
first the right
forefoot
carefully
then the hind
stepped down

into the pit of
the empty
flowerpot

Repr. from: R. Smith/M.F. Schulz (eds.), *Journeys, Delta,* Harcourt Brace, New York 1982, p. 245.

Assignments

1. What picture does this poem present? Is the presentation appropriate?
2. Why is pattern important in this poem?

Fog

CARL SANDBURG

The fog comes
on little cat feet.

It sits looking
over harbor and city
on silent haunches
and then moves on.

Repr. from: R.A. Bennet (ed.), *The World of Language, Book H,* Follett, Chicago 1972, p. 321.

Assignments

1. Compare *Fog* with the preceding poem.
2. What image does the poem rely on and what does it suggest?

6 Trends and Themes in Contemporary Poetry

American Poetry Today

American poetry at the present time exhibits great creative energy and a variety of styles and themes. As in the earlier decades of the century, poets continue to experiment with form and language, and poetry has become increasingly free in structure, increasingly "realistic" in subject matter. "Open" forms of "free" verse – that is, poetry without definite metrical pattern – is a characteristic mode of the period, although it is not the only one. Many outstanding poets still use meter and rhyme, but they, like their experimental contemporaries, are more influenced by the rhythms and textures of natural speech than by the old prosodic requirements. The prevalent feeling among most poets today is that all areas of human experience are appropriate for poetry. Hence, materials that in the past were considered at best too mundane for poetry and at worst offensive and improper are now freely used.

In preceding centuries critics and poets themselves were often concerned with the problem of an appropriate vocabulary for poetry – poetic diction. Slang and coarse expressions, common in recent poetry, were not approved by the arbiters of literary taste, although such major British poets as Shakespeare and William Blake frequently went beyond the limits of elegance and refinement. William Wordsworth, in the nineteenth-century England, held that poetry should be written in the language of "common men". The Scottish poet Robert Burns used dialect and folk expressions in his poems about Scottish life. Gerard Manley Hopkins (in late nineteenth-century England) frequently employed terms from the workaday world as well as outmoded and even made-up words.

Walt Whitman was undoubtedly the most daring of these early innovators. His *Leaves of Grass* offended many readers who considered his diction rough and "barbaric" and his references to the body, to sex, indelicate. In his efforts to encompass everything he did not hesitate to make use of slang and the vernacular – the language of "common men". And he was a pioneer in the use of free verse, rejecting conventional meters and stanza patterns in favor of a more flexible and individual kind of poetry.

Twentieth-century poets have gone much further in regard to diction and subject matter than Whitman. In order to get away from the "literary", poets like Allen Ginsberg and Le Roi Jones have employed slang and "fourletter" words, and they have sometimes consciously resorted to triteness and banality in order to bring their poems closer to everyday life and speech. The results are not always admirable or even interesting. Modern poets feel free to use any word that contributes to the expression of a theme or idea. The concept of a special vocabulary for poetry – "poetic diction" – has long since been abandoned.

Much of the poetry published in our country in recent years can be classified as the poetry of social awareness. It is poetry with a purpose and registers the social and moral pressures of our times. The Vietnam War, racial strife, such national tragedies as the assassinations of John and Robert Kennedy and Martin Luther King – all these have inspired poetic response.

The emergence of a so-called school of Black Poetry in America has been one of the significant literary developments of the modern period. Although the Harlem Renaissance of the 1920's brought certain Afro-American poets into prominence, it was not until the intensification of the civil rights struggle during the 1960's that a separate group of black poets began to take shape. Avowedly nationalistic (that is, racially proud) and scornful of western aesthetics, these poets continued the protest tradition, historically associated with Negro writers. But they were more radical in outlook than their predecessors. Unlike the Harlem group, they rejected entry into the mainstream of American literature as a desirable goal. They insisted that their poetry could not be judged by white standards, urging its importance as an expression of black consciousness.

Le Roi Jones – the most influential of the young activist poets – Don L. Lee, Nikki Giovanni, Sonia Sanchez, Mari Evans, Etheridge Knight, and David Henderson attune their lyres to the "black aesthetic". Not yet satisfactorily defined, this term, originating in the sixties, may be interpreted as a sense of the spiritual and artistic values of blackness. It is, perhaps, a logical (some would say "chauvinistic"), reaction to negative American racial attitudes. Perhaps the concept is best summarized by the slogan "Black is beautiful". Those who accept this point of view regard Negro subject matter as their exclusive domain, feeling that only those who have shared "black experience" can articulate it. Older poets whose work shows some alignment with the new Black Poetry include Margaret Walker and Gwendolyn Brooks, winner of the Pulitzer Prize in 1950.

Whether poetry should be valued primarily for the unique inner experience it can provide or for its effectiveness as political or social statement is a question that often recurs in discussions of the true function of the art today. (...)

American poets have frequently been criticized for their negative view of life in general and of American society in particular. It is true that many of them have given voice to doubt and pessimism. Yet the act of creation itself is an act of faith, a kind of affirmation, and the poetry of disillusionment often implies a moral concern with things as they ought to be, a vision of something better than we have.

R. Hayden in: J.E. Miller/R. Hayden (eds.), *The US in Literature,* Scott Foresman, Glenview, Ill. 1973, pp. 264–265.

Excess and Accuracy

If you are asked to picture mentally the last time you went swimming, you will probably "see" yourself in the act of swimming as though you were a witness somewhat at a distance from the swimmer, rather than "be" the swimmer and feel the water against your face, your arms extending from your shoulders, your body invisible behind you, the lake at eye-level before you. I take it to be a habit of brain (very familiar in dreams) to "see" oneself at a slight objective remove, as though you the rememberer were watching a film of the swimmer.

I believe this tendency to create a cinema in an "aesthetic distance" characterizes all intelligence, and that a poem is an event of intelligence which compresses all the techniques of mentation into a single rhythmic unit. To me the act of writing a poem gathers up and focuses sensualized forms of thought, just as memory gathers up and focuses the swimmer. A poem is brain in the act of braining. When the poem works it is a supreme pleasure for it is the objectified event of mind working well. When the poem fails (or when a year's worth of poems fails) it is a keen displeasure, for it is a model of indecision, vanity, and madness.

I think I am a religious poet. (My critics might argue that the tone of the poems in this anthology is that of a tent evangelist; I can hardly argue with them.) This "religion" is not to be confused with Christianity or Buddhism or Marxism or any other proscriptive belief system. By "religious" I mean an attitude toward matter and energy as intrinsically awesome. The goal of language, in my opinion, is to "worship" phenomena. The poem is always an act of homage, the intention of which is hallucination. The memory's objectified "view" of the self swimming is an hallucination of the swimmer. The trees vanish, the sky vanishes, the car you came to the lake in vanishes: what rises intensely to attention is the swimmer as Image, as emotionally charged icon, as "vision". The entire poem, for me, is a musicalized network of these religiously elevated vision-events. This is true of bombastic oratorical poems and murmured still-lifes-of-the-heart. I would contend that the very nature of intelligence is hallucinatory isolation of details. Every bush, intensely seen, is a burning bush.

Given this predisposition I have found myself struggling with a dilemma all my adult life, one that I have yet to resolve. I have found myself temperamentally at odds with most of the English and European verse which is my heritage. Most of it is, to my taste, overly concerned with what I would call "static harmony" – like the balance of equal weights on a seesaw – whereas I am inexorably drawn to "dynamic balance" – the mutually repulsive and attractive tensions which keep a solar system in coherence. The poems of my immediate tradition lack the teeth (not to mention the fangs) that I feel all objects and experiences have. They are *physically* dull to me. The nude intensity of phenomena seems untouched, even untouchable, by most English verse. The erotic complexity of phenomena seems to me an absolute given. The paper on which I write these words is *in fact* a furnace of molecular activity. How can a poetry dedicated to religious discovery (revelation) exclude (in its themes or in its language use) this feverish intensity, this aspiration in all entities to achieve as much as possible while still maintaining Livingness? My goal in every poem is to include as much as possible while remaining faithful to the parameters of the experience being examined and the poem itself. A poem has only one rule: to achieve and maintain livingness. The alternative is the death of the object. We say of such a poem "it doesn't work". We could as easily say "it failed to attain life".

The poems I wish to write always risk exaggeration, for this is the price of admission to the cinema of brain. The poems also willingly embrace the risk of theatricality. All thought is theatre. The nature of thinking is the transformation of sense impressions into Images which can be sorted, collated, and reassembled in insightful relationships. All "thinking" is "imagination" (image-making) or we could not figure-forth the image of the swimmer at all. The very chemistry of mental activity, we are gradually learning, is a tension of electrochemical accretion and release. This tension crests as the theatrical phenomenon known as Imagery. Poetry is an already theatrical and dramatic subjective process objectified. What falls on the remembered swimmer is the spotlight of Thought.

Stan Rice in: P. Dow (ed.),
19 New Poets of the Golden Gate,
Harcourt Brace, New York 1984,
pp. 269–270.

New Town Blues

John Cotton

I. Culture

Near half a week's pay on the blonde bouffant
and a pair of thigh length boots,
she queens the fore-court
to lighten many a darkness.
A workman, pasting posters
for the town's Arts Festival,
draws breath at the callipygian exposé
as she bends to remove a petrol cap.
He is not one for minority pursuits.
She thinks of what to get the kids for tea.

II. Environment

Grandma constantly tells how, as a girl,
she held the horses in the fields,
wiped them down at the end of the day
and slept by them in the stable.
While her grandson,
cut off by regiments of streets
and a technology that ostracises him,
each Saturday on the way back from the pub
kicks in the bus-shelter to show them.
And they, as regularly, repair it in reply.

III. Social Services

At the shopping centre they sit on benches,
a refuge from a hostile domesticity.
Grey stubble above grubby neckbands,
redolent of pipes and weak bladders,
they fumble for matches with thickly veined hands
while they soak in the last of the summer.
Memories revived by the young wives
with their sturdy hams, they recall places
the authorities considered unsuitable.

Repr. from: F.E.S. Finn (ed.), *Voices of Today,*
J. Murray, London 1980, p. 43.

Vocabulary

bouffant puffed-out hair – *to queen sic queen* (sl) prostitute – *callipygian* (of Venus) with finely shaped buttocks – *to ostracise* to refuse to have social dealings with – *redolent* (fml) smelling – *sturdy* strong and firm

Assignments

1. Outline what each of the sections deals with. What aspects of *culture, environment,* and *social services* are presented?
2. Discuss the connection among the three sections and relate them to the title of the poem.
3. Why may *contrast* be regarded as a structural principle in the poem?

Meditation on the A30

JOHN BETJEMAN

A man on his own in a car
  Is revenging himself on his wife;
He opens the throttle and bubbles with dottle
  And puffs at his pitiful life.

"She's losing her looks very fast,
  She loses her temper all day;
That lorry won't let me get past,
  This Mini is blocking my way.

"Why can't you step on it and shift her!
  I can't go on crawling like this!
At breakfast she said that she wished I was dead –
  Thank heavens we don't have to kiss.

"I'd like a nice blonde on my knee
  And one who won't argue or nag.
Who dares to come hooting at *me*?
  I only give way to a Jag.

"You're barmy or plastered, I'll pass you, you bastard –
  I *will* overtake you. I *will*!"
As he clenches his pipe, his moment is ripe
  And the corner's accepting its kill.

Repr. from: J. Murray, *J. Betjeman's Collected Poems,* London 1960, p. 352.

Vocabulary

throttle (of a car) part of a pipe which opens and closes to control the flow of gas, petrol, etc. – *dottle* partly burnt tobacco in a pipe – *barmy* (sl) foolish, mad

Assignments

1. Retell in your own words what happens in the poem.
2. Describe the form (sound and pattern, cf. text *Sound Patterns*, p. 15). To what extent is the rhythm particularly significant?
3. State the theme and comment on the tone of the poem.

The Man in the Bowler Hat

A.S.J. TESSIMOND

I am the unnoticed, the unnoticeable man:
The man who sat on your right in the morning train:
The man you looked through like a windowpane:
The man who was the colour of the carriage, the colour of the mounting
Morning pipe smoke.

I am the man too busy with a living to live,
Too hurried and worried to see and smell and touch:
The man who is patient too long and obeys too much
And wishes too softly and seldom.

I am the man they call the nation's backbone,
Who am boneless – playable catgut, pliable clay:
The Man they label Little lest one day
I dare to grow.

I am the rails on which the moment passes,
The megaphone for many words and voices:
I am graph, diagram,
Composite face.

I am the led, the easily-fed,
The tool, the not-quite-fool,
The would-be-safe-and-sound,
The uncomplaining, bound,
The dust fine-ground,
Stone-for-a-statue waveworn pebble-round.

Repr. from: M. Wollman (ed.), *Seven Themes in Modern Verse*, Harrap, London 1968, p. 25.

Vocabulary

pliable easily bent without breaking – *lest* (fml) in order that not

Assignments

1. What are the characteristics of *The Man in the Bowler Hat* and what does he stand for?
2. Discuss the use of language in the poem (pattern, lexical items, syntax).
3. What criticism is voiced in the poem?

I Am A Black Woman

MARI EVANS

I am a black woman
the music of my song
some sweet arpeggio of tears
is written in a minor key
and I
can be heard humming in the night
Can be heard
  humming
in the night

I saw my mate leap screaming to the sea
and I with these hands cupped the lifebreath
from my issue in the canebrake
I lost Nat's swinging body in a rain of tears
and heard my son scream all the way from Anzio
for Peace he never knew I
learned Da Nang and Pork Chop Hill
in anguish
Now my nostrils know the gas
and these trigger tired fingers
seek the softness in my warrior's beard

I
am a black woman
tall as a cypress
strong
beyond all definition still
defying place
and time
and circumstance
  assailed
    impervious
      indestructible
Look
  on me and be
renewed

Repr. from: A.J. Porter/H.L. Terrie (eds.), *American Literature*, Ginn/Lexington, Mass. 1981, p. 697.

Vocabulary

arpeggio notes of a musical chord played separately – *Nat Turner* hanged for leading a slave rebellion in 1831 – *Anzio* (Ital.) site of a battle in World War II – *Da Nang* site of US military base in Viet Nam – *Pork Chop Hill* battle site in Korea

Assignments

1. What is presented in the three parts of the poem?
2. Is the tone consistent or does it change in the course of the poem?
3. Describe the rhythm of the poem and its effect.

The Old Lady Under the Freeway

Diana O'Hehir

I've come down here to live on a bed of weeds.

Up there are white spaces with curving ceilings,
Harsh wide silver-fitted cars,
Marching squads of freckled-armed men.

My world is depths of green, a water of fern.
No one would guess that a safety hides here below,
Secretly jeweled, dropped in this special pocket.

I'm the mad old lady under the ledge. The good
Who fall headlong off the freeway bridge,
I salvage their nail files, pen knives;
I carve my way in with them;
I make a tunnel with green sides.

At night I lie on my back;
The ferns meet over my face like lover's hair.
They nestle my ear. Their words are unsafe.
The words they say are harsh and green.

I'm roasting shreds of leaf, roasting soup in a can.
My air is as solid as the inside of a honeydew melon.

Repr. from: P. Dow (ed.), *19 New Poets of the Golden Gate,*
Harcourt Brace, New York 1984, p. 30.

Assignments

1. Retell in your own words how the old lady lives.
2. What are the characteristics of the freeway and of the old lady's hiding place? To what extent might they have symbolic value?

Love Is ...

ADRIAN HENRI

Love is feeling cold in the back of vans
Love is a fanclub with only two fans
Love is walking holding paintstained hands
Love is

Love is fish and chips on winter nights
Love is blankets full of strange delights
Love is when you don't put out the light
Love is

Love is the presents in Christmas shops
Love is when you're feeling Top of the Pops
Love is what happens when the music stops
Love is

Love is white panties lying all forlorn
Love is a pink nightdress still slightly warm
Love is when you have to leave at dawn
Love is

Love is you and love is me
Love is a prison and love is free
Love's what's there when you're away from me
Love is ...

Repr. from: A. Henri/R. McGough/B. Patten, *The Mersey Sound,* Penguin, Harmondsworth 1967, p. 21.

Assignments

1. Describe the patterning of the poem. What is its effect?
2. Comment on some of the definitions of love in the poem.
3. What concept of love is presented in the poem?

Dreaming America

Joyce Carol Oates

When the two-lane highway was widened
the animals retreated.
Skunks, raccoons, rabbits – even their small corpses
disappeared from the road – transformed into rags
then into designs
then into stains
then nothing.

When the highway was linked to another
then to another
six lanes then nine then twelve rose
sweeping to the horizon
along measured white lines.
The polled Herefords were sold.
When the cornfields were bulldozed
the farmhouses at their edges turned into shanties;
the outbuildings fell.

When the fields were paved over
Frisch's Big Boy rose seventy-five feet in the air.
The *Sunoco* and *Texaco* and *Gulf* signs competed
on hundred-foot stilts
like eyeballs on stalks
white optic-nerves
miraculous.
Illuminated at night.

Where the useless stretch of trees lay
an orange sphere like a golf ball
announces the Shopping Mall, open
for Thursday evening shopping.
There, tonight, droves of teenagers hunt
one another, alert on the memorized pavement.

Where did the country go? – cry the travelers, soaring
past. *Where did the country go?* – ask the strangers.
The teenagers never ask.

Where horses grazed in a dream that had no history,
tonight a thirteen-year-old girl stands dreaming
into the window of Levitz's Record Shop.
We drive past, in a hurry. We disappear.
We return.

Repr. from: A.J. Porter/H.L. Terrie (eds.), *American Literature*, Ginn/Lexington, Mass. 1981, p. 711.

Vocabulary

raccoon (AE = Waschbär) – *to poll* (of animals) to cut the horns short – *Hereford* type of cow

Assignments

1. The poem mainly relies on the images of disappearance and replacement. Outline these images and their development.
2. What are the implications of the last three stanzas? What is the meaning of the title?
3. Compare this poem with *New Town Blues* by John Cotton.

The Skyjacker

STAN RICE

I am Tex Ritter. I am not Eldridge Cleaver.
I am approaching Havana.
I am carrying a pillow into the cockpit on which is embroidered
I am Tex Ritter. Howdy.
A calm falls over the cockpit.
The co-pilot takes off his extra ears and I tell them,
Relax. I tell the captain to tell the passengers
that this is not Eldridge Cleaver
this is Tex Ritter talkin
and we're going to Havana
and Relax. Then I hear the neighbor's black son's Pontiac
roar outside my window. I partly wake up. I look out.
He is wiping the water off the windows. Like a beast
out of the dream I just finished about living on a cliff
guarded by two white dogs with long flexible noses,
the Pontiac sits, its exhaust smoke
turns pink in the brakelights.

Does he know I am Tex Ritter? Does he realize
we have set down in Cuba, all of us, shrieking tires,
aluminum skin shuddering and windshield wipers
ferociously lapping the windows, the Cubans standing
behind the frosty reception room glass,
clipboards hanging from their belts, does he?
I'll bet he doesn't know.
I think I'll tell him.
But when I look back he and his Pontiac are gone. Oh well,
what's a skin-deep defeat to me, Tex Ritter?
Maybe it's better nobody knows who's talkin
when I kick in the cockpit door
and catch the pilots with their long soft black flexible noses
coiled in their laps, and slip
out of my embroidered pillow my gun and say, coolly,
We are going to Havana,
this is Tex Ritter,
this is not Eldridge Cleaver,
We are going to Havana forever!

Repr. from: P. Dow (ed.), *19 New Poets of the Golden Gate*, Harcourt Brace, New York 1984, p. 272.

Vocabulary

Tex Ritter (Woodward Ritter) American singing cowboy star

Assignments

1. What happens in the poem and to what extent is it real?
2. Why does the speaker insist that he is Tex Ritter and not Eldridge Cleaver? Why is he so keen on Havana?
3. What might be the deeper meaning of the poem?

Moon Rapture

M.A.B. Jones

Tonight the captured moon
Pouring her liquid silver over walls
Trees, buildings, patines inside floors
With candid light. At sight of her
High-riding over houses, mountains, moors
Clouds headstrong, boisterous
I can forget
The battery of silent armament
Assembled there. I can discard
News of soft landings, spacecraft
Circling insignificant earth
Soon to set off to the nearest stars.
And though I know
That unmanned capsules now explore
The solar system, may resolve
Unfathomed mysteries, tonight
My world drenched in this alabaster light
I can remember love
Among the ancient gods, Mount Latmos, myth
Think of romance, Endymion.

Repr. from: F.E.S. Finn (ed.), *Voices of Today*,
J. Murray, London 1980, p. 77.

Vocabulary

Mount Latmos mountain in Greece, near Milet – *Endymion* beautiful young man who was abducted and put to sleep forever on Mount Latmos

Assignments

1. How does the speaker experience the moonlight and what reaction does it evoke in him?
2. Discuss the patterning of the poem.
3. Compare this poem with Robert Hayden's *Astronauts* (p. 57) and Walter de la Mare's *Silver* (p. 40).

Astronauts

ROBERT HAYDEN

Armored in oxygen,
faceless in visors –
mirrormasks reflecting
the mineral glare and
shadow of moonscape –
they walk slowmotion
floating
the lifeless
dust of Taurus
Littrow. And Wow, they
exclaim, oh boy, this is it.

And sing, exulting
(though trained to be wary
of "emotion and
philosophy"), breaking
the calcined stillness
of once Absolute Otherwhere.

Risking edges, earthlings
to whom only
their machines are friendly
(and God's radar-
watching eye?), they
labor at gathering
proof of hypothesis;
in snowshine of sunlight
dangerous as radium
probe detritus for clues.

What is it we wish them
to find for us, as
we watch them on our
screens? They loom there
heroic antiheroes,
smaller than myth and
poignantly human.
Why are we troubled?
What do we want of these men?
What do we want of ourselves?

Repr. from:
A.J. Porter/H.L. Terrie (eds.),
American Literature,
Ginn/Lexington, Mass. 1981, p. XX.

Vocabulary

Littrow specific prism used in optics, here: beams of light produced by a prism

Assignments

1. What does each of the four sections of the poem deal with?
2. Why is the meaning of the poem largely based on the last stanza?
3. Discuss the tone of the poem. What techniques are used to achieve it? What role does the rhythm play in this respect?

7 Suggestions for Project Work

1. Give a complete analysis and appreciation of *Dreaming America* by J.C. Oates (p. 53), touching upon *pattern, imagery and figurative language, tone and meaning.*

2. Study the following poem and compare it in detail with *The Skyjacker* by S. Rice (p. 54).

Skyjack

M.A.B. Jones

Gun-toting men guard doors,
Gangways and exits of an innocent plane.
No more the mind is filled with business, holiday.
The purposed journey fails.

Terror takes over. Passengers,
Pilots in encapsulated seats
Cannot speak out. Fear has become
Companion alone, too close for confidence.

Travellers in a maze of glassed-in
Corridor watch distantly. Drama takes shape
Upon the airport apron. Suddenly
Drab truth appals. A body slumps, is flung

Flat to the tarmac, crumples in full sight
Of all obsessed spectators. Faces trapped
Freeze at the window. What is now the fate
Of those unfortunates who are within
Cannot be reckoned by a reasoned guess.
The unknown threatens – the last loneliness.

Repr. from: F.E.S. Finn (ed.), *Voices of Today,* J. Murray, London 1980, p. 32.

3. Study the poems in the section "Trends and Themes in Contemporary Poetry" regarding themes dealt with. With the help of poetry anthologies collect poems that deal with the same themes; present some of them in class and discuss similarities and differences.

4. Gather information on the development of English (American) poetry. Give a brief portrait of each period or school of poetry and illustrate it by analysing a representative poem.

5. Read *The Tiger* by W. Blake. Then study the following interpretations of the poem:
- H.J. Weiand, *The Tiger* in: Schiffer/Weiand, *Insight III,* Hirschgraben, Frankfurt 1969, pp. 39–48.
- W. Künne, *English and American Poetry – Interpretations,* Klett, Stuttgart 1982, pp. 25–26.
- B. Raffel, *How to Read a Poem,* New American Library, New York 1984, pp. 118–120.
- E. Werlich, *Poetry Analysis,* Lensing, Dortmund 1967, pp. 63–84.

Point out similarities and differences in approach and evaluation.

6. Read the monographs on Charles Causley, Ted Hughes and John Betjeman in: M. Schmidt, *50 Modern British Poets,* Pan, London 1982, and give a short talk in class, concentrating on essentials only and stating what these poets have contributed to modern English poetry.

Gerhard Haefner

The Short Story

Contents

"Plot and theme: future tense; past tense; present tense. The story of our life. Try to fill the blank. This is a story? I can't fnish anything. Yet it's these interruptions that make it a story. Can't you read between the lines?"

John Barth, *Title* (1968)

1 On Short Stories – Approach

Nathaniel Hawthorne

A skilful literary artist has constructed a tale. If wise, he has not fashioned his thoughts to accomodate his incidents; but having conceived, with deliberate care, a certain unique or single *effect* to be wrought out, he then invents such incidents – he then combines such events as may best aid him in establishing this preconceived effect. If his very initial sentence tend not to the outbringing of this effect, then he has failed in his first step. In the whole composition there should be no word written, of which the tendency, direct or indirect, is not to the one pre-established design. And by such means, with such care and skill, a picture is at length painted which leaves in the mind of him who contemplates it with a kindred art, a sense of the fullest satisfaction. The idea of the tale has been presented unblemished, because undisturbed; and this is an end unattainable by the novel. Undue brevity is just as exceptionable here as in the poem; but undue length is yet more to be avoided. (1842)

E.A. Poe, *Tales, Poems, Essays,* Collins, London/Glasgow 1952, p. 521.

The Philosophy of the Short Story

The difference between a Novel and a Novelette is one of length only: a Novelette is a brief Novel. But the difference between a Novel and a Short-story is a difference of kind. A true Short-story is something other and something more than a mere story which is short. A true Short-story differs from the Novel chiefly in its essential unity of impression. In a far more exact and precise use of the word, a Short-story has unity as a Novel cannot have it. Often, it may be noted by the way, the Short-story fulfils the three false unities of the French classic drama: it shows one action in one place on one day. A Short-story deals with a single character, a single event, a single emotion, or the series of emotions called forth by a single situation. (1885)

Brander Matthews, in: A. Weber/W.F. Greiner (eds.), *Short-Story-Theorien 1573–1973,* Athenäum, Kronberg 1977, pp. 45–46.

The Modern Short Story

The basis of almost every argument or conclusion I can make is the axiom that the short story can be anything the author decides it shall be; it can be anything from the death of a horse to a young girl's first love affair, from the static sketch without plot to the swiftly moving machine of bold action and climax, from the prose poem, painted rather than written, to the piece of straight reportage in which style, colour, and elaboration have no place, from the piece which catches like a cobweb the light subtle iridescence of emotions that can never be really captured or measured to the solid tale in which all emotion, all action, all reaction is measured, fixed, puttied, glazed, and finished, like a well-built house, with three coats of shining and enduring paint. In that infinite flexibility, indeed, lies the reason why the short story has never been adequately defined. (1941)

H.E. Bates, *The Modern Short Story,* Thomas Nelson and Sons, London/Edinburgh et al. 1941, pp. 15–16.

What Makes a Short Story Short?

... a story may be short because its action is intrinsically small; or because its action, being large, is reduced in length by means of the devices of selection, scale, and/or point of view. No one can tell in advance that, if a story is short, it is short because it has a certain number of words, or because it has more unity, or because it focuses upon culmination rather than development. All we can do, upon recognizing its shortness, is to ask how and why, keeping balanced simultaneously in our minds the alternative ways of answering these questions and their possible combinations. And then we may win increased understanding and hence appreciation of the specific artistic qualities of this curious and splendid but vastly underrated art. (1959)

N. Friedman, in: *Modern Fiction Studies,* IV, a critical quarterly published by the Modern Fiction Club of the Purdue University of English, West Lafayette, Indiana, 1958/59, p. 117.

The International Symposium on the Short Story

The novelist has to exhaust his action, while keeping enough sense of touch to halt it before it metamorphoses completely into a new action. And this is why we define the short-story writer by negatives. He is not under this obligation. He begins, as the novelist begins, by imagining people in a certain situation. But he need not go until the situation is completely explored. It is enough for him to present the people and the situation vividly, to indicate, deftly, some of the possible ways in which they might react to it, and the reader is left with a new experience, a fresh sense of the variety and interest of life, which would be lost if he had to sit down and follow, page by page, as the writer took up all the slack in the situation. (1969)

J. Wain, *The International Symposium on the Short Story: Part Two,* in: A. Weber/W.F. Greiner (eds.), op. cit., pp. 198–199.

The International Symposium on the Short Story

... length is not the most distinguishing and significant feature of a short story. Length is merely the most obviously marked feature. The short story differs *conceptually* from the novel, though a story can achieve effects similar to those of a novel. ... However, there is a difference in scale. Details, characters, the manner in which meanings are concretely conceived are significant. It might be said that a short story is a flash of life, and that a novel is a floodlight that illuminates a segment of life for more than a flash. But this is an analogical metaphor that suggests the obvious. I present it here in order to emphasize that this differentiation is simple. Less simple is the matter of conceiving something happening, some kind of change, some movement – psychological or physical or social – some conflict within a relatively limited space. (1970)

J.T. Farrell, *The International Symposium on the Short Story: Part Four,* in: A. Weber/W.F. Greiner (eds.), op. cit., p. 202.

The Birth of a Story

And how to write a story?

There are no set rules. Like the novel, the short story is elastic in form. Broadly, the novel relates the interplay of a number of characters, whereas the short story is concerned with one episode or tendency in the lives of one or two people. The short story is really nearer to a poem than its apparent prose-brother, the novel. It is usually about one thing, blown up big or refined beneath the microscope. It can take the form of a moody piece occurring in one person's mind, or a stream of consciousness in the author's mind, or a classic narrative with a beginning, a middle and an end: to adopt this latter technique, it does not follow that the story is old fashioned, it can taste as fresh as tomorrow. (1972)

W. Sansom in: A. Weber/W.F. Greiner (eds.), op. cit., pp. 213–214.

2 A Psychological Short Story

The Boarding House

JAMES JOYCE (1882–1941)

Mrs Mooney was a butcher's daughter. She was a woman who was quite able to keep things to herself: a determined woman. She had married her father's foreman and opened a butcher's shop near Spring Gardens. But as soon as his father-in-law was dead Mr Mooney began to go to the devil. He drank, plundered the till, ran headlong into debt. It was no use making him take the pledge: he was sure to break out again a few days after. By fighting his wife in the presence of customers and by buying bad meat he ruined his business. One night he went for his wife with the cleaver and she had to sleep in a neighbour's house.

After that they lived apart. She went to the priest and got a separation from him with care of the children. She would give him neither money nor food nor house-room; and so he was obliged to enlist himself as a sheriff's man. He was a shabby stooped little drunkard with a white face and a white moustache and white eyebrows, pencilled above his little eyes, which were pink-veined and raw; and all day long he sat in the bailiff's room, waiting to be put on a job. Mrs Mooney, who had taken what remained of her money out of the butcher business and set up a boarding house in Hardwicke Street, was a big imposing woman. Her house had a floating population made up of tourists from Liverpool and the Isle of Man and, occasionally, *artistes* from the music halls. Its resident population was made up of clerks from the city. She governed her house cunningly and firmly, knew when to give credit, when to be stern and when to let things pass. All the resident young men spoke of her as *The Madam*.

Mrs. Mooney's young men paid fifteen shillings a week for board and lodgings (beer or stout at dinner excluded). They shared in common tastes and occupations and for this reason they were very chummy with one another. They discussed with one another the chances of favourites and outsiders. Jack Mooney, the Madam's son, who was clerk to a commission agent in Fleet Street, had the reputation of being a hard case. He was fond of using soldiers' obscenities: usually he came home in the small hours. When he met his friends he had always a good one to tell them and he was always sure to be on to a good thing – that is to say, a likely horse or a likely *artiste*. He was also handy with the mits and sang comic songs. On Sunday nights there would often be a reunion in Mrs Mooney's front drawing-room. The music-hall *artistes* would oblige; and Sheridan played waltzes and polkas and vamped accompaniments. Polly Mooney, the Madam's daughter, would also sing. She sang:

I'm a ... naughty girl.
You needn't sham:
You know I am.

Polly was a slim girl of nineteen, she had light soft hair and a small full mouth. Her eyes, which were grey with a shade of green through them, had a habit of glancing upwards when she spoke with anyone, which made her look like a little perverse madonna. Mrs Mooney had first sent her daughter to be a typist in a corn-factor's office but, as a disreputable sheriff's man used to come every other day to the office, asking to be allowed to say a word to his daughter, she had taken her daughter home again and set her to do housework. As Polly was very lively the intention was to give her the run of the young men. Besides, young men like to feel that there is a young woman not very far away. Polly, of course, flirted with the young men but Mrs Mooney, who was a shrewd judge, knew that the young men were only passing the time away: none of them meant business. Things went on so for a long time and Mrs Mooney began to think of sending Polly back to typewriting when she noticed that something was going on between Polly and one of the young men. She watched the pair and kept her own counsel.

Polly knew that she was being watched, but still her mother's persistent silence could not be misunderstood. There had been no open complicity between mother and daughter, no open understanding but, though people in the house began to talk of the affair, still Mrs Mooney did not intervene. Polly began to grow a little strange in her manner and the young man was evidently perturbed. At last, when she judged it to be the right moment, Mrs Mooney intervened. She dealt with moral problems as a cleaver deals with meat: and in this case she had made up her mind.

It was a bright Sunday morning of early summer, promising heat, but with a fresh breeze blowing. All the windows of the boarding house were open and the lace curtains ballooned gently towards the street beneath the raised sashes. The belfry of George's Church sent out constant peals and worshippers, singly or in groups, traversed the little circus before the church, revealing their purpose by their self-contained demeanour no less than by the little volumes in their gloved hands. Breakfast was over in the boarding house and the table of the breakfast-room was covered with plates on which lay yellow streaks of eggs with morsels of bacon-fat and bacon-rind. Mrs Mooney sat in the straw arm-chair and watched the servant Mary remove the breakfast things. She made Mary collect the crusts and pieces of broken bread to help to make Tuesday's bread-pudding. When the table was cleared, the broken bread collected, the sugar and butter safe under lock and key, she began to reconstruct the interview which she had had the night before with Polly. Things were as she had suspected: she had been frank in her questions and Polly had been frank in her answers. Both had been somewhat awkward, of course. She had been made awkward by her not wishing to receive the news in too cavalier a fashion or to seem to have connived and Polly had been made awkward not merely because allusions of that kind always made her awkward but also because she did not wish it to be thought that in her wise innocence she had divined the intention behind her mother's tolerance.

Mrs Mooney glanced instinctively at the little gilt clock on the mantelpiece as soon as she had become aware through her revery that the bells of George's Church had stopped ringing. It was seventeen minutes past eleven: she would have lots of time to have the matter out with Mr Doran and then catch short twelve at Marlborough Street. She was sure she would win. To begin with she had all the weight of social opinion on her side: she was an outraged mother. She had allowed him to live beneath her roof, assuming that he was a man of honour, and he had simply abused her hospitality. He was thirty-four or thirty-five years of age, so that youth could not be pleaded as his excuse; nor could ignorance be his excuse since he was a man who had seen something of the world. He had simply taken advantage of Polly's youth and inexperience: that was evident. The question was: What reparation would he make? There must be reparation made in such cases. It is all very well for the man: he can go his ways as if nothing had happened, having had his moment of pleasure, but the girl has to bear the brunt. Some mothers would be content to patch up such an affair for a sum of money; she had known cases of it. But she would not do so. For her only one reparation could make up for the loss of her daughter's honour: marriage.

She counted all her cards again before sending Mary up to Mr Doran's room to say that she wished to speak with him. She felt sure she would win. He was a serious young man, not rakish or loud-voiced like the others. If it had been Mr Sheridan or Mr Meade or Bantam Lyons her task would have been much harder. She did not think he would face publicity. All the lodgers in the house knew something of the affair; details had been invented by some. Besides, he had been employed for thirteen years in a great Catholic wine-merchant's office and publicity would mean for him, perhaps, the loss of his sit. Whereas if he agreed all might be well. She knew he had a good screw for one thing and she suspected he had a bit of stuff put by.

Nearly the half-hour! She stood up and surveyed herself in the pier-glass. The decisive expression of her great florid face satisfied her and she thought of some mothers she knew who could not get their daughters off their hands.

Mr Doran was very anxious indeed this Sunday morning. He had made two attempts to shave but his hand had been so unsteady that he had been obliged to desist. Three days' reddish beard fringed his jaws and every two or three minutes a mist gathered on his glasses so that he had to take them off and polish them with his pocket-handkerchief. The recollection of his confession of the night before was a cause of acute pain to him; the priest had drawn out every ridiculous detail of the affair and in the end had so magnified his sin that he was almost thankful at being afforded a loophole of reparation. The harm was done. What could he do now but marry her or run away? He could not brazen it out. The affair would be sure to be talked of and his employer would be certain to hear of it. Dublin is such a small city: everyone knows everyone else's business. He felt his heart leap warmly in his throat as he heard in his excited imagination old Mr Leonard calling out in his rasping voice: *Send Mr Doran here, please.*

All his long years of service gone for nothing! All his industry and diligence thrown away! As a young man he had sown his wild oats, of course; he had boasted of his free-thinking and denied the existence of God to his companions in public-houses. But that was all passed and done with ... nearly. He still bought a copy of *Reynolds's Newspaper* every week but he attended to his religious duties and for nine-tenths of the year lived a regular life. He had money enough to settle down on; it was not that. But the family would look down on her. First of all there was her disreputable father and then her mother's boarding house was beginning to get a certain fame. He had a notion that he was being had. He could imagine his friends talking of the affair and laughing. She *was* a little vulgar; sometimes she said *I seen* and *If I had've known*. But what would grammar matter if he really loved her? He could not make up his mind whether to like her or despise her for what she had done. Of course, he had done it too. His instinct urged him to remain free, not to marry. Once you are married you are done for, it said.

While he was sitting helplessly on the side of the bed in shirt and trousers she tapped lightly at his door and entered. She told him all, that she had made a clean breast of it to her mother and that her mother would speak with him that morning. She cried and threw her arms round his neck, saying:

– O, Bob! Bob! What am I to do? What am I to do at all? She would put an end to herself, she said.

He comforted her feebly, telling her not to cry, that it would be all right, never fear. He felt against his shirt the agitation of her bosom.

It was not altogether his fault that it had happened. He remembered well, with the curious patient memory of the celibate, the first casual caresses her dress, her breath, her fingers had given him. Then late one night as he was undressing for bed she had tapped at his door, timidly. She wanted to relight her candle at his for hers had been blown out by a gust. It was her bath night. She wore a loose open combing-jacket of printed flannel. Her white instep shone in the opening of her furry slippers and the blood glowed warmly behind her perfumed skin. From her hands and wrists too as she lit and steadied her candle a faint perfume arose.

On nights when he came in very late it was she who warmed up his dinner. He scarcely knew what he was eating, feeling her beside him alone, at night, in the sleeping house. And her thoughtfulness! If the night was anyway cold or wet or windy there was sure to be a little tumbler of punch ready for him. Perhaps they could be happy together ...

They used to go upstairs together on tiptoe, each with a candle, and on the third landing exchange reluctant goodnights. They used to kiss. He remembered well her eyes, the touch of her hand and his delirium ...

But delirium passes. He echoed her phrase, applying it to himself: *What am I to do?*

The instinct of the celibate warned him to hold back. But the sin was there; even his sense of honour told him that reparation must be made for such a sin.

While he was sitting with her on the side of the bed Mary came to the door and said that the missus wanted to see him in the parlour. He stood up to put on his coat and waistcoat, more helpless than ever. When he was dressed he went over to her to comfort her. It would be all right, never fear. He left her crying on the bed and moaning softly: *O my God!*

Going down the stairs his glasses became so dimmed with moisture that he had to take them off and polish them. He longed to ascend through the roof and fly away to another country where he would never hear again of his trouble, and yet a force pushed him downstairs step by step. The implacable faces of his employer and of the Madam stared upon his discomfiture. On the last flight of stairs he passed Jack Mooney who was coming up from the pantry nursing two bottles of *Bass*. They saluted coldly; and the lover's eyes rested for a second or two on a thick bulldog face and a pair of thick short arms. When he reached the foot of the staircase he glanced up and saw Jack regarding him from the door of the return-room.

Suddenly he remembered the night when one of the music hall *artistes*, a little blond Londoner, had made a rather free allusion to Polly. The reunion had been almost broken up on account of Jack's violence. Everyone tried to quiet him. The music-hall *artiste*, a little paler than usual, kept smiling and saying that there was no harm meant: but Jack kept shouting at him that if any fellow tried that sort of a game on with *his* sister he'd bloody well put his teeth down his throat, so he would.

...

Polly sat for a little time on the side of the bed, crying. Then she dried her eyes and went over to the looking-glass. She dipped the end of the towel in the water-jug and refreshed her eyes with the cool water. She looked at herself in profile and readjusted a hairpin above her ear. Then she went back to the bed again and sat at the foot. She regarded the pillows for a long time and the sight of them awakened in her mind secret amiable memories. She rested the nape of her neck against the cool iron bed-rail and fell into a revery. There was no longer any perturbation visible on her face. She waited on patiently, almost cheerfully, without alarm, her memories gradually giving place to hopes and visions of the future. Her hopes and visions were so intricate that she no longer saw the white pillows on which her gaze was fixed or remembered that she was waiting for anything.

At last she heard her mother calling. She started to her feet and ran to the banisters.

– Polly! Polly!

– Yes, mamma?

– Come down, dear. Mr Doran wants to speak to you.

Then she remembered what she had been waiting for.

Repr. from: James Joyce, *Dubliners,* A Bantam Classic, New York / Toronto / London / Sydney / Auckland 1990, pp. 45–51.

Vocabulary

to take the pledge to abstain from alcoholic drink – *pink-veined* with pink-coloured veins – *chummy* friendly – *a likely horse* a horse that will probably win a race – *a likely artiste* an artiste worth watching – *mit* boxing glove – *to oblige* here: to sing or play songs – *to vamp accompaniments* to improvise a musical accompaniment to a song or dance – *corn-factor* corn-trader – *to keep one's own counsel* to keep one's opinions or intentions secret – *sash* sash window (one that slides up and down) – *to connive* to work together secretly (for some wrong or illegal purpose) – *to have the matter out* to discuss the matter – *rakish* dissolute, evil – *sit* job – *screw* (BE sl) amount of salary or wages – *stuff* here: money – *pier-glass* large, long mirror – *loophole* way of escape – *to brazen it out* to behave as if one has nothing to be ashamed of – *to sow one's wild oats* to lead a life of pleasure and gaiety while young before settling down seriously – *missus* mistress – *discomfiture* confusion – *Bass* a brand of beer – *nape* back of the neck – *banisters* upright supports with a bar along the top guarding the open side of a stairway

Assignments

1. Describe the three main characters in the story and their relations with each other!
2. What narrative means are used to give characterizations of Mrs Mooney, Mr Doran and Polly?
3. Describe and discuss the different ideas and vocabulary of Mrs Mooney's and Mr Doran's reflections concerning the love-affair!
4. Why does Mrs Mooney regard *social opinion* and *publicity* as her allies in the affair? What does this attitude show?
5. Try to explain the discrepancy between Polly's remark that she would commit suicide and her oblivion at the end of the story!
6. It is Polly who asks the question: "What am I to do?" This question applies to Mr Doran's situation, too. Why does he not ask it?
7. The crucial interviews between Mrs Mooney and her daughter and Mrs Mooney and Mr Doran do not appear in the text. What might be the significance of these omissions?

James Joyce
"My intention was to write a chapter of the moral history of my country and I chose Dublin for the scene because that city seemed to me the centre of paralysis."

Richard Ellmann (ed.), *Selected Letters of James Joyce,* Faber and Faber, London 1975, p. 83.

"The most frequent form of paralysis is captivity, both imposed by the deadening environment and produced by the characters' own moral weaknesses ... in "The Boarding House" Bob Doran longs 'to ascend through the roof and fly away to another country', but is instead trapped into marriage."

Peter K. Garrett (ed.), *Twentieth Century Interpretations of Dubliners,* Prentice-Hall, A Spectrum Book, Englewood Cliffs, New Jersey 1968, p. 4.

"Occasionally we do find traditional, omniscient commentary, such as the observation in "The Boarding House" that Mrs Mooney, the butcher's wife, 'dealt with moral problems as a cleaver deals with meat', but such epigrammatic, authorial analysis soon yields to a style which reflects the vulgar, mercenary mind of "the Madam" herself: 'She knew he had a good screw for one thing and she suspected he had a bit of stuff put by'. Joyce's style scrupulously registers the meanness of his subject."

Ibid., p. 14.

The last two sentences of "The Boarding House" read in an earlier version as follows:
"She remembered now what she had been waiting for. This was it."

"This is the precarious instant of focus. The story is at that point of balance where the smallest touch will send its extremes into oscillation. In these final lines the exact mode of understanding that exists between Polly and her mother is to be revealed, and Polly herself is to be exactly placed on the scale between narcissism and acumen. 'This was it' implies too crude a prearrangement, and too explicit an awareness of her own feelings. For the printed text, Joyce deleted it, and made the last line read simply, 'Then she remembered what she had been waiting for'."

Hugh Kenner, *Dubliners,* in: Peter K. Garrett (ed.), op. cit., p. 39.

3 A Short Story of Unfamiliar Perspectives

The Voyage

KATHERINE MANSFIELD (1888–1923)

The Picton boat was due to leave at half past eleven. It was a beautiful night, mild, starry, only when they got out of the cab and started to walk down the Old Wharf that jutted out into the harbour, a faint wind blowing off the water ruffled under Fenella's hat, and she put up her hand to keep it on. It was dark on the Old Wharf, very dark; the wool sheds, the cattle trucks, the cranes standing up so high, the little squat railway engine, all seemed carved out of solid darkness. Here and there on a rounded wood-pile, that was like the stalk of a huge black mushroom, there hung a lantern, but it seemed afraid to unfurl its timid, quivering light in all that blackness; it burned softly, as if for itself.

Fenella's father pushed on with quick, nervous strides. Beside him her grandma bustled along in her crackling black ulster; they went so fast that she had now and again to give an undignified little skip to keep up with them. As well as her luggage strapped into a neat sausage, Fenella carried clasped to her her grandma's umbrella, and the handle, which was a swan's head, kept giving her shoulder a sharp little peck as if it too wanted her to hurry ... Men, their caps pulled down, their collars turned up, swung by; a few women all muffled scurried along; and one tiny boy, only his little black arms and legs showing out of a white woolly shawl, was jerked along angrily between his father and mother; he looked like a baby fly that had fallen into the cream.

Then suddenly, so suddenly that Fenella and her grandma both leapt, there sounded from behind the largest wool shed, that had a trail of smoke hanging over it, *Mia-oo-oo-O-O!*

"First whistle," said her father briefly, and at that moment they came in sight of the Picton boat. Lying beside the dark wharf, all strung, all beaded with round golden lights, the Picton boat looked as if she was more ready to sail among stars than out into the cold sea. People pressed along the gangway. First went her grandma, then her father, then Fenella. There was a high step down on to the deck, and an old sailor in a jersey standing by gave her his dry, hard hand. They were there; they stepped out of the way of the hurrying people, and standing under a little iron stairway that led to the upper deck they began to say goodbye.

"There, mother, there's your luggage!" said Fenella's father, giving Grandma another strapped-up sausage.

"Thank you, Frank."

"And you've got your cabin tickets safe?"

"Yes, dear."

"And your other tickets?"

Grandma felt for them inside her glove and showed him the tips.

"That's right."

He sounded stern, but Fenella, eagerly watching him, saw that he looked tired and sad. *Mia-oo-oo-O-O!* The second whistle blared just above their heads, and a voice like a cry shouted, "Any more for the gangway?"

"You'll give my love to Father," Fenella saw her father's lips say. And her grandma, very agitated, answered, "Of course I will, dear. Go now. You'll be left. Go now, Frank. Go now."

"It's all right, Mother. I've got another three minutes." To her surprise Fenella saw her father take off his hat. He clasped Grandma in his arms and pressed her to him. "God bless you, Mother!" she heard him say.

And Grandma put her hand, with the black thread glove that was worn through on her ring finger, against his cheek, and she sobbed, "God bless you, my own brave son!"

This was so awful that Fenella quickly turned her back on them, swallowed once, twice, and frowned terribly at a little green star on a mast head. But she had to turn round again; her father was going.

"Good-bye, Fenella. Be a good girl." His cold wet moustache brushed her cheek. But Fenella caught hold of the lapels of his coat.

"How long am I going to stay?" she whispered anxiously. He wouldn't look at her. He shook her off gently, and gently said, "We'll see about that. Here! Where's your hand?" He pressed something into her palm. "Here's a shilling in case you should need it."

A shilling! She must be going away for ever! "Father!" cried Fenella. But he was gone. He was the last off the ship. The sailors put their shoulders to the gangway. A huge coil of dark rope went flying through the air and fell "thump" on the wharf. A bell rang; a whistle shrilled. Silently the dark wharf began to slip, to slide, to edge away from them. Now there was a rush of water between. Fenella strained to see with all her might. "Was that Father turning round?" – or waving? – or standing alone? – or walking off by himself? The strip of water grew broader, darker. Now the Picton boat began to swing round steady, pointing out to sea. It was no good looking any longer. There was nothing to be seen but a few lights, the face of the town clock hanging in the air, and more lights, little patches of them, on the dark hills.

The freshening wind tugged at Fenella's skirts; she went back to her grandma. To her relief Grandma seemed no longer sad. She had put the two sausages of luggage one on top of the other, and she was sitting on them, her hands folded, her head a little on one side. There was an intent, bright look on her face. Then Fenella saw that her lips were moving and guessed that she was praying. But the old woman gave her a bright nod as if to say the prayer was nearly over. She unclasped her hands, sighed, clasped them again, bent forward, and at last gave herself a soft shake.

“And now, child,” she said, fingering the bow of her bonnet-strings, “I think we ought to see about our cabins. Keep close to me, and mind you don't slip.”

“Yes, Grandma!”

“And be careful the umbrellas aren't caught in the stair rail. I saw a beautiful umbrella broken in half like that on my way over.”

“Yes, Grandma.”

Dark figures of men lounged against the rails. In the glow of their pipes a nose shone out, or the peak of a cap, or a pair of surprised-looking eyebrows. Fenella glanced up. High in the air, a little figure, his hand thrust in his short jacket pockets, stood staring out to sea. The ship rocked ever so little, and she thought the stars rocked too. And now a pale steward in a linen coat, holding a tray high in the palm of his hand, stepped out of a lighted doorway and skimmed past them. They went through that doorway. Carefully over the high brass-bound step on to the rubber mat and then down such a terribly steep flight of stairs that Grandma had to put both feet on each step, and Fenella clutched the clammy brass rail and forgot all about the swan-necked umbrella.

At the bottom Grandma stopped; Fenella was rather afraid she was going to pray again. But no, it was only to get out the cabin tickets. They were in the saloon. It was glaring bright and stifling; the air smelled of paint and burnt chop-bones and india-rubber. Fenella wished her grandma would go on, but the old woman was not to be hurried. An immense basket of ham sandwiches caught her eye. She went up to them and touched the top one delicately with her finger.

“How much are the sandwiches?” she asked.

“Tuppence!” bawled a rude steward, slamming down a knife and fork.

Grandma could hardly believe it.

“Twopence *each*?” she asked.

“That's right,” said the steward, and he winked at his companion.

Grandma made a small, astonished face. Then she whispered primly to Fenella. “What wickedness!” and they sailed out at the further door and along a passage that had cabins on either side. Such a very nice stewardess came to meet them. She was dressed all in blue, and her collar and cuffs were fastened with large brass buttons. She seemed to know Grandma well.

“Well, Mrs Crane,” said she, unlocking their washstand. “We've got you back again. It's not often you give yourself a cabin.”

“No,” said Grandma. “But this time my dear son's thoughtfulness –”

“I hope –” began the stewardess. Then she turned round and took a long mournful look at Grandma's blackness and at Fenella's black coat and skirt, black blouse, and hat with a crape rose.

Grandma nodded. “It was God's will,” said she.

The stewardess shut her lips and, taking a deep breath, she seemed to expand.

“What I always say is,” she said, as though it was her own discovery, “sooner or later each of us has to go, and that's a certingty.” She paused. “Now, can I bring you anything, Mrs Crane? A cup of tea? I know it's no good offering you a little something to keep the cold out."

Grandma shook her head. "Nothing, thank you. We've got a few wine biscuits, and Fenella has a very nice banana."

"Then I'll give you a look later on," said the stewardess, and she went out, shutting the door.

What a very small cabin it was! It was like being shut up in a box with Grandma. The dark round eye above the washstand gleamed at them dully. Fenella felt shy. She stood against the door, still clasping her luggage and the umbrella. Were they going to get undressed in here? Already her grandma had taken off her bonnet, and, rolling up the strings, she fixed each with a pin to the lining before she hung the bonnet up. Her white hair shone like silk; the little bun at the back was covered with a black net. Fenella hardly ever saw her grandma with her head uncovered; she looked strange.

"I shall put on the woollen fascinator your dear mother crocheted for me," said Grandma, and, unstrapping the sausage, she took it out and wound it round her head; the fringe of grey bobbles danced at her eyebrows as she smiled tenderly and mournfully at Fenella. Then she undid her bodice, and something under that, and something else underneath that. Then there seemed a short, sharp tussle, and Grandma flushed faintly. Snip! Snap! She had undone her stays. She breathed a sigh of relief, and sitting on the plush couch, she slowly and carefully pulled off her elastic-sided boots and stood them side by side.

By the time Fenella had taken off her coat and skirt and put on her flannel dressing-gown Grandma was quite ready.

"Must I take off my boots, Grandma? They're lace."

Grandma gave them a moment's deep consideration. "You'd feel a great deal more comfortable if you did, child," said she. She kissed Fenella. "Don't forget to say your prayers. Our dear Lord is with us when we are at sea even more than when we are on dry land. And because I am an experienced traveller," said Grandma briskly, "I shall take the upper berth."

"But, Grandma, however will you get up there?"

Three little spider-like steps were all Fenella saw. The old woman gave a small silent laugh before she mounted them nimbly, and she peered over the high bunk at the astonished Fenella.

"You didn't think your grandma could do that, did you?" said she. And as she sank back Fenella heard her light laugh again.

The hard square of brown soap would not lather, and the water in the bottle was like a kind of blue jelly. How hard it was, too, to turn down those stiff sheets; you simply had to tear your way in. If everything had been different, Fenella might have got the giggles ... At last she was inside, and while she lay there panting, there sounded from above a long, soft whispering, as though someone was gently, gently rustling among tissue paper to find something. It was Grandma saying her prayers ...

A long time passed. Then the stewardess came in; she trod softly and leaned her hand on Grandma's bunk.

"We're just entering the Straits," she said.

"Oh!"

"It's a fine night, but we're rather empty. We may pitch a little."

And indeed at that moment the Picton boat rose and rose and hung in the air just long enough to give a shiver before she swung down again, and there was the sound of heavy water slapping against her sides. Fenella remembered she had left that swan-necked umbrella standing up on the little couch. If it fell over, would it break? But Grandma remembered too, at the same time.

"I wonder if you'd mind, stewardess, laying down my umbrella," she whispered.

"Not at all, Mrs Crane." And the stewardess, coming back to Grandma, breathed, "Your little granddaughter's in such a beautiful sleep."

"God be praised for that!" said Grandma.

"Poor little motherless mite!" said the stewardess. And Grandma was still telling the stewardess all about what happened when Fenella fell asleep.

But she hadn't been asleep long enough to dream before she woke up again to see something waving in the air above her head. What was it? What could it be? It was a small grey foot. Now another joined it. They seemed to be feeling about for something; there came a sigh.

"I'm awake, Grandma," said Fenella.

"Oh, dear, am I near the ladder?" asked Grandma. "I thought it was this end."

"No, Grandma, it's the other. I'll put your foot on it. Are we there?" asked Fenella.

"In the harbour," said Grandma. "We must get up, child. You'd better have a biscuit to steady yourself before you move."

But Fenella had hopped out of her bunk. The lamp was still burning, but night was over, and it was cold. Peering through that round eye, she could see far off some rocks. Now they were scattered over with foam; now a gull flipped by; and now there came a long piece of real land.

"It's land, Grandma," said Fenella, wonderingly, as though they had been at sea for weeks together. She hugged herself; she stood on one leg and rubbed it with the toes of the other foot; she was trembling. Oh, it had all been so sad lately. Was it going to change? But all her Grandma said was, "Make haste, child. I should leave your nice banana for the stewardess as you haven't eaten it." And Fenella put on her black clothes again, and a button sprang off one of her gloves and rolled to where she couldn't reach it. They went up on deck.

But if it had been cold in the cabin, on deck it was like ice. The sun was not up yet, but the stars were dim, and the cold pale sky was the same colour as the cold pale sea. On the land a white mist rose and fell. Now they could see quite plainly dark bush. Even the shapes of the umbrella ferns showed, and those strange silvery withered trees that are like skeletons ... Now they could see the landing-stage and some little houses, pale too, clustered together, like shells on the lid of a box. The other passengers tramped up and down, but more slowly than they had the night before, and they looked gloomy.

And now the landing-stage came out to meet them. Slowly it swam towards the Picton boat, and a man holding a coil of rope, and a cart with a small drooping horse and another man sitting on the step, came too.

"It's Mr Penreddy, Fenella, come for us," said Grandma. She sounded pleased. Her white waxen cheeks were blue with cold, her chin trembled, and she had to keep wiping her eyes and her little pink nose.

"You've got my –"

"Yes, Grandma." Fenella showed it to her.

The rope came flying through the air, and "smack" it fell on to the deck. The gangway was lowered. Again Fenella followed her grandma on to the wharf over to the little cart, and a moment later they were bowling away. The hooves of the little horse drummed over the wooden piles, then sank softly into the sandy road. Not a soul was to be seen; there was not even a feather of smoke. The mist rose and fell, and the sea still sounded asleep as slowly it turned on the beach.

"I seen Mr Crane yestiddy," said Mr Penreddy. "He looked himself then. Missus knocked him up a batch of scones last week."

And now the little horse pulled up before one of the shell-like houses. They got down. Fenella put her hand on the gate, and the big, trembling dewdrops soaked through her glovetips. Up a little path of round white pebbles they went, with drenched sleeping flowers on either side. Grandma's delicate white picotees were so heavy with dew that they were fallen, but their sweet smell was part of the cold morning. The blinds were down in the little house; they mounted the steps on to the veranda. A pair of old bluchers was on one side of the door, and a large red water-can on the other.

"Tut! tut! Your grandpa," said Grandma. She turned the handle. Not a sound. She called, "Walter!" And immediately a deep voice that sounded half stifled called back, "Is that you, Mary?"

"Wait, dear," said Grandma. "Go in there." She pushed Fenella gently into a small dusky sitting-room.

On the table a white cat, that had been folded up like a camel, rose, stretched itself, yawned, and then sprang on to the tips of its toes. Fenella buried one cold little hand in the white, warm fur, and smiled timidly while she stroked and listened to Grandma's gentle voice and the rolling tones of Grandpa.

A door creaked. "Come in, dear." The old woman beckoned, Fenella followed. There, lying to one side of an immense bed, lay Grandpa. Just his head with a white tuft, and his rosy face and long silver beard showed over the quilt. He was like a very old wide-awake bird.

"Well, my girl!" said Grandpa. "Give us a kiss!" Fenella kissed him. "Ugh!" said Grandpa. "Her little nose is as cold as a button. What's that she's holding? Her grandma's umbrella?"

Fenella smiled again, and crooked the swan neck over the bed-rail. Above the bed there was a big text in a deep-black frame:

Lost! One Golden Hour
Set with Sixty Diamond Minutes.
No Reward Is Offered
For It Is GONE FOR EVER!

"Yer grandma painted that," said Grandpa. And he ruffled his white tuft and looked at Fenella so merrily she almost thought he winked at her.

Repr. from: Christopher Dolley (ed.), *The Penguin Book of English Short Stories,* Penguin Book, Harmondsworth 1978, pp. 224–232.

Vocabulary

to jut out to stand out – *to muffle* to wrap or cover for warmth or protection – *lapel* [lə'pel] part of the breast of a coat folded back – *tuppence* twopence – *cuff* end of a shirt sleeve at the wrist – *certingty* (corrupt pronunciation of) certainty – *bun* a hairknot – *to crochet* [krəʊ'ʃei] (= häkeln) – *tussle* hard struggle or fight – *straits* (pl. = Meerenge) – *mite* small child – yestiddy (corrupt pronunciation of) yesterday – *batch* group, number – *picotee* here: gilly-flower (= Levkoje) – *blucher* a kind of boots

Assignments

1. What information is the reader given at the beginning, and what is the reader not told?
2. The short story is largely told from Fenella's point of view. How does this become apparent, and what are the implications for the reader and the reading process?
3. How does the reader realize what events have preceded the point in time of the story?
4. What do the girl's animal associations (swan, spider) and her awareness of the *swan-necked umbrella* show?
5. Why does the description of surroundings play such an important part in this story?

"Some of the more obvious features of Katherine Mansfield's style can ... be seized: a swift fantasy which delights in simile and metaphor, witty in the linking of the unexpected alike, usually – though not always – enough controlled for the figures to serve the immediate purpose of the story; a sensibility almost morbidly alert to detail and to the evidence of the senses, to colour and shape, to the feel, smell, and sound of things."

D.M. Davin (ed.), *Katherine Mansfield: Selected Stories,* Oxford University Press, London / Oxford / New York 1969, p. XIV.

"What is to Fenella an adventure contains almost no action at all: her father puts a shilling into her hand (to her a great sum), and he brushes her cheek with his wet moustache, wet presumably with his tears. The grandmother takes Fenella on board, they descend some steps, the grandmother refuses to buy a sandwich because it costs two pence. "What wickedness!" she exclaims. Fenella is put to bed, and wakes next morning to be taken off the ferry and brought to her grandparents' house. That is all that happens in the story.

But something more happens in the reader. For even the youngest reader will be superior to Fenella by virtue of age and experience. This reader is obliged (and by virtue of his knowledge of the world enabled) to reinterpret the information which Fenella passes on to him. This information is not conveyed by what Fenella says. Primarily it is the grandmother that speaks, whereas Fenella thinks and feels. So their means of expression stand in complementary distribution to one another: although the grandmother does most of the talking, we know almost nothing of what goes on in her head; on the other hand, Fenella says almost nothing, although the story is largely a vehicle to convey her lively and individual impressions. The reader needs to interpret these impressions, for Fenella seems unaware of their significance – occasionally she is even mistaken about what she experiences – and neither she nor a narrator gives us a cogent commentary. The vehicles for conveying Fenella's sense of the world are her sense perceptions, similes and metaphors."

H. Bonheim, *Teaching Katherine Mansfield's "The Voyage": Metaphor Boxes,* LWU XX, 1987/1, Würzburg 1987, p. 99.

4 A Political Short Story

Brother

GRAHAM GREENE (1904–1991)

The Communists were the first to appear. They walked quickly, a group of about a dozen, up the boulevard which runs from Combat to Ménilmontant; a young man and a girl lagged a little way behind because the man's leg was hurt and the girl was helping him along. They looked impatient, harassed, hopeless, as if they were trying to catch a train which they knew already in their hearts they were too late to catch.

The proprietor of the café saw them coming when they were still a long way off; the lamps at that time were still alight (it was later that the bullets broke the bulbs and dropped darkness all over that quarter of Paris), and the group showed up plainly in the wide barren boulevard. Since sunset only one customer had entered the café, and very soon after sunset firing could be heard from the direction of Combat; the Métro station had closed hours ago. And yet something obstinate and undefeatable in the proprietor's character prevented him from putting up the shutters; it might have been avarice; he could not himself have told what it was as he pressed his broad yellow forehead against the glass and stared this way and that, up the boulevard and down the boulevard.

But when he saw the group and their air of hurry he began immediately to close his café. First he went and warned his only customer, who was practising billiard shots, walking round and round the table, frowning and stroking a thin moustache between shots, a little green in the face under the low diffused lights.

"The Reds are coming," the proprietor said, "you'd better be off. I'm putting up the shutters."

"Don't interrupt. They won't harm me," the customer said. "This is a tricky shot. Red's in baulk. Off the cushion. Screw on spot." He shot his ball straight into a pocket.

"I knew you couldn't do anything with that," the proprietor said, nodding his bald head. "You might just as well go home. Give me a hand with the shutters first. I've sent my wife away." The customer turned on him maliciously, rattling the cue between his fingers. "It was your talking that spoilt the shot. You've cause to be frightened, I dare say. But I'm a poor man. I'm safe. I'm not going to stir." He went across to his coat and took out a dry cigar. "Bring me a bock." He walked round the table on his toes and the balls clicked and the proprietor padded back into the bar, elderly and irritated. He did not fetch the beer but began to close the shutters; every move he made was slow and clumsy. Long before he had finished the group of Communists was outside.

He stopped what he was doing and watched them with furtive dislike. He was afraid that the rattle of the shutters would attract their attention. If I am very quiet and still, he thought, they may go on, and he remembered with malicious pleasure the police barricade across the Place de la République. That will finish them. In the meanwhile I must be very quiet, very still, and he felt a kind of warm satisfaction at the idea that worldly wisdom dictated the very attitude most suited to his nature. So he stared through the edge of a shutter, yellow, plump, cautious, hearing the billiard balls crackle in the other room, seeing the young man come limping up the pavement on the girl's arm, watching them stand and stare with dubious faces up the boulevard towards Combat.

But when they came into the café he was already behind the bar, smiling and bowing and missing nothing, noticing how they had divided forces, how six of them had begun to run back the way they had come.

The young man sat down in a dark corner above the cellar stairs and the others stood round the door waiting for something to happen. It gave the proprietor an odd feeling that they should stand there in his café not asking for a drink, knowing what to expect, when he, the owner, knew nothing, understood nothing. At last the girl said "Cognac," leaving the others and coming to the bar, but when he had poured it out for her, very careful to give a fair and not a generous measure, she simply took it to the man sitting in the dark and held it to his mouth.

"Three francs," the proprietor said. She took the glass and sipped a little and turned it so that the man's lips might touch the same spot. Then she knelt down and rested her forehead against the man's forehead and so they stayed.

"Three francs," the proprietor said, but he could not make his voice bold. The man was no longer visible in his corner, only the girl's back, thin and shabby in a black cotton frock, as she knelt, leaning forward to find the man's face. The proprietor was daunted by the four men at the door, by the knowledge that they were Reds who had no respect for private property, who would drink his wine and go away without paying, who would rape his women (but there was only his wife, and she was not there), who would rob his bank, who would murder him as soon as look at him. So with fear in his heart he gave up the three francs as lost rather than attract any more attention. Then the worst that he contemplated happened.

One of the men at the door came up to the bar and told him to pour out four glasses of cognac. "Yes, yes," the proprietor said, fumbling with the cork, praying secretly to the Virgin to send an angel, to send the police, to send the Gardes Mobiles, now, immediately, before the cork came out, "that will be twelve francs."

"Oh, no," the man said, "we are all comrades here. Share and share alike. Listen," he said, with earnest mockery, leaning across the bar, "all we have is yours just as much as it's ours, comrade," and stepping back a pace he presented himself to the proprietor, so that he might take his choice of stringy tie, of threadbare trousers, of starved features. “And it follows from that, comrade, that all you have is ours. So four cognacs. Share and share alike.”

“Of course,” the proprietor said, “I was only joking.” Then he stood with bottle poised, and the four glasses tingled upon the counter. “A machine-gun,” he said, “up by Combat,” and smiled to see how for the moment the men forgot their brandy as they fidgeted near the door. Very soon now, he thought, and I shall be quit of them.

“A machine-gun,” the Red said incredulously, “they’re using machine-guns?”

“Well,” the proprietor said, encouraged by this sign that the Gardes Mobiles were not very far away, “you can’t pretend that you aren’t armed yourselves.” He leant across the bar in a way that was almost paternal. “After all, you know, your ideas – they wouldn’t do in France. Free love.”

“Who’s talking of free love?” the Red said.

The proprietor shrugged and smiled and nodded at the corner. The girl knelt with her head on the man’s shoulder, her back to the room. They were quite silent and the glass of brandy stood on the floor beside them. The girl’s beret was pushed back on her head and one stocking was laddered and darned from knee to ankle.

“What, those two? They aren’t lovers.”

“I,” the proprietor said, “with my bourgeois notions would have thought ...”

“He’s her brother,” the Red said.

The men came clustering round the bar and laughed at him, but softly as if a sleeper or a sick person were in the house. All the time they were listening for something. Between their shoulders the proprietor could look out across the boulevard; he could see the corner of the Faubourg du Temple.

“What are you waiting for?”

“For friends,” the Red said. He made a gesture with open palm as if to say, You see, we share and share alike. We have no secrets.

Something moved at the corner of the Faubourg du Temple.

“Four more cognacs,” the Red said.

“What about those two?” the proprietor asked.

“Leave them alone. They’ll look after themselves. They’re tired.”

How tired they were. No walk up the boulevard from Ménilmontant could explain the tiredness. They seemed to have come farther and fared a great deal worse than their companions. They were more starved; they were infinitely more hopeless, sitting in their dark corner away from the friendly gossip, the amicable desperate voices which now confused the proprietor’s brain, until for a moment he believed himself to be a host entertaining friends.

He laughed and made a broad joke directed at the two of them; but they made no sign of understanding. Perhaps they were to be pitied, cut off from the camaraderie round the counter; perhaps they were to be envied for their deeper comradeship. The proprietor thought for no reason at all of the bare grey trees of the Tuileries like a series of exclamation marks drawn against the winter sky. Puzzled, disintegrated, with all his bearings lost, he stared out through the door towards the Faubourg.

It was as if they had not seen each other for a long while and would soon again be saying good-bye. Hardly aware of what he was doing he filled the four glasses with brandy. They stretched out worn blunted fingers for them.

"Wait," he said. "I've got something better than this"; then paused, conscious of what was happening across the boulevard. The lamplight splashed down on blue steel helmets; the Gardes Mobiles were lining out across the entrace to the Faubourg, and a machine-gun pointed directly at the café windows.

So, the proprietor thought, my prayers are answered. Now I must do my part, not look, not warn them, save myself. Have they covered the side door? I will get the other bottle. Real Napoleon brandy. Share and share alike.

He felt a curious lack of triumph as he opened the trap of the bar and came out. He tried not to walk quickly back towards the billiard room. Nothing that he did must warn these men; he tried to spur himself with the thought that every slow casual step he took was a blow for France, for his café, for his savings. He had to step over the girl's feet to pass her; she was asleep. He noted the sharp shoulder blades thrusting through the cotton, and raised his eyes and met her brother's, filled with pain and despair.

He stopped. He found he could not pass without a word. It was as if he needed to explain something, as if he belonged to the wrong party. With false bonhomie he waved the corkscrew he carried in the other's face. "Another cognac, eh?"

"It's no good talking to them," the Red said. "They're German. They don't understand a word."

"German?"

"That's what's wrong with his leg. A concentration camp."

The proprietor told himself that he must be quick, that he must put a door between him and them, that the end was very close, but he was bewildered by the hopelessness in the man's gaze. "What's he doing here?" Nobody answered him. It was as if his question were too foolish to need a reply. With his head sunk upon his breast the proprietor went past, and the girl slept on. He was like a stranger leaving a room where all the rest are friends. A German. They don't understand a word; and up, up through the heavy darkness of his mind, through the avarice and the dubious triumph, a few German words remembered from very old days climbed like spies into the light: a line from the *Lorelei* learnt at school, *Kamerad* with its war-time suggestion of fear and surrender, and oddly from nowhere the phrase *mein Bruder*. He opened the door of the billiard room and closed it behind him and softly turned the key.

"Spot in baulk," the customer explained and leant across the great green table, but while he took aim, wrinkling his narrow peevish eyes, the firing started. It came in two bursts with a rip of glass between. The girl cried out something, but it was not one of the words he knew. Then feet ran across the floor, the trap of the bar slammed.

The proprietor sat back against the table and listened and listened for any further sound; but silence came in under the door and silence through the keyhole.

"The cloth. My God, the cloth," the customer said, and the proprietor looked down at his own hand which was working the corkscrew into the table.

"Will this absurdity ever end?" the customer said. "I shall go home."

"Wait," the proprietor said. "Wait." He was listening to voices and footsteps in the other room. These were voices he did not recognize. Then a car drove up and presently drove away again. Somebody rattled the handle of the door.

"Who is it?" the proprietor called.

"Who are you? Open that door."

"Ah," the customer said with relief, "the police. Where was I now? Spot in baulk."

He began to chalk his cue. The proprietor opened the door. Yes, the Gardes Mobiles had arrived; he was safe again, though his windows were smashed. The Reds had vanished as if they had never been. He looked at the raised trap, at the smashed electric bulbs, at the broken bottle which dripped behind the bar. The café was full of men, and he remembered with odd relief that he had not had time to lock the side door.

"Are you the owner?" the officer asked. "A bock for each of these men and a cognac for myself. Be quick about it."

The proprietor calculated: "Nine francs fifty," and watched closely with bent head the coins rattle down upon the counter.

"You see," the officer said with significance, "we pay." He nodded towards the side door. "Those others: did they pay?"

No, the proprietor admitted, they had not paid, but as he counted the coins and slipped them into the till, he caught himself silently repeating the officer's order – "A bock for each of these men." Those others, he thought, one's got to say that for them, they weren't mean about the drink. It was four cognacs with them. But, of course, they did not pay. "And my windows," he complained aloud with sudden asperity, "what about my windows?"

"Never you mind," the officer said, "the government will pay. You have only to send in your bill. Hurry up now with my cognac. I have no time for gossip."

"You can see for yourself," the proprietor said, "how the bottles have been broken. Who will pay for that?"

"Everything will be paid for," the officer said.

"And now I must go to the cellar to fetch more."

He was angry at the reiteration of the word pay. They enter my café, he thought, they smash my windows, they order me about and think that all is well if they pay, pay, pay. It occurred to him that these men were intruders.

"Step to it," the officer said and turned and rebuked one of the men who had leant his rifle against the bar.

At the top of the cellar stairs the proprietor stopped. They were in darkness, but by the light from the bar he could just make out a body half-way down. He began to trem-

ble violently, and it was some seconds before he could strike a match. The young German lay head downwards, and the blood from his head had dropped on to the step below. His eyes were open and stared back at the proprietor with the old despairing expression of life. The proprietor would not believe that he was dead. "Kamerad," he said bending down, while the match singed his fingers and went out, trying to recall some phrase in German, but he could only remember, as he bent lower still, "mein Bruder." Then suddenly he turned and ran up the steps, waved the match-box in the officer's face, and called out in a low hysterical voice to him and his men and to the customer stooping under the low green shade, "Cochons. Cochons."
"What was that? What was that?" the officer exclaimed. "Did you say that he was your brother? It's impossible," and he frowned incredulously at the proprietor and rattled the coins in his pocket.

Repr. from: W.H. New/H.J. Rosengarten (eds.), *Modern Stories in English*, Copp Clark Publishing, Toronto 1977, pp. 108–114.

Vocabulary

baulk balk (= Quartier, Raum zwischen Bande und Begrenzungslinie beim Billard) – *cushion* (= Billardbande) – *screw* (Effet, Drehbewegung) – *frock* (oldfashioned) a woman's dress – *beret* ['bereɪ] flat, round cap – *ladder* (= Laufmasche) – *to lose one's bearings* to become confused – *asperity* harshness, severity – *cochon* (French) pig

Assignments

1. This story has an immediate beginning. How does this affect the reader?
2. How is the historical background conveyed to the reader?
3. What does the reader learn of the proprietor's political standpoint? What thoughts dominate his thinking? What does he mean by *bourgeois notions* and where can they be found in the text? In what way does he alter his first view?
4. Where do the author's sympathies lie? Where can tokens of his sympathy be detected in the text?
5. On what levels are the differences between the Reds and the police conveyed to the reader? How is the process of reading and understanding affected by the various levels and perspectives?
6. Greene once declared that it is the writer's task "to act as the devil's advocate, to elicit sympathy and a measure of understanding for those who lie outside the boundaries of State approval". In which way has he tried to fulfil this aim in the short story?

"This singularity of Greene's technique is attributable also to his recurring images and to the use of a diction alternately plain and rhetorical. Many of his effects are achieved by juxtaposing these two levels of diction. His use of imagery is more complex, for it contributes not only to the atmosphere, but informs character and theme as well; it is a means of communicating the emotion in an attempt to get at the truth."

R.O. Evans (ed.), *Graham Greene: Some Critical Considerations,* University of Kentucky Press, 1963, p. 64.

"... Greene's early fiction clearly belongs to the thirties. It presents a vivid picture of that period of economic depression and the threat of war ... The writers of the thirties characteristically confronted these circumstances by committing themselves to Marxist political solutions, ... Greene was a Party member for only four weeks in early youth, but the sympathies in his fiction go out to the underprivileged and the characters who are ideologically on the left ... his development of a fictional mode that was serious without being highbrow, using devices of journalism and the cinema, shot through with the sense of social and political crisis, were in accord with the literary program of Auden, Isherwood, and their associates."

D. Lodge, *Graham Greene,* Columbia University Press, New York/London 1966, pp. 16–17.

5 *An Allegory, a Fable and a Parable*

The Jewbird

BERNARD MALAMUD (1914–1986)

The window was open so the skinny bird flew in. Flappity-flap with its frazzled black wings. That's how it goes. It's open, you're in. Closed, you're out and that's your fate. The bird wearily flapped through the open window of Harry Cohen's top-floor apartment on First Avenue near the lower East River. On a rod on the wall hung an escaped canary cage, its door wide open, but this black-type long-beaked bird – its ruffled head and small eyes, crossed a little, making it look like a dissipated crow – landed if not smack on Cohen's thick lamb chop, at least on the table, close by. The frozen foods salesman was sitting at supper with his wife and young son on a hot August evening a year ago. Cohen, a heavy man with hairy chest and beefy shorts; Edie, in skinny yellow shorts and red halter; and their ten-year-old Morris (after her father) – Maurie, they called him, a nice kid though not overly bright – were all in the city after two weeks out, because Cohen's mother was dying. They had been enjoying Kingston, New York, but drove back when Mama got sick in her flat in the Bronx.

"Right on the table," said Cohen, putting down his beer glass and swatting at the bird. "Son of a bitch."

"Harry, take care with your language," Edie said, looking at Maurie, who watched every move.

The bird cawed hoarsely and with a flap of its bedraggled wings – feathers tufted this way and that – rose heavily to the top of the open kitchen door, where it perched staring down.

"Gevalt, a pogrom!"

"It's a talking bird," said Edie in astonishment.

"In Jewish," said Maurie.

"Wise guy," muttered Cohen. He gnawed on his chop, then put down the bone. "So if you can talk, say what's your business. What do you want here?"

"If you can't spare a lamb chop," said the bird, "I'll settle for a piece of herring with a crust of bread. You can't live on your nerve for ever."

"This ain't a restaurant," Cohen replied. "All I'm asking is what brings you to this address?"

"The window was open," the bird sighed; adding after a moment, "I'm running. I'm flying but I'm also running."

"From whom?" asked Edie with interest.

"Anti-Semeets."

"Anti-Semites?" they all said.

"That's from whom."

"What kind of anti-Semites bother a bird?" Edie asked.

"Any kind," said the bird, "also including eagles, vultures, and hawks. And once in a while some crows will take your eyes out."

"But aren't you a crow?"

"Me? I'm a Jewbird."

Cohen laughed heartily. "What do you mean by that?"

The bird began dovening. He prayed without Book or tallith, but with passion. Edie bowed her head though not Cohen. And Maurie rocked back and forth with the prayer, looking up with one wide-open eye.

When the prayer was done Cohen remarked, "No hat, no phylacteries?"

"I'm an old radical."

"You're sure you're not some kind of ghost or dybbuk?"

"Not a dybbuk," answered the bird, "though one of my relatives had such an experience once. It's all over now, thanks God. They freed her from a former lover, a crazy jealous man. She's now the mother of two wonderful children."

"Birds?" Cohen asked slyly.

"Why not?"

"What kind of birds?"

"Like me. Jewbirds."

Cohen tipped back in his chair and guffawed. "That's a big laugh. I've heard of a Jewfish but not a Jewbird."

"We're once removed." The bird rested on one skinny leg, then on the other. "Please, could you spare maybe a piece of herring with a small crust of bread?"

Edie got up from the table.

"What are you doing?" Cohen asked her.

"I'll clear the dishes."

Cohen turned to the bird. "So what's your name, if you don't mind saying?"

"Call me Schwartz."

"He might be an old Jew changed into a bird by somebody," said Edie, removing a plate.

"Are you?" asked Harry, lighting a cigar.

"Who knows?" answered Schwartz. "Does God tell us everything?"

Maurie got up on his chair. "What kind of herring?" he asked the bird in excitement.

"Get down, Maurie, or you'll fall," ordered Cohen.

"If you haven't got matjes, I'll take schmaltz," said Schwartz.

"All we have is marinated, with slices of onion – in a jar," said Edie.

"If you'll open for me the jar I'll eat marinated. Do you have also, if you don't mind, a piece of rye bread – the spitz?"

Edie thought she had.

"Feed him out on the balcony," Cohen said. He spoke to the bird. "After that take off."

Schwartz closed both bird eyes. "I'm tired and it's a long way."

"Which direction are you headed, north or south?"

Schwartz, barely lifting his wings, shrugged.

"You don't know where you're going?"

"Where there's charity I'll go."

"Let him stay, papa," said Maurie. "He's only a bird."

"So stay the night," Cohen said, "but no longer."

In the morning Cohen ordered the bird out of the house but Maurie cried, so Schwartz stayed for a while. Maurie was still on vacation from school and his friends were away. He was lonely and Edie enjoyed the fun he had, playing with the bird.

"He's no trouble at all," she told Cohen, "and besides his appetite is very small."

"What'll you do when he makes dirty?"

"He flies across the street in a tree when he makes dirty, and if nobody passes below, who notices?"

"So all right," said Cohen, "but I'm dead set against it. I warn you he ain't gonna stay here long."

"What have you got against the poor bird?"

"Poor bird, my ass. He's a foxy bastard. He thinks he's a Jew."

"What difference does it make what he thinks?"

"A Jewbird, what a chuzpah. One false move and he's out on his drumsticks."

At Cohen's insistence Schwartz lived out on the balcony in a new wooden birdhouse Edie had bought him.

"With many thanks," said Schwartz, "though I would rather have a human roof over my head. You know how it is at my age. I like the warm, the windows, the smell of cooking. I would also be glad to see once in a while the *Jewish Morning Journal* and have now and then a schnapps because it helps my breathing, thanks God. But whatever you give me, you won't hear complaints."

However, when Cohen brought home a bird feeder full of dried corn, Schwartz said, "Impossible."

Cohen was annoyed. "What's the matter, crosseyes, is your life getting too good for you? Are you forgetting what it means to be migratory? I'll bet a helluva lot of crows you happen to be acquainted with, Jews or otherwise, would give their eyeteeth to eat this corn."

Schwartz did not answer. What can you say to a grubber yung?

"Not for my digestion," he later explained to Edie. "Cramps. Herring is better even if it makes you thirsty. At least rainwater don't cost anything." He laughed sadly in breathy caws.

And herring, thanks to Edie, who knew where to shop, was what Schwartz got, with an occasional piece of potato pancake, and even a bit of soupmeat when Cohen wasn't looking.

When school began in September, before Cohen would once again suggest giving the bird the boot, Edie prevailed on him to wait a little while until Maurie adjusted.

"To deprive him right now might hurt his school work, and you know what trouble we had last year."

"So okay, but sooner or later the bird goes. That I promise you."

Schwartz, though nobody had asked him, took on full responsibility for Maurie's performance in school. In return for favours granted, when he was let in for an hour or two at night, he spent most of his time overseeing the boy's lessons. He sat on top of the dresser near Maurie's desk as he laboriously wrote out his homework. Maurie was a restless type and Schwartz gently kept him to his studies. He also listened to him practise his screechy violin, taking a few minutes off now and then to rest his ears in the bathroom. And they afterwards played dominoes. The boy was an indifferent checkers player and it was impossible to teach him chess. When he was sick, Schwartz read him comic books though he personally disliked them. But Maurie's work improved in school and even his violin teacher admitted his playing was better. Edie gave Schwartz credit for these improvements though the bird pooh-poohed them.

Yet he was proud there was nothing lower than C minuses on Maurie's report card, and on Edie's insistence celebrated with a little schnapps.

"If he keeps up like this," Cohen said, "I'll get him in an Ivy League college for sure."

"Oh I hope so," sighed Edie.

But Schwartz shook his head. "He's a good boy – you don't have to worry. He won't be a shicker or a wifebeater, God forbid, but a scholar he'll never be, if you know what I mean, although maybe a good mechanic. It's no disgrace in these times."

"If I were you," Cohen said, angered, "I'd keep my big snoot out of other people's private business."

"Harry, please," said Edie.

"My goddamn patience is wearing out. That crosseyes butts into everything."

Though he wasn't exactly a welcome guest in the house, Schwartz gained a few ounces although he did not improve in appearance. He looked bedraggled as ever, his feathers unkempt, as though he had just flown out of a snowstorm. He spent, he admitted, little time taking care of himself. Too much to think about. "Also outside plumbing," he told Edie. Still there was more glow to his eyes so that though Cohen went on calling him crosseyes he said it less emphatically.

Liking his situation, Schwartz tried tactfully to stay out of Cohen's way, but one night when Edie was at the movies and Maurie was taking a hot shower, the frozen foods salesman began a quarrel with the bird.

"For Christ sake, why don't you wash yourself sometimes? Why must you always stink like a dead fish?"

"Mr Cohen, if you'll pardon me, if somebody eats garlic he will smell from garlic. I eat herring three times a day. Feed me flowers and I will smell like flowers."

"Who's obligated to feed you anything at all? You're lucky to get herring."

"Excuse me, I'm not complaining," said the bird. "You're complaining."

"What's more," said Cohen, "even from out on the balcony I can hear you snoring away like a pig. It keeps me awake at night."

"Snoring," said Schwartz, "isn't a crime, thanks God."

"All in all you are a goddamn pest and free loader. Next thing you'll want to sleep in bed next to my wife."

"Mr Cohen," said Schwartz, "on this, rest assured. A bird is a bird."

"So you say, but how do I know you're a bird and not some kind of a goddamn devil?"

"If I was a devil you would know already. And I don't mean because your son's good marks."

"Shut up, you bastard bird," shouted Cohen.

"Grubber yung," cawed Schwartz, rising to the tips of his talons, his long wings outstretched.

Cohen was about to lunge for the bird's scrawny neck but Maurie came out of the bathroom, and for the rest of the evening until Schwartz's bedtime on the balcony, there was pretended peace.

But the quarrel had deeply disturbed Schwartz and he slept badly. His snoring woke him, and awake, he was fearful of what would become of him. Wanting to stay out of Cohen's way, he kept to the birdhouse as much as possible. Cramped by it, he paced back and forth on the balcony ledge, or sat on the birdhouse roof, staring into space. In the evenings, while overseeing Maurie's lessons, he often fell asleep. Awakening, he nervously hopped around exploring the four corners of the room. He spent much time in Maurie's closet, and carefully examined his bureau drawers when they were left open. And once when he found a large paper bag on the floor, Schwartz poked his way into it to investigate what possibilities were. The boy was amused to see the bird in the paper bag.

"He wants to build a nest," he said to his mother.

Edie, sensing Schwartz's unhappiness, spoke to him quietly.

"Maybe if you did some of the things my husband wants you, you would get along better with him."

"Give me a for instance," Schwartz said.

"Like take a bath, for instance."

"I'm too old for baths," said the bird. "My feathers fall out without baths."

"He says you have a bad smell."

"Everybody smells. Some people smell because of their thoughts or because who they are. My bad smell comes from the food I eat. What does his comes from?"

"I better not ask him or it might make him mad," said Edie.

In late November Schwartz froze on the balcony in the fog and cold, and especially on rainy days he woke with stiff joints and could barely move his wings. Already he felt twinges of rheumatism. He would have liked to spend more time in the warm house, particularly when Maurie was in school and Cohen at work. But though Edie was good-hearted and might have sneaked him in in the morning, just to thaw out, he was afraid to ask her. In the meantime Cohen, who had been reading articles about the migration of birds, came out on the balcony one night after work when Edie was in the kitchen preparing pot roast, and peeking into the birdhouse, warned Schwartz to be on his way soon if he knew what was good for him. "Time to hit the flyways."

"Mr Cohen, why do you hate me so much?" asked the bird. "What did I do to you?"

"Because you're an A-number-one trouble maker, that's why. What's more, whoever heard of a Jewbird? Now scat or it's open war."

But Schwartz stubbornly refused to depart so Cohen embarked on a campaign of harassing him, meanwhile hiding it from Edie and Maurie. Maurie hated violence and Cohen didn't want to leave a bad impression. He thought maybe if he played dirty tricks on the bird he would fly off without being physically kicked out. The vacation was over, let him make his easy living off the fat of somebody else's land. Cohen worried about the effect of the bird's departure on Maurie's schooling but decided to take the chance, first because the boy now seemed to have the knack of studying – give the black bird-bastard credit – and second, because Schwartz was driving him bats by being there always, even in his dreams.

The frozen foods salesman began his campaign against the bird by mixing watery cat food with the herring slices in Schwartz's dish. He also blew up and popped numerous paper bags outside the birdhouse as the bird slept, and when he had got Schwartz good and nervous, though not enough to leave, he brought a full-grown cat into the house, supposedly a gift for little Maurie, who had always wanted a pussy. The cat never stopped springing up at Schwartz whenever he saw him, one day managing to claw out several of his tailfeathers. And even at lesson time, when the cat was usually excluded from Maurie's room, though somehow or other he quickly found his way in at the end of the lesson, Schwartz was desperately fearful of his life and flew from pinnacle to pinnacle – light fixture to clothestree to door-top – in order to elude the beast's wet jaws.

Once when the bird complained to Edie how hazardous his existence was, she said, "Be patient, Mr Schwartz. When the cat gets to know you better he won't try to catch you any more."

"When he stops trying we will both be in Paradise," Schwartz answered. "Do me a favour and get rid of him. He makes my whole life worry. I'm losing feathers like a tree loses leaves."

"I'm awfully sorry but Maurie likes the pussy and sleeps with it."

What could Schwartz do? He worried but came to no decision, being afraid to leave. So he ate the herring garnished with cat food, tried hard not to hear the paper bags bursting like fire crackers outside the birdhouse at night, and lived terror-stricken closer to the ceiling than the floor, as the cat, his tail flicking, endlessly watched him.

Weeks went by. Then on the day after Cohen's mother had died in her flat in the Bronx, when Maurie came home with a zero on an arithmetic test, Cohen, enraged, waited until Edie had taken the boy to his violin lesson, then openly attacked the bird. He chased him with a broom on the balcony and Schwartz frantically flew back and forth, finally escaping into his birdhouse. Cohen triumphantly reached in, and grabbing both skinny legs, dragged the bird out, cawing loudly, his wings wildly beating. He whirled the bird around and around his head. But Schwartz, as he moved in circles, managed to swoop down and catch Cohen's nose in his beak, and hung on for dear life. Cohen cried out in great pain, punched the bird with his fist, and tugging at its legs with all his might, pulled his nose free. Again he swung the yawking Schwartz around until the bird grew dizzy, then with a furious heave, flung him into the night. Schwartz sank like stone into the street. Cohen then tossed the birdhouse and feeder after him, listening at the ledge until they crashed on the sidewalk below. For a full hour, broom in hand, his heart palpitating and nose throbbing with pain, Cohen waited for Schwartz to return but the broken-hearted bird didn't.

That's the end of that dirty bastard, the salesman thought and went in. Edie and Maurie had come home.

"Look," said Cohen, pointing to his bloody nose swollen three times its normal size, "what that sonofabitchy bird did. It's a permanent scar."

"Where is he now?" Edie asked, frightened.

"I threw him out and he flew away. Good riddance."

Nobody said no, though Edie touched a handkerchief to her eyes and Maurie rapidly tried the nine-times table and found he knew approximately half.

In the spring when the winter's snow had melted, the boy, moved by a memory, wandered in the neighbourhood, looking for Schwartz. He found a dead black bird in a small lot near the river, his two wings broken, neck twisted, and both bird-eyes plucked clean.

"Who did it to you, Mr Schwartz?" Maurie wept.

"Anti-Semeets," Edie said later.

James Cochrane (ed.), *The Penguin Book of American Short Stories,* Penguin Book, Harmondsworth 1979, pp. 391–399.

Vocabulary

to swat to hit with a flat object or the hand – *to caw* to make a rough, loud cry – *bedraggled* made wet and dirty by mud – *pogrom* [ˈpɒgrəm] organized killing and plunder of a group or class of people – *to doven* to utter Jewish prayers – *phylactery* (= Phylakterion, Gebetsriemen der Juden) – *dybbuk* (Yiddish) the soul of a dead person which possesses another human and lives through this person – *to guffaw* to give a noisy laugh – *to marinate* to marinade (to keep (meat or fish) in a marinade) – *chuzpah* (Yiddish) impertinence – *drumstick* lower part of the leg of a chicken or similar bird – *helluva* hell of a – *grubber yung* (Yiddish) coarse, impolite young man – *screechy* making a harsh piercing sound – *to pooh-pooh* to treat with contempt – *shicker* (Yiddish) drunkard – *garlic* (= Knoblauch) – *scat* to go away fast – *sonofabitchy* like a son of a bitch, i.e., s.o. one strongly dislikes – *good riddance* said rudely when one is glad that someone or something has gone

Assignments

1. *The Jewbird* is a difficult story to classify. The following questions deal with the issue of whether it should be seen as a fable, a parable, or an allegory. Look up the precise meanings of these terms first.
   Animals that can talk often appear in fables with a didactic aim. Can this story be regarded as a fable? If so, what is it out to teach us?
   Can this story be considered a parable? If so, where is its crucial point?
   Do you think this story is an allegory of the historical fate of the Jews? What is, in this connection, the importance of the fact that the Cohens are themselves Jews?

Is it possible to regard the story as a mixture of all three forms? How would this affect interpretation?

2. Describe the function of these sentences at the beginning: "That's how it goes. It's open, you're in. Closed, you're out and that's your fate."
3. Examine the role of clichés in the story.
4. Do you see any remnants of Nazi power in this story?
5. When Malamud received the National Book Award in 1959, he said in his speech: "The purpose of the writer is to keep civilization from destroying itself." Can this comment be used as a key in understanding *The Jewbird*?

6 An Ethnic Short Story

Advancing Luna and Ida B. Wells

ALICE WALKER (1944)

I met Luna the summer of 1965 in Atlanta where we both attended a political conference and rally. It was designed to give us the courage, as temporary civil rights workers, to penetrate the small hamlets farther South. I had taken a bus from Sarah Lawrence in New York and gone back to Georgia, my home state, to try my hand at registering voters. It had become obvious from the high spirits and sense of almost divine purpose exhibited by black people that a revolution was going on, and I did not intend to miss it. Especially not this summery, student studded version of it. And I thought it would be fun to spend some time on my own in the South.

Luna was sitting on the back of a pickup truck, waiting for someone to take her from Faith Baptist, where the rally was held, to whatever gracious black Negro home awaited her. I remember because someone who assumed I would also be traveling by pickup introduced us. I remember her face when I said, "No, no more back of pickup trucks for me. I know Atlanta well enough, I'll walk." She assumed of course (I guess) that I did not wish to ride beside her because she was white, and I was not curious enough about what she might have thought to explain it to her. And yet I was struck by her passivity, her *patience* as she sat on the truck alone and ignored, because someone had told her to wait there quietly until it was time to go.

This look of passively waiting for something changed very little over the years I knew her. It was only four or five years in all that I did. It seems longer, perhaps because we met at such an optimistic time in our lives. John Kennedy and Malcolm X had already been assassinated, but King had not been and Bobby Kennedy had not been. Then too, the lethal, bizarre elimination by death of this militant or that, exiles, flights to Cuba, shoot-outs between former Movement friends sundered forever by lies planted by the FBI, the gunning down of Mrs Martin Luther King, Sr., as she played the Lord's Prayer on the piano in her church (was her name Alberta?), were still in the happily unfathomable future.

We believed we could change America because we were young and bright and held ourselves *responsible* for changing it. We did not believe we would fail. That is what lent fervor (revivalist fervor, in fact; we would *revive* America!) to our songs, and lent sweetness to our friendships (in the beginning almost all interracial), and gave a wonderful fillip to our sex (which, too, in the beginning, was almost always interracial).

What first struck me about Luna when we later lived together was that she did not own a bra. This was curious to me, I suppose, because she also did not need one. Her chest was practically flat, her breasts like those of a child. Her face was round, and she suffered from acne. She carried with her always a tube of that "skin-colored" (if one's skin is pink or eggshell) medication designed to dry up pimples. At the oddest times – waiting for a light to change, listening to voter registration instructions, talking about her father's new girlfriend she would apply the stuff, holding in her other hand a small brass mirror the size of her thumb, which she also carried for just this purpose.

We were assigned to work together in a small, rigidly segregated South Georgia town whose city fathers, incongruously and years ago, had named Freehold, Georgia. Luna was slightly asthmatic and when overheated or nervous she breathed through her mouth. She wore her shoulder-length black hair with bangs to her eyebrows and the rest brushed behind her ears. Her eyes were brown and rather small. She was attractive, but just barely and with effort. Had she been the slightest bit overweight, for instance, she would have gone completely unnoticed, and would have faded into the background where, even in a revolution, fat people seem destined to go. I have a photograph of her sitting on the steps of a house in South Georgia. She is wearing tiny pearl earrings, a dark sleeveless shirt with Peter Pan collar, Bermuda shorts, and a pair of those East Indian sandals that seem to adhere to nothing but a big toe.

The summer of '65 was as hot as any other in that part of the South. There was an abundance of flies and mosquitoes. Everyone complained about the heat and the flies and the hard work, but Luna complained less than the rest of us. She walked ten miles a day with me up and down those straight Georgia highways, stopping at every house that looked black (one could always tell in 1965) and asking whether anyone needed help with learning how to vote. The simple mechanics: writing one's name, or making one's "X" in the proper column. And then, though we were required to walk, everywhere, we were empowered to offer prospective registrants a car in which they might safely ride down to the county courthouse. And later to the polling places. Luna, almost overcome by the heat, breathing through her mouth like a dog, her hair plastered with sweat to her head, kept looking straight ahead, and walking as if the walking itself was her reward.

I don't know if we accomplished much that summer. In retrospect, it seems not only minor, but irrelevant. A bunch of us, black and white, lived together. The black people who took us in were unfailingly hospitable and kind. I took them for granted in a way that now amazes me. I realize that at each and every house we visited I *assumed* hospitality, I *assumed* kindness. Luna was often startled by my "boldness". If we walked up to a secluded farmhouse and half a dozen dogs ran up barking around our heels and a large black man with a shotgun could be seen whistling to himself under a tree, she would become nervous. I, on the other hand, felt free to yell at this stranger's dogs, slap a couple of them on the nose, and call over to him about his hunting.

That month with Luna of approaching new black people every day taught me something about myself I had always suspected: I thought black people superior people. Not simply superior to white people, because even without thinking about it much, I assumed almost everyone was superior to them; but to everyone. Only white people, after all, would blow up a Sunday school class and grin for television over their "victory", *i.e.*, the death of four small black girls. Any atrocity, at any time, was expected from them. On the other hand, it never occurred to me that black people *could* treat Luna and me with anything but warmth and concern. Even their curiosity about the sudden influx into their midst of rather ignorant white and black Northerners was restrained and courteous. I was treated as a relative, Luna as a much welcomed guest.

Luna and I were taken in by a middle-aged couple and their young school-age daughter. The mother worked outside the house in a local canning factory, the father worked in the paper plant in nearby Augusta. Never did they speak of the danger they were in of losing their jobs over keeping us, and never did their small daughter show any fear that her house might be attacked by racists because we were there. Again, I did not expect this family to complain, no matter what happened to them because of us. Having understood the danger, they had assumed the risk. I did not think them particularly brave, merely typical.

I think Luna liked the smallness – only four rooms – of the house. It was in this house that she ridiculed her mother's lack of taste. Her yellow-and-mauve house in Cleveland, the eleven rooms, the heated garage, the new car every year, her father's inability to remain faithful to her mother, their divorce, the fight over the property, even more so than over the children. Her mother kept the house and the children. Her father kept the car and his new girlfriend, whom he wanted Luna to meet and "approve". I could hardly imagine anyone disliking her mother so much. Everything Luna hated in her she summed up in three words: *"yellow-and-mauve."*

I have a second photograph of Luna and a group of us being bullied by a Georgia state trooper. This member of Georgia's finest had followed us out into the deserted countryside to lecture us on how misplaced – in the South – was our energy, when "the Lord knew" the North (where he thought all of us lived, expressing disbelief that most of us were Georgians) was just as bad. (He had a point that I recognized even then, but it did not seem the point where we were.) Luna is looking up at him, her mouth slightly open as always, a somewhat dazed look on her face. I cannot detect fear on any of our faces, though we were all afraid. After all, 1965 was only a year after 1964 when three civil rights workers had been taken deep into a Mississippi forest by local officials and sadistically tortured and murdered. Luna almost always carried a flat black shoulder bag. She is standing with it against her side, her thumb in the strap.

At night we slept in the same bed. We talked about our schools, lovers, girlfriends we didn't understand or missed. She dreamed, she said, of going to Goa. I dreamed of going to Africa. My dream came true earlier than hers: an offer of a grant from an unsuspected source reached me one day as I was writing poems under a tree. I left Freehold, Georgia, in the middle of summer, without regrets, and flew from New York to London, to Cairo, to Kenya, and finally, Uganda, where I settled among black people with the same assumptions of welcome and kindness I had taken for granted in Georgia. I was taken on rides down the Nile as a matter of course, and accepted all invitations to dinner, where the best local dishes were superbly prepared in my honor. I became, in fact, a lost relative of the people, whose ancestors had foolishly strayed, long ago, to America.

I wrote to Luna at once.

But I did not see her again for almost a year. I had graduated from college, moved into a borrowed apartment in Brooklyn Heights, and was being evicted after a month. Luna, living then in a tenement on East Ninth Street, invited me to share her two-bedroom apartment. If I had seen the apartment before the day I moved in I might never have agreed to do so. Her building was between Avenues B and C and did not have a front door. Junkies, winos, and others often wandered in during the night (and occasionally during the day) to sleep underneath the stairs or to relieve themselves at the back of the first-floor hall.

Luna's apartment was on the third floor. Everything in it was painted white. The contrast between her three rooms and kitchen (with its red bathtub) and the grungy stairway was stunning. Her furniture consisted of two large brass beds inherited from a previous tenant and stripped of paint by Luna, and a long, high-backed church pew which she had managed somehow to bring up from the South. There was a simplicity about the small apartment that I liked. I also liked the notion of extreme contrast, and I do to this day. Outside our front window was the decaying neighborhood, as ugly and ill-lit as a battleground. (And allegedly as hostile, though somehow we were never threatened with bodily harm by the Hispanics who were our neighbors, and who seemed, more than anything, *bewildered* by the darkness and filth of their surroundings.) Inside was the church pew, as straight and spare as Abe Lincoln lying down, the white walls as spotless as a monastery's, and a small, unutterably pure patch of blue sky through the window of the back bedroom. (Luna did not believe in curtains, or couldn't afford them, and so we always undressed and bathed with the lights off and the rooms lit with candles, causing rather nun-shaped shadows to be cast on the walls by the long-sleeved high-necked nightgowns we both wore to bed.)

Over a period of weeks, our relationship, always marked by mutual respect, evolved into a warm and comfortable friendship which provided a stability and comfort we both needed at that time. I had taken a job at the Welfare Department during the day, and set up my typewriter permanently in the tiny living room for work after I got home. Luna worked in a kindergarten, and in the evenings taught herself Portuguese.

It was while we lived on East Ninth Street that she told me she had been raped during her summer in the South. It is hard for me, even now, to relate my feeling of horror and incredulity. This was some time before Eldridge Cleaver wrote of being a rapist/revolutionary; of "practicing" on black women before moving on to white. It was also, unless I'm mistaken, before LeRoi Jones (as he was then known; now of course Imamu Baraka, which has an even more presumptuous meaning than "the King") wrote his advice to young black male insurrectionaries (women were not told what to do with *their* rebelliousness): "Rape the white girls. Rape their fathers." It was clear that he meant this literally and also as: to rape a white girl *is* to rape her father. It was the misogynous cruelty of this latter meaning that was habitually lost on black men (on men in general, actually), but nearly always perceived and rejected by women of whatever color.

"Details?" I asked.

She shrugged. Gave his name. A name recently in the news, though in very small print.

He was not a Movement star or anyone you would know. We had met once, briefly. I had not liked him because he was coarse and spoke of black women as "our" women. (In the early Movement, it was pleasant to think of black men wanting to own us as a group; later it became clear that owning us meant exactly *that* to them.) He was physically unattractive, I had thought, with something of the hoodlum about him: a swaggering, unnecessarily mobile walk, small eyes, rough skin, a mouthful of wandering or absent teeth. He was, ironically, among the first persons to shout the slogan everyone later attributed solely to Stokeley Carmichael – Black Power! Stokeley was chosen as the originator of this idea by the media, because he was physically beautiful and photogenic and articulate. Even the name – Freddie Pye – was diminutive, I thought, in an age of giants.

"What did you do?"

"Nothing that required making a noise."

"Why didn't you scream?" I felt I would have screamed my head off.

"You know why."

I did. I had seen a photograph of Emmett Till's body just after it was pulled from the river. I had seen photographs of white folks standing in a circle roasting something that had talked to them in their own language before they tore out its tongue. I knew why, all right.

"What was he trying to prove?"

"I don't know. Do you?"

"Maybe you filled him with unendurable lust," I said.

"I don't think so," she said.

Suddenly I was embarrassed. Then angry. Very, very angry. *How dare she tell me this!* I thought.

Who knows what the black woman thinks of rape? Who has asked her? Who *cares*? Who has even properly acknowledged that *she* and not the white woman in this story is the most likely victim of rape? Whenever interracial rape is mentioned, a black woman's first thought is to protect the lives of her brothers, her father, her sons, her lover. A history of lynching has bred this reflex in her. I feel it as strongly as anyone. While writing a fictional account of such a rape in a novel, I read Ida B. Wells's autobiography three times, as a means of praying to her spirit to forgive me.

My prayer, as I turned the pages, went like this: *"Please forgive me. I am a writer."* (This self-revealing statement alone often seems to me sufficient reason to require perpetual forgiveness; since the writer is guilty not only of always wanting to know – like Eve – but also of trying – again like Eve – to find out.) *"I cannot write contrary to what life reveals to me. I wish to malign no one. But I must struggle to understand at least my own tangled emotions about interracial rape. I know, Ida B. Wells, you spent your whole life protecting, and trying to protect, black men accused of raping white women, who were lynched by white mobs, or threatened with it. You know, better than I ever will, what it means for a whole people to live under the terror of lynching. Under the slander that their men, where white women are concerned, are creatures of uncontrollable sexual lust. You made it so clear that the black men accused of rape in the past were innocent victims of white criminals that I grew up believing black men literally did not rape white women. At all. Ever. Now it would appear that some of them, the very twisted, the terribly ill, do. What would you have me write about them?"*

Her answer was: *"Write nothing. Nothing at all. It will be used against black men and therefore against all of us. Eldridge Cleaver and LeRoi Jones don't know who they're dealing with. But you remember. You are dealing with people who brought their children to witness the murder of black human beings, falsely accused of rape. People who handed out, as trophies, black fingers and toes. Deny! Deny! Deny!"*

And yet, I have pursued it, *"some black men themselves do not seem to know what the meaning or raping someone is. Some have admitted rape in order to denounce it, but others have accepted rape as a part of rebellion, of 'paying whitey back'. They have gloried in it."*

"They know nothing of America," she says. *"And neither, apparently, do you. No matter what you think you know, no matter what you feel about it, say nothing. And to your dying breath!"*

Which, to my mind, is virtually useless advice to give to a writer.

Freddie Pye was the kind of man I would not have looked at then, not even once. (Throughout that year I was more or less into exotica: white ethnics who knew languages were a peculiar weakness; a half-white hippie singer; also a large Chinese mathematician who was a marvelous dancer and who taught me to waltz.) There was no question of belief.

But, in retrospect, there was a momentary *suspension* of belief, a kind of *hope* that perhaps it had not really happened; that Luna had made up the rape, "as white women have been wont to do." I soon realized this was unlikely. I was the only person she had told.

She looked at me as if to say: "I'm glad *that* part of my life is over." We continued our usual routine. We saw every interminable, foreign, depressing, and poorly illuminated film ever made. We learned to eat brown rice and yogurt and to tolerate kasha and odd-tasting teas. My half-black hippie singer friend (now a well-known reggae singer who says he is from "de *I*-lands" and not Sheepshead Bay) was "into" tea and kasha and Chinese vegetables.

And yet the rape, the knowledge of the rape, out in the open, admitted, pondered over, was now between us. (And I began to think that perhaps – whether Luna had been raped or not – it had always been so; that her power over my life was exactly the power *her word on rape* had over the lives of black men, over *all* black men, whether they were guilty or not, and therefore over my whole people.)

Before she told me about the rape, I think we had assumed a lifelong friendship. The kind of friendship one dreams of having with a person one has known in adversity; under heat and mosquitoes and immaturity and the threat of death. We would each travel, we would write to each other from the three edges of the world.

We would continue to have an "international list" of lovers whose amorous talents or lack of talents we would continue (giggling into our dotage) to compare. Our friendship would survive everything, be truer than everything, endure even our respective marriages, children, husbands – assuming we *did*, out of desperation and boredom someday, marry, which did not seem a probability, exactly, but more in the area of an amusing idea.

But now there was a cooling off of our affection for each other. Luna was becoming mildly interested in drugs, because everyone we knew was. I was envious of the open-endedness of her life. The financial backing to it. When she left her job at the kindergarten because she was tired of working, her errant father immediately materialized. He took her to dine on scampi at an expensive restaurant, scolded her for living on East Ninth Street, and looked at me as if to say: "Living in a slum of this magnitude must surely have been your idea." As a cullud, of course.

For me there was the welfare department every day, attempting to get the necessary food and shelter to people who would always live amid the dirty streets I knew I must soon leave. I was, after all, a Sarah Lawrence girl "with talent". It would be absurd to rot away in a building that had no front door.

I slept late one Sunday morning with a painter I had met at the welfare department. A man who looked for all the world like Gene Autry, the singing cowboy, but who painted wonderful surrealist pictures of birds and ghouls and fruit with *teeth*. The night before, three of us – me, the painter, and "an old Navy buddy" who looked like his twin and who had just arrived in town – had got high on wine and grass.

That morning the Navy buddy snored outside the bedrooms like a puppy waiting for its master. Luna got up early, made an immense racket getting breakfast, scowled at me as I emerged from my room, and left the apartment, slamming the door so hard she damaged the lock. (Luna had made it a rule to date black men almost exclusively. My insistence on dating, as she termed it "anyone", was incomprehensible to her, since in a politically diseased society to “sleep with the enemy” was to become “infected” with the enemy’s “political germs”. There is more than a grain of truth in this, of course, but I was having too much fun to stare at it for long. Still, coming from Luna it was amusing, since she never took into account the risk her own black lovers ran by sleeping with “the white woman”, and she had apparently been convinced that a summer of relatively innocuous political work in the South had cured her of any racial, economic, or sexual political disease.)

Luna never told me what irked her so that Sunday morning, yet I remember it as the end of our relationship. It was not, as I at first feared, that she thought my bringing the two men to the apartment was inconsiderate. The way we lived allowed us to *be* inconsiderate from time to time. Our friends were varied, vital, and often strange. Her friends especially were deeper than they should have been into drugs.

The distance between us continued to grow. She talked more of going to Goa. My guilt over my dissolute if pleasurable existence coupled with my mounting hatred of welfare work, propelled me in two directions. South, or to West Africa. When the time came to choose, I discovered that *my* summer in the South had infected me with the need to return, to try to understand, and write about, the people I’d merely lived with before.

We never discussed the rape again. We never discussed, really, Freddie Pye or Luna’s remaining feelings about what had happened. One night, the last month we lived together, I noticed a man’s blue denim jacket thrown across the church pew. The next morning, out of Luna’s bedroom walked Freddie Pye. He barely spoke to me – possibly because as a black woman I was expected to be hostile toward his presence in a white woman’s bedroom. I was too surprised to exhibit hostility, however, which was only a part of what I felt, after all. He left.

Luna and I did not discuss this. It is odd, I think now, that we didn’t. It was as if he were never there; as if he and Luna had not shared the bedroom that night. A month later, Luna went alone to Goa, in her solitary way. She lived on an island and slept, she wrote, on the beach. She mentioned she’d found a lover there who protected her from the local beachcombers and pests.

Several years later, she came to visit me in the South and brought a lovely piece of pottery which my daughter much later dropped and broke, but which I glued back together in such a way that the flaw improves the beauty and fragility of the design.

Repr. from: M.H. Washington (ed.), *Midnight Birds,*
Anchor Book, Anchor Press/Doubleday, New York 1980, pp. 63–75.

Vocabulary

student-studded with many students – *lethal* causing death – *fillip* stimulus – *bra* a woman's close-fitting undergarment worn to support the breasts – *acne* ['ækni] skin disease in which the face is covered with pimples – *canning factory* (= Konservenfabrik) – *mauve* [məʊv] pale purple – *trooper* soldier – *Goa* region on the western coast of India – *tenement* large building divided into flats; found in poorer areas of a city – *junky* (sl) a heroin addict – *wino* (sl) someone who habitually gets drunk on wine – *grungy* (AE sl) run-down, dirty – *pew* bench in a church – *insurrectionary* man in open resistance to the government – *misogynous* [mɪ'sɒdʒənəs] woman-hating –*hoodlum* (sl) a violant or criminal person – *slander* ['sla:ndə] false statement that damages a person's reputation – *kasha* (= Buchweizenbrei) – *reggae* music from Jamaica – *cullud* (suggesting corrupt pronunciation) a coloured person – *ghoul* [gu:l] a monster eating living or dead humans – *racket* loud noise – *denim* (= grober Baumwolldrillich)

Assignments

1. What is the story's political background and how is it presented?
2. Examine the narrator's point of view. Why is it so important in this story?
3. Describe and discuss the different meanings of *rape* in this story.
4. How does Alice Walker show that race relations are both important and difficult?
5. Examine the symbols in the story and their use.
6. Analyse the role of prejudice in the story.
7. Alice Walker wrote postscripts to this story, trying to account for the inexplicable occurrence. Write a postscript of your own, explaining Luna's behaviour.

7 Suggestions for Project Work

1. Study the short story *The Boarding House* carefully and compare its subject and structure with other short stories in Joyce's *Dubliners* (especially *The Sisters, Araby, Eveline, Two Gallants, A Little Cloud* and *The Dead*).
What position and function does *The Boarding House* have in the whole collection?

2. Examine the themes of love and alienation as they relate to *The Boarding House* in particular and *Dubliners* in general. Describe the overall structure of the collection of stories.

3. Compare the story *The Voyage* with others in Mansfield's collection *The Garden Party.* Analyse the similarities and differences. What do these tell us about Mansfield's art?

4. Compare the points of view in *The Voyage* and short stories written at about the same time by Virginia Woolf, such as *Kew Gardens* or *The Mark on the Wall.* What different problems are posed by Katherine Mansfield and Virgina Woolf? What effects do the unusual points of view in these stories have on the reading process?

5. Examine Greene's story *Brother* as a political and historical document. What does it show, and what is it unable to show?

6. Compare the theme and structure of *Brother* with that of Greene's most famous novel, *The Power and the Glory* (1940). What similarities and differences do you see? Which of the differences may be due to the different subjects and which to the different literary genres? How are the different political standpoints shown in the two texts?

7. Find other short stories or novels by US Jewish writers (such as Saul Bellow or Philip Roth) and examine the ways in which Jewish and minority problems are approached.

8. Compare two texts which appear to have little in common, Malamud's story *The Jewbird* and Erich Segal's bestselling novel *Love Story* (1970). Segal's heroine, Jennifer Cavilleri, also comes from an ethnic minority (Italo-American). How can the approach to minority problems in the story and the novel be compared? Does the attitude to the problems have any bearing on the artistic value of the text? Discuss this problem.

9. Compare Alice Walker's short story with her novel *The Color Purple* in terms of setting, background, plot, structure, major theme and language.

10. Compare Walker's *Advancing Luna and Ida B. Wells* with other short stories by contemporary black women writers in the United States (such as Ntozake Shange, Alexis Deveaux, Gayl Jones and Toni Morrison). Analyse their various racial or feminist views.

Friedhold Schmidt
T. Lothar Wullen

The Novel

Contents

1 What is a Novel? – Approach

The Novel

Fiction vs. non-fiction

The novel (like the short story, drama, and poetry) belongs to the fictional text group as opposed to the non-fictional text group. Generally speaking, a fictional text is rather the product of a writer's imagination than a reference to facts, i.e. it generally deals with imaginary or fictitious characters or events. The non-fictional text, on the other hand, is usually based on facts. It is, however, not always easy to clearly distinguish between a non-fictional and a fictional text.

If a work deals mainly with fact it becomes history; if it primarily recounts the writer's experiences, it may be an autobiography or a memoir; if it restricts itself to a factual record of the life of some real person, it becomes biography. But fiction is both imagination and truth, contained and made real by its similarity to, or reflection of, real life. In a work of fiction the artist must form from the chaos and the realities of daily life a work that is ordered and aesthetically satisfying. In order to do so, he may distort time, compress, re-arrange, or omit details. He may dramatically emphasize those actions or features of characters that will best demonstrate his views.

Fiction is, in a sense, dramatic. The writer creates a world of its own, presenting it through action, dialogue, and images. Modern fiction is usually *objective*, that is, the writer does not tell us what to think about the characters or the situation they are in; rather than telling us *about* a story, the writer presents it through action; it will then be the task of the reader to study the artist's presentation of that action and the involvement of the characters within it. When, however, the artist's presence is obvious in his fiction, i.e. by open references to his personal experiences or attitudes, his method may be called *subjective*.

In fiction, focus is on the narrative, i.e. the presentation of events, of an experience or of an emotion or situation. Fictional narration may take the form of a short story or a novel. Critics debate the fundamental differences between these forms, because there are no essential criteria that truly distinguish the short story from the novel; the novel is an extended narrative and differs from the short story in length and potential for more elaboration and complexity. It is claimed that a short story seldom exceeds fifteen thousand words, while a novel traditionally exceeds one hundred pages. (A narrative that seems too long for a short story and too short for a novel is often called *novella*.) Though a novel must be organized through some unity of time, place, character development, or series of connected events, the novelist is free in his presentation and exploration of characters and settings, so that his plot may operate on an extended or multiple level. On the other hand, by restrictions in length, the short story writer is forced to limit his actions and settings and cannot extend the character presentation. Thus, the short story writer often begins his story somewhere near or even at the climax (crisis/conflict) and restricts the action to a single but crucial episode.

Categories

When studying narratives it is often helpful to determine whether the artist has laid emphasis on action (incident, adventure) or character (character presentation / character revelation).
Furthermore, fiction may be classified according to type or genre: it is *picaresque* or *episodic* if the characters proceed from one adventure to another (Fielding's Tom Jones or Twain's Adventures of Huckleberry Finn); *sociological* if the social or economic influences of a particular period are stressed (Stowe's Uncle Tom's Cabin, Steinbeck's Grapes of Wrath); *historical* if the author takes his characters or setting from history (Dickens' Tale of Two Cities); *psychological* if the emphasis is on the mental state or development of the characters (Dostoevsky's Crime and Punishment); *autobiographical* if the writer refers to his own life experience (Lawrence's, Sons and Lovers).

Development

The novel is one of the most popular of all literary forms; people have always appreciated story-telling and enjoy being able to identify with the human problems and emotions with which the novel has always been concerned. Through its scope of a longish story, usually with many characters and more than one plot, the novel has enabled authors to present a broad picture of life and it has remained close to the changes of society, reflecting the particular circumstances of the period in which it was produced.
The novel came into being when a new social class of merchants, bankers and shopkeepers started to rise in the seventeenth century and established itself in the eighteenth century. Up to this time, literature centered around noblemen and legendary heroes, and their poetic and high-sounding language referred to something remote in time and spirit from the mind of the ordinary people. The new social class wanted to read about people like themselves in their own everyday language. One of the first authors to meet the new demand was Daniel Defoe (c. 1660–1731); the hero in Robinson Crusoe (1719) is an ordinary merchant, whose picaresque story focusses on the problems and experiences of ordinary people. Both the urge to reform public behaviour by revealing social ills and the people's demand for stories from which they could learn some lesson or truth about life, was answered by Richardson's Pamela (1740). In this work, a servant girl, writing letters to her friends, narrates how her master pursues her, how she reforms and eventually marries him. Pamela,

often regarded as the first English novel, describes the dilemmas, moral concerns and daily problems of its characters. It has a definite plot and a central theme – the idea of virtue rewarded – is presented and developed. Although, in the course of time, the novel has changed a great deal in technique, style and theme, it has retained certain fundamental elements.

Elements

Among these are the plot and subplots of a novel, its characters, and its central idea, or theme. The plot of the novel, the pattern of events which form the story, entangles the characters in increasing conflicts so that the story develops towards a climax, or point of culmination. The novel ends with the denouement or resolution (disentanglement) of the conflicts, or it may have an open end. Characterization is intricately connected with the plot and can be developed to varying degrees, ranging from superficial to multidimensional in scope. In novels of action, suspense, and mystery, there may be greater emphasis on plot, while the characters are rather sketchily drawn. In other types of novels, the characters may be fully developed and contrasted with each other, with minor characters being less fully developed. One way to present characters is to describe their physical appearance and to give them outstanding traits; the English novel is rich in "great characters", figures who are larger than life and represent an idea or concept. An author may also try to create characters by examining their thoughts and feelings, or by describing their actions, gestures, talk, or (physical) surroundings. The language and style used by a character play an important part for the reader's understanding. Also, the use of imagery (symbols, metaphors etc.), which often represents an idea on a different level, may be important in this context.

Another basic element of the novel is the theme, which contains a central idea or attitude about life which is developed in the course of the work. The theme of a novel may sometimes be used to point out and criticize certain (social) conditions, concepts, or attitudes.

Further important structural elements are point of view and narrative order (cf. Glossary, p. 235).

The Novel Today

We live in an age in which fiction has conspicuously grown more provisional, more anxious, more self-questioning, than it was a few years ago. Looking about us at the novel now, it must seem that many questions about the nature of fictionality and about its constituent parts – the role of plot and story, the nature of character, the relationship between realism and fantasy or fabulation – have come to the forefront of attention. Indeed, ideas about what the novel is, and what it might be, have shifted so markedly in recent years that we might well judge that a serious aesthetic shift is taking place; that, in fact, there are signs of a distinctive new era of style. This is something that happens from time to time in fiction, as part of the novel's ongoing business, its development. And so in many respects the present debate, though it is intensified, is not original. Most of the questions and issues in discussion go right back to the novel's full emergence as a form in the seventeenth and eighteenth centuries, when the novel was indeed novel, when it evolved as a distinct species and as a significant social institution, and when its nature was much considered. And they especially bear on polar distinctions that have long been made – between, on the one hand, the novel's propensity toward realism, social documentation and interrelation with historical events and movements, and on the other with its propensity toward form, fictionality, and reflexive self-examination. The novel has always had two reputations – as a relatively innocent affair, an instrument for expressing our pleasure in tale and our delight in social fact through the one literary language, prose, that we all speak and write; and as a complex verbal invention, in which the ambiguities of narrative, the complexities of structure-making, the problems of making a grammar for experience, the perplexities of creating a sense of truth from falsehood, have been explored. The two reputations have both contested and consorted with each other, and helped make the novel the very various form it is: a form highly implicated in history, much concerned with representation, yet with an essential bias toward self-questioning and 'reflexiveness'. In some periods the one side of fiction has been emphasized, in some criticism began to grant the novel the greatness and centrality James had claimed for it; but then, until the present time, the novel does indeed seem to have become, in criticism, the exemplary literary object, displacing the poem, and, to a lesser extent, the play, as the type of literary experience, an ultimate example of what we do when we tell a story, report a fact, devise an order for events.

By this time, it seemed, much of the impetus of the modern movement had been exhausted; the postwar years saw the revival of the liberal and realist novel. The writers who emerged after 1945 are, of course, very much our novelists, and their development is very much related to our development, our contemporary history. After 1945 the novel showed every sign of reasserting its realistic potential, its moral and social concern, its sense of life as progress. The lessons of the great moderns – Dostoevsky and Mann, Joyce and Proust, Musil and Kafka, Faulkner and Virginia Woolf – had been taken, but they were assimilated back into a spirit of relative realism, and technical and epistemological questions were not strongly pressed; the novel was the book of life, the quintessence of experience. But as the revived liberal and historical hopes of the 1950s began to falter in the 1960s, the mood began to change. Formal and epistemological questions about the novel began to reassert themselves; many of the novelists who had begun writing after the war began to change in manner; and certain constituents of the modernist impulse, especially its tendency toward play and game, its stress on art as forgery, and its surreal and fabulous dimension, began to appear significant again. Again a stress on the insubstantiality or corruptibility of history became evident, the problems of establishing solid character, in a world in which humanism was threatened, in which man was held by many to be the sum of his roles, was felt, and the idea of the novel as realistic tale was challenged. Some writers systematically and self-consciously elaborated the referential character of the novel, using the modes of reportage, documentary, and journalism, as in the non-fiction novel; others emphasized the one-dimensionality of character and the flattening of plot by apeing popular forms or inventing the technetronic novel; others insisted on the elusiveness or the unreliability of text, creating novels where the dominant narrator asserting the truth of his tale either disappeared from sight into text or reappeared in the overt guise of the game-player or impresario, displaying the lie he had made, the fictionality he commanded. In general, then, the realistic centre tended to disappear; the stable text lost its stability; the reader was invited into the novel in novel ways. These developments appeared to occur, at roughly the same rhythm, on an international scale; and even in England, where the realistic and the liberal tradition in fiction has been notably strong, the consequences have been striking.

M. Bradbury, *The Novel Today,* Fontana, London 1977, pp. 8–11.

2 The Psychological Novel

I'm the King of the Castle

Susan Hill

Edmund Hooper is used to being 'master' of the large, lonely country house in which he lives with his widowed father. When his father's lady friend, a Mrs Kingshaw, moves in with her son, Charles, Edmund defends his position by trying to drive Charles away. He seems to be successful at first, when he scares Charles on several occasions, but Charles builds up his own defence system by fortifying himself psychologically. He gains the upper hand when one day the two boys lose their way in a nearby forest: Charles proves to be more courageous, while Edmund is deeply frightened. The conflict between the two boys becomes even harsher, until, during a visit to a castle, they climb on the high castle walls.
Misjudging a movement of Charles to help him, Edmund falls down deep from a wall, is thought dead at first but recovers in hospital. Meanwhile, Charles makes friends with Fielding, a boy from the neighbourhood. He dreads Edmund's return, and his despair and helplessness increase when later Edmund tries to gain influence with Fielding and when the forthcoming marriage of his mother to Edmund's father is announced. And while Mrs Kingshaw thinks about the prospects of her future, Charles drowns himself in a nearby stream, which leads to Edmund's personal triumph, supported by Mrs Kingshaw's comforting words: "Now it's all right, Edmund dear, everything is all right."

"Some people are coming here today," said Joseph Hooper, "now you will have a companion."
For he had been much impressed by the graceful letters of Mrs Helena Kingshaw, by their honesty and lightness of tone, and by her voice over the telephone, later. She was widowed, she was thirty-seven, and she was to become what he had termed an informal housekeeper. There would be Mrs Boland for the cleaning and some cooking.
"Perhaps you might agree to come for the summer, just at first," he had written, "to see how you and your boy settle, and how we all of us rub along."
"Warings," Mrs Kingshaw had replied, "sounds so much like the home we have been looking for."
Joseph Hooper had been greatly touched. That night, he examined his own, thin

figure in the cheval mirror. "I am a lonely man," he had said, and was not ashamed, afterwards, of having admitted it.

"His name is Charles Kingshaw, and he is just your age, he is almost eleven. You must make a good effort to welcome him and be friendly."

Edmund Hooper went slowly up the four flights of stairs to his own bedroom. It was raining hard again, and great, bruisecoloured clouds hung low over the copse. He had thought of going in there today, but the grass would be too wet.

And another boy was coming, after all, with his mother, so that there would always be someone about the house to notice him. She would start making them play games and go on expeditions, that was how the mothers of some boys at school were. Once, recently, he had wondered if he ought to feel his own mother's absence, to want things that only she might provide. But he had been unable to imagine what these things might be. He remembered nothing at all about her.

His father had said, "I know that you are not quite happy, that we are only making the best of a bad job. But you must come to me and tell me about things, you must not be afraid to admit when something is wrong."

"I'm quite all right. There isn't anything wrong at all." For he hated his father to talk to him in that way, wanted to stop his ears to keep him out. "There's nothing wrong." And he only spoke the truth. But Joseph Hooper looked for subtleties beneath the surface of things, anxious, because he had been warned of how much the boy would suffer.

Hooper began to mould plasticine between his hands, for another layer to the geological model, standing on a board beside the window. He thought of the boy called Kingshaw, who was coming.

"It is my house," he thought, "it is private, I got here first. Nobody should come here."

Still, he would not give anything of himself away, the other boy could be ignored, or evaded, or warned off. It depended what he was like. All sorts of things could be done.

He laid down a flat strip of dark red plasticine, following the colouring of strata on a map. The model was humped in the shape of a barrow, like one of those on the downs. When it was finished, he would slice it down like a cake, and all the layers would be revealed. Then he could get on with his Battle of Waterloo map. There were so many things to do, and he wanted to do them by himself, he did not want the boy called Kingshaw here. That afternoon, when they arrived by car, he locked his door. But he watched them, tilting the mirror so that he could look down into the drive without being seen himself. They all stood about nervously. Kingshaw had red hair. "Edmund!" his father had been calling, up and down the house. "Edmund! Now your friend is here, I wish you would not lurk about the place, it is so very ill-mannered. Come out here, please. Edmund!"

Joseph Hooper busied himself, for he was suddenly alarmed at the arrival of this woman, alarmed by what he had done. They were to make their home here, they were all to live together in the same house, and he might suffer from it, might know the consequences of a terrible mistake.

He is very uncertain of himself, thought Mrs Helena Kingshaw, who had also, for some years past, been much alone.

"Edmund, you will come down here at once!"

Edmund Hooper took up a small piece of paper from the table, wrote something on it and attached the paper carefully to a lump of grey plasticine. He looked out of the window again. The boy, Charles Kingshaw, was glancing up, seeing the sudden flash of the mirror. Hooper dropped the plasticine, it fell straight as a stone. He moved back from the window. Kingshaw bent down.

"Come along, Charles dear, you must help me with the cases, we cannot leave everything to Mr Hooper." Mrs Helena Kingshaw wore a jade green suit and worried about it, lest it should be thought too smart.

"Oh – what is it, what have you found?" She was anxious that he should like it here, should very soon feel at home.

Kingshaw thought, I didn't want to come, I didn't want to come, it is one more strange house in which we do not properly belong. But he had dropped the lump of plasticine. "Nothing, it's nothing. It's only a pebble."

Walking behind his mother, into the dark hall, he managed to open out the scrap of paper.

"I DIDN'T WANT YOU TO COME HERE" was written.

"Now let me show you to your rooms," said Mr Joseph Hooper.

Kingshaw stuffed the message fearfully into his trouser pocket.

Hooper said, "Why have you come here?" facing him across the room. Kingshaw flushed brick red. He stood his ground, not speaking. There was a small round table between them. His trunk and a suitcase stood on the floor. "Why did you have to find somewhere new to live?"

Silence. Hooper thought, now I see why it is better to have a house like Warings, I see why my father goes about clutching the big bunch of keys. We live here, it is ours, we belong. Kingshaw has nowhere.

He walked round the table, towards the window. Kingshaw stepped back as he came.

"Scaredy!"

"No."

"When my father dies," Hooper said, "this house will belong to me, I shall be master. It'll all be mine."

"That's nothing. It's only an old house."

Hooper remembered bitterly the land that his grandfather had been forced to sell off. He said quietly, "Downstairs is something very valuable. Something you've never seen."

"What then?"

Hooper smiled, looking away out of the window, choosing not to tell. And he was uncertain how impressive the moth collection might really be.

"My grandfather died in this room. Not very long ago, either. He lay and died in that bed. Now it's your bed." This was not true.

Kingshaw went to the suitcase and squatted down.

"Where did you live before?"

"In a flat."

"Where?"

"London."

"Your *own* flat?"

"Yes – no. Well, it was in somebody's house."

"You were only *tenants*, then."

"Yes."

"It wasn't really yours."

"No."

"Why didn't your father buy you a proper house?"

Kingshaw stood up. "My father's dead." He was angry, not hurt. He wanted to put his fists up to Hooper, and dared not.

Hooper raised his eyebrows. He had learned to do it from a master at school. It seemed an impressive way of looking.

"Well, my mother can't afford to buy us a house, can she? We can't help that."

"Your father should have left you some money, then, shouldn't he? Didn't *he* have a house."

"Yes, he did, it had to be sold."

"Why?"

"I don't know."

"To pay off all his debts."

"No, no."

"Do you remember your father?"

"Oh, yes. Well – a bit. He was a pilot, once. He was in the Battle of Britain. I've got ..." Kingshaw went down on his knees again, and began to search feverishly through the tartan suitcase.

"... I've got a picture of him."

"Is it a picture of him in the Battle?"

"No. But ..."

"I don't believe you, anyway, you're a liar, the Battle of Britain was in the war."

"Well, I know that, everybody knows that."

"It was years ago, dozens of years. It was history. He couldn't have been in it."

"He was, he was."

"When did he die, then?"

"Here's the picture, look – that's my father."

"*When did he die,* I said." Hooper moved nearer, menacing.

"A few years ago. I was about five. Or six."

"He would have been pretty old by then. How old was he?"

"I don't know. Quite old, I suppose. Look, then, there's the photograph." Kingshaw held out a small, brown wallet. He was desperate for Hooper to see it, to believe him, he felt that he must make some mark on this house, must be believed about something. After a second, Hooper bent down slightly, and took the picture. He had expected someone different, courageous-looking, interesting. But it was only a bald, cadaverous man with a mole on his chin.

"He's old," he said.

"I told you. When he was in the Battle of Britain, he was twenty. That was the war."

Hooper said nothing. He threw the photograph down into the suitcase and walked back to the window. Kingshaw knew that he had won, but he did not *feel* the winner; Hooper had conceded him nothing.

"Where do you go to school?"

"In Wales."

Hooper raised his eyebrows, "I should think there would be about a hundred schools in Wales. More than a hundred."

"It's called St Vincent's."

"Is it a proper school?"

Kingshaw did not answer. He was still on the floor beside his case. He had been going to start unpacking, but now he would not, unpacking would make it seem final, as though he had accepted the fact that he was going to stay here, as though there were a future to be considered. He had been brought up sharp, by Hooper. He said, "You needn't think I wanted to come, anyway."

Hooper considered this. He remembered when he had been told of his grandfather's death. He had said, "I don't want to live in that house."

He pushed open the window. It had stopped raining. The sky was the colour of dirty sixpences. The rhododendrons still shone with wetness, all down the drive.

"You'd better shut the window," Kingshaw said, "it's my window now."

Hooper turned, hearing the new note in his voice, considering what it meant, and hearing the tremor of anxiety, too. He raised his fists and came at Kingshaw.

The scrap was brief and wordless and violent. It died down quite quickly. Kingshaw wiped his bloody nose and then examined the handkerchief. His heart was thumping. He had never fought another boy like that before. He wondered what the future would be like now.

Outside, in the corridor below, he heard the voice of his mother, answering Mr Hooper gaily, and then the banging of a door. He thought, it's her fault that we came here, it's her fault.

Hooper was beside the window again. It was still open. For some time, neither of them spoke. Kingshaw wished that he would go.

Hooper said, "You needn't think you've got to stick about the place with mie, I've got my own things to do."

"I'm supposed to, that's what your father said."
"You do what I say."
"Don't be stupid."
"I'll bash you again, just watch it."
Kingshaw backed. He said, "Look, you needn't think I wanted to come here, you needn't think I like it."
Though he had expected to get used to things. He had not bargained for Hooper. He began to pick up the things which had fallen out of his tartan suitcase.
"Is your school a proper boarding school?"
"Yes."
"Well how does your mother afford to pay for you at a boarding school if she can't afford for you to live in a house?"
"I think ... I don't know. I think it's free."
"No schools are free."
"Yes, they are."
"Only schools for poor people. Boarding schools aren't free."
"It's ... I don't know. I daresay my father paid them a lot of money when I first went there. I daresay he paid all of the fees at once, and so now it doesn't cost anything. Yes, yes, he did do that, I know he did."
Hooper looked at him coldly. He had won, and Kingshaw knew it. He could afford to turn away, letting the subject drop.
Kingshaw wondered whether there might now be some sort of truce between them, whether he might somehow have won his right to stay here. He had come prepared to get on with Hooper, as he got on with most people, because it was safer to do so. He was too vulnerable to let himself indulge in the making of enemies.
But Hooper was something different again, he had never faced this sort of hostility. He was unbalanced by it, and by Hooper's self-possession, not knowing what to do, and ashamed because he did not know. It was like the first time of going away to school, trying to find his way around, watching other people to see what they did.
He wanted to say, I've come here and I don't like it, I don't want to stay, I want to be somewhere by myself, in our own place, not in somebody else's place, we always go to live in somebody else's place. But I can't, I've got to stay here, why can't we make the best of things? He was willing to put himself out, he would even, just at this moment, have said he would do whatever Hooper wanted, would acknowledge him as master of his own territory. But he couldn't put any of it into words, not even to himself, it was only a series of feelings, overlapping one another like small waves. He was confused.
Hooper was looking at him across the table. A bruise was coming up on his left cheekbone, and swelling slightly, where Kingshaw's fist had struck. He looked the older of the two boys, though in height he was shorter. There was something about the way he walked, about the cast of his eyes.
He waited for a moment, and then walked slowly out of the room. But at the door,

he turned. "You still needn't think you're wanted here," he said, "this isn't your place."

Kingshaw stood for a long time after Hooper had gone. He thought, there is nobody. The whole summer stretched ahead of him. After a while, he began to cry, though without making any sound, and swallowing hard to try and stop himself. He couldn't stop. But there was nothing that he would say, nobody to say it to.

In the end, he stopped. He might as well get the rest of his things out, and put them away. His mother had brought him here, she had been very excited about it, she had told him it was the answer to a prayer. He was ashamed of the way she had spoken.

He walked deliberately over to the window. "It is my window, now," he said, and pulled it tight shut.

Turning back into the room, he remembered what Hooper had told him about his grandfather, that it was here, in this room, in this bed, that he had died. It did not occur to Kingshaw to question the truth of it. He tried not to think of his own fears to come.

Susan Hill, *I'm the King of the Castle,* Penguin, Harmondsworth 1974, pp. 16–23.

Vocabulary

to rub along to succeed in living together – *cheval mirror* long mirror in an upright frame – *copse* wood of small trees – *to lurk* to wait in hiding – *scaredy* timid person – *cadaverous* [kə'dævərəs] looking like a dead body – *mole* small dark mark on the skin – *to bring up* (infml) to speak severely to – *sixpence* old currency, now 2,5 pence – *scrap* short quarrel – *to bash* (infml) to hit hard – *tartan* plaid pattern of the type worn by Scottish clans – *truce* stopping the fighting for a period – *vulnerable* easily attacked, not well protected – *to indulge in* to enjoy

Assignments

1. What is the situation presented? Who are the main characters and how do they react to the situation?
2. In what narrative sequences is the text developed? How do they differ?
3. Examine in detail how the characters are portrayed. In this connection, discuss the importance of point of view and its shifts.
4. What, in your opinion, is the theme / subject of the passage? State why the passage appeals or does not appeal to you.

3 The Symbolic Novel

The Viaduct

DAVID WHELDON

After his dismissal from the prison where he had been serving a sentence for seditious activities, A., the protagonist of the novel, tries to get away from the city. But he is reproached with fresh charges of sedition and only escapes his pursuers by passing the city boundary.

On his journey he meets a "small man" and a "tall man" and they continue the journey together. While they march along the unused railway line, information is revealed about their background and about the manuscript which A. is carrying: it describes, among other things, some supposedly secret religious practices of the state.

When the small man dies in an accident, A. is heard as a witness by the mayor of the nearest town. The inquest develops into a somewhat vague discussion of the object of A.'s journey, leading to frequent conversations between A. and the tall man about travelling and travellers in general; they find out that they are both outcasts, the tall man because of his epileptic fits and A. because he was in prison for something that now has no meaning to him. Travelling seems to be the only possible existence for both men and for several other people, too, as is confirmed by an old man and some travellers they meet later on.

When the old man eventually dies and A. takes his body to the nearest town, he is welcomed with respect, since he is now regarded as an experienced traveller. At the same time he is shattered by the vision dawning upon him that all his hopes, including the purpose of his travelling, might prove futile. This becomes evident when the railway line takes A. back to the city that he was so desperate to leave behind him.

A. is arrested and marched to prison but feels slightly elated because he regards himself as more experienced now, more able to stand his ground in a trial. The trial, however, has taken place in his absence and he has been sentenced to death. After hearing that he has been absolved **in absentia** *A. is executed.*

The range of hills was perceptibly closer. The air was colder. The embankment of the railway had risen to meet the lowest of the valleys with a slow and steady gradient. The track still ran on, straight and without deviation, as if it were the permanent part of the landscape and the valley had been later created for the railway to travel through.

In the shadow of a roofless stone hut, such as might once have been used by the permanent waymen of the Eastern Privincial Railway, an old man sat by a fire. It was clear that he had been travelling alone, for he had an air of self-contained independence about him. His pack was close to his side. He had this travelling worked out; his steady grey eyes beneath their bushes of grey brows were always on the lookout. The direction in which his eyes gazed had no correlation with anything he was saying, as if he looked with half his brain and saw with half his brain and, with the whole of the cerebrum he mixed the input of his failing five senses with the sureness of experience. It was obvious that he had been travelling for many years. *A.* sat across the fire from him, looking at him. His observations of the old man were very much the observations which have just been told, but it is very probable that he observed much more; he must have seen things that, when written, would have been laborious in their reading and unimportant in their communication. Following this statement, therefore, it is necessary to say that *A.* was in a much better position to ascertain the truth or otherwise of what the old man was saying. The old man was clearly no fool, for all the fact of his years' travel. Perhaps, though, that was not strictly true; some degree of foolishness, of senile futility might have been apparent in the fact that he had been eager to speak and that he had been less than eager to listen to anything that *A.* might have had to say or to comment on.

"I have been making my way along this track for well over ten years," said the old man. His voice was lively and virile and at variance with his apparent age. "I made my way out before the railway first closed ten years ago I think, though it may have been longer."

"Ten years," said *A.*

"Ten years," repeated the old man, making something profound out of the simple statement. "Since that time I've spoken to many and listened to many and all I can say is that no place is a place to stay. Stay in one place and you might as well be travelling backwards." He jerked his head back in the direction of the city. "Once I stayed for a year or more in a stone hut, out there. It was a stone hut, like this thing here, but it had a roof to it." He indicated the structure behind him. "But that was no good. I soon found that as I stayed, and the longer I stayed, the more I drifted, in thought at least, to my old home."

"Why did you start travelling?"

For the first time the old man put on a look of vagueness; he feigned deafness, cupping a hand to his large ear, though it was clear from his expression that he had heard *A.*'s question. "Yes," he said at length, judging the lapse of time since he had last spoken, "I did a foolish thing in staying in that one place for so long. You get a feeling of security which can never be real. Why, it's like accumulating things; gathering them up; making an estate; getting things together. You know that you might be considered prosperous and many of them are, down in the plain, but equally well you know that there'll come a time when your will is read out, with you dead and your prosperity in vain. Though there's more to it than that. Of course there is; there's many a justification for a man to take this track. Probably there are as many reasons as there are men travelling. I have only to think back to the times when the railway ran. Do you remember that?"

"I was told that I had once travelled on the train as a child, yes, but I remember nothing of that. It was only what I was told."

The old man leaned forward to tend his small fire; never before had *A*. seen so small a fire glow so hotly and yet be so conservative of the scant fuel that was to be found in the environs of the railway. The old man was about to speak again; there was a premonitory trembling of the lips, some inward rehearsal of the coming words. "I remember the days of the old railway," said the old man. "I remember them. The signal boxes, with their great glass windows and their white painted finials; the signalmen themselves, seen vaguely through the glass of those windows. Why, I remember at the end of the great viaduct, over the city, there was such a signal box. I remember it well. Perhaps the base of it, the stonework, still stands?" He looked questioningly at *A*.

"I didn't notice it," said the young traveller.

"No, perhaps not. Time may have altered things. But I remember that box, because it was high up; high above the viaduct and the viaduct was high above the city. I got to know the signalman there well. He was, well, he would have been, when I was your age, I suppose, a middle-aged man. I remember him talking about his retirement. He used to talk about his retirement and his garden, down in the city, and the church he used to go to and the allotment he was on the list for. I could never understand all this. After all, he was the highest of all things; he looked down at the embankment and the viaduct and the city. He was above all things. The city was spread out below him, like a map, or as though seen from an aeroplane. But that did not concern him. Perhaps his years there, in that box, had taken away any feeling of awe that inevitably overcame a stranger such as myself. He would sit and look at me, half amused, as I peered from the window of his signal box. The height of it was frightening to me. The steps ran in a long zigzag up the white-painted posts to his box." The old man shook his head. "But there was never a man more conscientious. Have you ever seen the inside of a signal box?"

"No."

"Well, I don't know. I don't know much about these things. The telegraph system. The coded ringing of the bells. There were two bells and two dials, I think, all mounted on a dark wooden panel. And the signal levers." The old man allowed his head to sway from side to side, a curious senile mannerism that gave his voice a sing-song quality, as though he were intoning rather than speaking his words. "Theirs was a solitary life, the old signalmen. They sometimes used to go odd with solitude. The very neatness with which their boxes were kept; nothing to be touched with the fingers, only through a cloth; all the brasswork polished and all the woodwork likewise. And the gleam of the windows! I remember the man I was speaking of, one day when he was cleaning his windows with some white liquid. He didn't mind the height. He was concerned with the neatness, the cleanness within the box. And who can blame him? It was his home. He was no traveller. He was due for retirement and he was looking forward to the time when he could retire to his city cottage in some terrace. He told me his address, but that I can't remember. His name also escapes me, now. But it was the feeling of his proprietorial pride, his air of satisfaction at the neatness of the signal box of which he was master. His logging of the trains. He would only allow certain travellers up there ..."

"There were travellers even while the railway was still running?"

The old man seemed surprised at the question. "Of course," he said. "Didn't you know that? The travellers used to walk along the platelayers' track. It was illegal then, of course. You had to get down when you came to a signal box that was manned by an officious bastard. Not all signalmen were like that, of course; some of them liked your company, and they kept an eye open for you: you could go up to their signal box with some small present, perhaps a few eggs that you'd found, or something like that, and they'd allow you to have a brew up on their stoves and get yourself warm by their fire in winter. Some of them used to allow you to sleep in the lower storey of the signal boxes, the room where the mechanism was. It was a better place to sleep than under a bridge or in a culvert." He smiled slightly, the reminiscence being pleasant to him. "It was good, that. You'd hear the man pacing the floorboards above your head. You'd hear the grate of the signal levers; in the moonlight you'd see the rods move, in your half sleep. You'd hear the single tang of the signal bell. The tapped reply. The distant clack of the semaphore arms. The coming thunder of the train.

"Of course, in my youth the railway was even more important. There were few travellers then. The railway seemed so permanent then. Way beyond your city ..."

A. leaned forward. "I thought the railway stopped at my city. That the city station was a terminus."

The old man laughed. "No, never. That was never so. In your lifetime maybe, but I come from far beyond ..."

The old man began speaking again, talking about the isolation of the signalmen; of the fact that even the permanent way employees regarded the signalmen as being solitary and idiosyncratic. Now the old man was talking of rumours of accidents; now he was talking of individual men he had once known, describing them in detail, and apologising for his forgetfulness as to their names. But *A.*'s thought was directed elsewhere. He had for the last day or two entertained the perturbing notion that perhaps his own city had not been a terminus or a starting-off point. Now he knew the fact to be true.

He did not know why the fact should fill him with a sudden fear, but fear was there. He looked across at the old man, wondering how much of his sudden fear he had transmitted; the old man was still speaking, though his eyes were slyly fixed on the young traveller's face.

Why a sudden fear?

A. had known since the beginning of his travelling that the end of the railway would be an unknown thing. All his questions on that point had provided no adequate answer. Now, and only now, he knew that he had started out from no definite starting point. The railway ran as far backwards as it did forwards.

A. suddenly looked at the old man. He looked at the aged face; the mouth was still muttering. "Tell me," said *A.*, interrupting, "where the terminus is."

The old man had been speaking; he recognised the interruption, and his voice stopped. The sounds of the growing evening impinged on the two sitting men. The graveness of a tranquil evening had fallen, and the two men, one old and one young, were revealed as being no more than an old man and a young man. There was nothing more. The old man, interrupted in his speaking, stood up. Now, standing, he was revealed as being of a far greater age than an observer might previously have reckoned. He bent down and picked up his few belongings.

"Where does the railway originate?" *A.* asked the question, but expected no answer.

"Keep the fire, if you like. There's a bit of wood behind the hut." His voice was not unkind. Perhaps he had heard *A.*'s question so often that he no longer saw any point in making an attempt to answer it. He looked down at the young man. His attitude might have been the attitude of a tolerant sage to a youth who has yet much to learn, but it was difficult to tell; the light was failing.

And then, with a slowness during which the darkness deepened, he made his way down the track, towards the distant hills.

David Wheldon, *The Viaduct*,
Penguin, Harmondsworth 1984, pp. 14–21.

Vocabulary

gradient amount of inclination – *cerebrum* ['serɪbrəm] front part of the brain – *laborious* needing great effort – *to feign* [feɪn] to pretend to have – *conservative* here: tending to save – *scant* short, not present in large supply – *finial* ornament or gable on a roof – *allotment* here: small portion of (usually) public land let out for cultivation – *proprietorial* [prəpraɪə'tɔ:rɪəl] belonging to or typical of an owner – *to log* to write into an official record (here: of the trains) – *platelayer* (BE) workman who puts down or repairs railway tracks – *semaphore* signal with lights and a movable arm

Assignments

1. Point out the plot and the setting of the passage and discuss their relative importance.
2. Describe the two characters and their relationship.
3. Analyse the communication between the two characters. What is it about, why is it so peculiar and what is the outcome?
4. By what means is the effect of mysteriousness brought about?
5. Discuss the symbolical value of the passage.

Travelling blindly
Linda Taylor

David Wheldon
The Viaduct
175 pp. Bodley Head.
£ 5.95.
0 370 30519

The viaduct spans the city and provides a diminished view of it. In the days of the railway, trains sped across its arches. For a man in prison, who can see it from his cell window, it represents distance and freedom, and it is on its overgrown track that we meet "the freed man" (or Alexander or A.) as David Wheldon's first novel opens. It might be the beginning of a thriller (A. is being pursued) or something Kafkaesque (the crime was an unspecified sedition; people and places are nameless). More the latter than the former, the book is, in fact, a long extended metaphor – the one about life being a journey. For, as A. follows the track away from the city (his pursuers cease their pursuit at something called the boundary line), he discovers many more travellers like himself. Though none of them knows why (and, indeed, questions about where one is going are taboo on the railway), they are all heading in the same direction – towards the beautiful but illusory hills. The parallels, between travelling and life, are not hard to construct – as the tall man tells A. when he describes a conversation he once had with a trackside philosopher: "He was telling me the usual things. He was drawing the analogy between the length of the railway and the passing of time. That's an old story." As old as the hills, in fact.

The journey along the track (like life's?) is tedious but compulsive. The travellers think about food; they talk, when they happen upon one another, in repetitive snatches; they are superstitious about the towns and villages that they pass – the inhabitants, A. is told, are fiercely hostile to travellers, or vagrants as they call them. Wheldon shows what a thin line there is between notions of the glorious freedom of travelling and the parasitical banality of vagrancy. And A., while conscientiously learning all the rules of escape, keeps his options open. He knows, though he doggedly follows the track away from the city, that it will, inevitably, return there. That is his fate.

Thus *The Viaduct* poses the problem of how we should live our lives. On the one hand, there is the static life of the unit – the order, persecution, industry, dependence and caring of the towns and cities. Or, there is the independence, solitariness (or loneliness) and transience of the traveller, the rolling stone. Though little attention is paid to the virtues, or otherwise, of stasis, Wheldon doesn't seem to think that there's much of any value going on on the railway either. He is good, however, at conveying the way in which the apparent freedom and honesty of the transient life ultimately lead to a lack of communication and dullness. Either route leads to death, of course, and the novel begs the question as to which one is preferable. Inconclusiveness provides its own momentum, though, and one is compelled to turn the pages of this book in much the same way as the travellers feel the blind urge to put one foot in front of the other. Gradually we begin to realize that the terminus really doesn't exist but, still, there must be something, mustn't there?

Apparently not, Stevenson, who knew a great deal about travelling, said "To travel hopefully is a better thing than to arrive, and the true success is the labour." Wheldon, in his grinding onward, replaces "hopefully" by "blindly" and in his dim vision (life, simply, leads to death), omits to take account of the labour involved. A., once he is, as it were, on the road, rapidly gives up any remaining shreds of faith he has in the only thing in life that had caused him effort and pain – his seditious manuscript. While he escapes from the static zombies, who still want to persecute him for it, he merely joins another set of travelling automatons. David Wheldon's vision is bleak, but it is oddly soporific.

Times Literary Supplement,
1/4/1983, p. 324.

Assignments

1. What aspects of Wheldon's novel does critic Linda Taylor focus on? To what extent is her review a summary, to what extent is it an interpretation of the novel?
2. What is her evaluation of the novel?

4 The Sociological Novel

The Ice Age

MARGARET DRABBLE

The Ice Age *is, to a large extent, a portrait of the England of the 1970s. Its scanty plot focusses on the attempt of the characters to respond to the economic and social situation. The protagonist is Anthony Keating, a middle-aged former TV editor of economic affairs, who has turned into a property developer and has had several severe economic setbacks due to the general state of Britain. He now suffers from poor health due to a heart attack. He is divorced from his wife, Babs, and more or less leads the life of a recluse, which gives him plenty of time to ponder on his situation, and the general state of Britain. This is presented through encounters with and visits of his friends and relations.*
The situation changes when Jane, the daughter of his lady friend Alison, is arrested in Walachia, and Anthony is talked into travelling there in order to look after Jane and work towards her dismissal. He manages to put her on the last plane to fly home before a revolution starts, but he himself ends up in a state prison and is not allowed to leave the country.

Not everybody in Britain on that night in November was alone, incapacitated or in jail. Nevertheless, over the country depression lay like fog, which was just about all that was missing to lower spirits even further, and there was even a little of that in East Anglia. All over the nation, families who had listened to the news looked at one another and said 'Goodness me' or 'Whatever next' or 'I give up' or 'Well, fuck that', before embarking on an evening's viewing of colour television, or a large hot meal, or a trip to the pub, or a choral society evening. All over the country, people blamed other people for all the things that were going wrong – the trades unions, the present government, the miners, the car workers, the seamen, the Arabs, the Irish, their own husbands, their own wives, their own idle good-for-nothing offspring, comprehensive education. Nobody knew whose fault it really was, but most people managed to complain fairly forcefully about somebody: only a few were stunned into honourable silence. Those who had been complaining for the last twenty years about the negligible rise in the cost of living did not of course have the grace to wish that they had saved their breath to cool their porridge, because once a complainer, always a complainer, so those who had complained most when there was nothing to complain about were having a really wonderful time now.
Expansionist plans were, it is true, here and there being checked: for a second holiday, a three-piece suite, a new car. But very few people were having to work out how

to do without what they had already got, though they were puzzled by the way their hard-won wage increases had got them nowhere at all. The old headline phrases of freeze and squeeze had for the first time become for everyone – not merely for the old and unemployed – a living image, a reality: millions who had groaned over them in steadily increasing prosperity were now obliged to think again. A huge icy fist, with large cold fingers, was squeezing and chilling the people of Britain, that great and puissant nation, slowing down their blood, locking them into immobility, fixing them in a solid stasis, like fish in a frozen river: there they all were in their large houses and their small houses, with their first mortgages and second mortgages, in their rented flats and council flats and basement bedsits and their caravans: stuck, congealed, amongst possessions, in attitudes, in achievements they had hoped next month to shed, and with which they were now condemned to live. The flow had ceased to flow: the ball had stopped rolling: the game of musical chairs was over. *Rien ne va plus*, the croupier had shouted.

Some, who had thought they understood, were more bewildered than others. An economist, who had just received a salary increase of £2,000 in expectation of next year's inflation, pondered the problem of growth over a supper of macaroni cheese. He was one of those who had tried to work out an anti-growth policy. He had signally failed to communicate his enthusiasm for this concept to others: and, indeed, recognizing his sigh of relief at the salary increase, to himself. Man needs a prospect of increase. Only static, stagnant, hopeless communities can live without it. The poor must get rich, the rich must get richer. He prodded his static macaroni cheese, a satisfying but fattening dish in pleasant tones of cream, yellow and brown, in pleasantly graded smooth affiliated doughy textures: one of the favourite dishes of his childhood, as of his manhood. His real tastes had changed little with the years. Why then the elation at an extra £2,000 a year when he of all people knew how little that could mean?

There were, of course, a few perverse souls who enjoyed the prospect of a little austerity. They had been happiest during the war, and had returned to a life of cheese-rind-paring and carrot-growing with alacrity. To them, affluence had always been an unreal delusion: there was nothing in it against which one could pit one's wits. And now once more, with a sense of virtue, they could go round switching off fires and lowering the power of electric light bulbs, bathing in water three inches deep, using up old crusts and thinning sauces in the bottoms of old bottles with vinegar. Some of them even wanted to reintroduce rationing, and were disappointed when first sugar, then petrol, then salt, then lavatory rolls dropped off the economic hook. According to their enemies, their philosophy was: *it is wrong to enjoy oneself, it is right to sit in the cold by a candle end.* But they, in fact, enjoyed sitting by a candle end.

This generation had produced another minority group, their spiritual and often their physical offspring: the war babies. They had accepted recession with a balanced cheerfulness, for they had always been astonished at their own purchasing power each time they bought a pound of bananas or a small pot of double cream. Hearing the gusts of anguish that shook the country, they shook their heads in mild amusement. Early childhood had solved for these lucky few the economic problem of growth: they would never be able to regard growth, or indeed survival, as anything other than an astonishing blessing.

Others enjoyed the crisis for more indirect reasons. Odd new groups of the far left hoped that each rise in the bank rate and each strike in a car factory heralded the final collapse of capitalism. Sociologists expressed approval of the rate of social change, the radicalizing influence of increasing confrontations of worker and management. Out of this, some sincerely believed, would rise a new order, of selfless, social, greedless beings. So they applauded disruptive strikes for more pay, and, illogically, snapped crossly at their children when their children told them that yes, it really did cost 15p to get to the football match on the bus, and yes, that really did make 30p there and back, and yes there were 3 of them, and yes, 3 times 30 was 90, and could they also have at least 50p each for a hamburger and 20p each for a coke?

There were also the real poor: the old, the unemployed, the undesirable immigrants. They were better off than they would have been in the thirties, for Britain is, after all, a welfare state, and not many slip through its net. Let us not think of them. Their rewards will be in heaven.

Finally, there was the small communion of saints, who truly hoped that from this crisis would come a better sharing among the nations of the earth: who truly in their hearts applauded the rise in price of raw materials from the poorer countries of the earth: who thought of the poor, and of themselves rarely, and included themselves among the rich, which most of them, by Western European standards, were not. They tried now to repress their horror and their satisfaction at the unedifying spectacle of the death-throes of greed in their own so-privileged nation. Amongst these, one might record an elderly Quaker in Keighley, who sent every spare penny of her small income to a school in Africa where she had once worked; a one-time Member of Parliament, who had lost his job through lack of charisma and was prepared to spend the rest of his life working, ill paid, for the Child Poverty Action Group; a bishop, who had taken in youth a vow of poverty and celibacy, in fear of his own too great charisma, and who prayed nightly for the country of his birth, where most people were so much richer than he, where the needs of others, compared to his own, seemed to be so great.

There are not many people like the bishop, the ex-MP, and the elderly Quaker. It is just as well that there are not more. Self-sacrifice is all very well, in the eyes of God, but where would the country be, without self-interest? Two and a half centuries ago the poet Pope expressed the optimistic view, which maybe he believed, that God ordained that self-love and social should be the same. But which self, which society? The population of Britain then was only five and a half million: now it is sixty million.

Pity the bishop, on his knees on the cold linoleum. His love is strained, dilute, insufficient. Could even God's love suffice this multitude?
It must be said that even the bishop cannot find it in his heart to regret that Britain has struck oil.
This is the state of the nation.

Margaret Drabble, *The Ice Age,* Penguin, Harmondsworth 1979, pp. 62–65.

Vocabulary

to incapacitate to make incapable – *fuck* (sl) damn – *to stun* to shock (into helplessness) – *stasis* stagnation – *to congeal* (of a liquid) to become thick and solid – *musical chairs* game in which one has to move around a number of chairs and try to sit down when the music stops – *to prod* to push or press – *afiliated* joined or connected – *elation* pride and joy – *austerity* lack of comfort – *to herald* to be a sign of s.th. coming – *disruptive* bringing into disorder – *unedifying* not improving, not impressing – *throes* (lit) severe pains – *strained* weakened

Assignments

1. What is the state of the nation? How do various groups of society respond to it and for what reasons?
2. Evaluate the tone of the passage. What techniques are used to bring it about and how can it be described?
3. What may be the function of this passage within the framework of the novel?
4. *The Ice Age* may be considered as a novel of social criticism. To what extent is this confirmed by the above passage?

The Novels of M. Drabble

In comparison with *The Realms of Gold*, Drabble's next novel, *The Ice Age* (1977) seems to confront the human condition more relentlessly but ultimately evades it too. The novel explores the effects of the economic crisis in Britain in the mid-seventies through the experience of several figures, especially that of its main character, the property developer Anthony Keating, who is made bankrupt by the crisis, suffers a heart attack and retreats to his country house hoping there to work out a perspective on his situation. And he is not disappointed:

He was feeling exceptionally well: country life was suiting him. And it reassured him, that all this landscape had stood up so well to the onslaughts. England. It would never shake to the roots, surely. An old tree might crash, but the rest endured.

Keating's identification of nature with the process of history is Drabble's own. It is reiterated in nature images to describe the economic situation throughout the novel and the equation with the natural process not only "inexcusably flattens the difficulties of the human and social environment" it also shirks any human responsibility. Although the novel contains a good deal of criticism of the dominant concept of progress and makes one aware that modern (British) society is living by false values, these issues are not dwelled upon. Through her main character Drabble provides a solution without having investigated any causes of the social problems alluded to. By a rather surprising twist in the plot, Anthony Keating winds up leaving Britain and capitalism as well as his lover Alison and her brain damaged child far behind to search for God and nature in different realms. Keating escapes and the nagging social questions which the novel purports to explore quietly escape with him. Drabble's pitiless and sombre epilogue "Alison, there is no leaving. Alison can neither live nor die. Alison has Molly. Her life is beyond imagining. It will not be imagined. Britain will recover, but not Alison Murray" stands out awkwardly, almost as an afterthought or an idea for a different novel, but with no real connection with the main subject of *The Ice Age*. Basically *The Ice Age* is, like most of Drabble's novels, a story of salvation and reinforces a belief which Sarah Bennett already voiced in *A Summer Bird-Cage*, "I do believe that people can't be changed: they can only be saved or enlightened or renewed, one by one, which is a different thing and not one that can be affected by legislation".

Gudrun G. Boch in: H. Bock/A. Wertheim (eds.), *Essays on the Contemporary British Novel*, Hueber, München 1986, pp. 255–256.

Assignments

1. What aspects of *The Ice Age* does G. Boch focus on?
2. What evidence of G. Boch's view does the extract from *The Ice Age* contain?

5 The Comic/Phantasy Novel

Sweet Dreams

MICHAEL FRAYN

While waiting in his car in front of a stop-light, Howard Baker, 37, an architect and designer, has a long dream. He imagines situations and experiences in which his secret wishes come true. He sees fascinating places, meets interesting people, and he can do whatever he wants to do.
Besides growing younger every day, he is successful in his career, and is surrounded by a host of friends. At fashionable dinner parties he is the centre of everybody's attention. He leads a happy family life and is on good terms with his wife Felicity, which even allows him to confess to her that he is in love with another woman, Rose. Felicity takes it very calmly and comforts Howard in his emotional state, especially when his attempt to seduce Rose fails. Howard is happy about a travelling fellowship to investigate aspects of the Third World (which turns out to be Britain). His final report on the human condition is welcomed with enthusiasm and is even going to be filmed.
Reality seems to creep into his dream, when, in a scene of the film, his friend Phil seems to be attracted to Rose, and, in fact, is married to her. As a consequence of this disappointment, Harold turns his back on the life he has led in this society, because "its moral confusion disgusts him". He moves into a ramshackle farmhouse and becomes a poet and revolutionary, which, in turn, leads to inevitable changes: a new film crew, a new film (strictly revolutionary stuff) and infatuation with another woman. Harold has become a celebrity again, he is surrounded by fans and friends who try to imitate his life style.
"His understanding of the world continues to deepen, and so does his understanding of himself." He is even to have lunch with the Japanese Prime Minister. He wants to go out to offer his friend Phil a job, so he gets in the car to go there, and suddenly finds himself waiting in front of a stop-light, just as at the beginning of his dream.

A man sits in his car at the traffic-lights, waiting for them to go green.
He is thirty-seven years old, with high forehead, and thin hair that stands on end in the slightest breeze. His eyes are a little protuberant, and his lips are set in a faint smile, so that as he leans forward against the wheel, gazing straight ahead through the windscreen, he seems to be waiting for the green light with eagerness.
In fact the light has been green for some time already.
Howard Baker (this is his name) is sit-

ting in front of a green light waiting for a green light because he is thinking. He is wondering:

– whether he is adequately insured;

– whether it's Hornsey Lane he is about to enter on the other side of Highgate Hill, or whether he has confused Highgate Hill with Highgate West Hill once again;

– whether life might really be coming to an end, as ecologists say;

– whether he should kiss Rose, the wife of the man he is on his way to see, when she opens the front door to him;

– whether, conceptually, it would be helpful to try regarding the house as an extension of the car, rather than the other way about, and experimenting with an internal trim based upon black simulated leather, with built-in ashtrays;

– whether he will be invited to lunch with Rose and Phil, and if not, whether to get a sandwich in a pub, or go straight back to the office, send out for sandwiches, and catch up on the plans for the Manchester Marina scheme; and if so, whether to order egg and tomato sandwiches, or cheese and chutney, or some of each;

– whether the girl standing on the opposite side of Highgate Hill (or Highgate West Hill) with the long dark hair blowing forwards over her shoulders will turn so that he can see her face; and if so whether the face will be the revelation that the long dark hair promises; and what a face would have to be *like* to be the revelation that one always expects …

Another car pulls up behind him, and hoots discreetly – pup-pup. He does not hear it.

The lights go yellow.

The girl is just about to turn. She is gazing up Highgate Hill (or Highgate West Hill), waiting for someone. At any moment she will turn round and check that her friend is not coming from the opposite direction.

The lights go red.

Howard Baker now recalls an unanalysed sound waiting in his memory for attention – a pup-pup, a sound of hooting. He looks quickly in his mirror, and sees the head of the man in the car behind move from side to side with sardonic patience. Smiling foolishly, he puts the car into gear, and violently accelerates away, taking one last look at the girl, just in case she turns.

And she does. She turns to look at *him*. Her face is astonished – blank with astonishment. An attractive face, with dark eyes and dark eyebrows, but no revelation. Just amazed, with the mouth a little open, as if preparing to formulate some cry.

So that's one thing settled. The problem of lunch he doesn't resolve, nor whether to kiss Rose, nor the question of internal trim in public housing. But he does find out whether it's Hornsey Lane on the other side of Highgate Hill (or Highgate West Hill).

It's not. It's a ten-lane expressway, on a warm midsummer evening, with the sky clearing after a day of rain.

The expressway! Of course! How obvious everything is when once it's happened.

He drives with the windows down, warm air streaming around him, swept along in a jewelled red river of taillights five lanes wide.

They are approaching some great metropolis. The expressway flies over quiet suburban streets with oldfashioned lamps coming on among the elms. A pagoda is silhouetted against the golden west, then a windmill with sails turning, picked out with coloured lights, then a floodlit château with pink pigs standing outside it on their hind legs, sharpening knives and holding up menus. Neon signs flash and shift, ghostly pale against the sunset, brilliant against the piled black clouds in the north. He recognizes some of them – the Pan-Am symbol, *Dagens Nyheter*, the Seven Names of God. Electric characters announce the temperature and humidity, closing prices on the stock market, and the latest digits reached in the computation of the value of II. There is a smell of coffee in the air. In the forecourt of a pancake house the gigantic figure of a woman revolves on top of a pylon, picked out by spotlights, standing on tiptoe, high-kicking. He cranes to catch sight of her face, and as she turns towards him he sees that it is St Julian of Norwich. 'And all shall be well,' she tells him softly, over the car radio, 'and all manner of things shall be well.'

He knows that she is right; all matter of things *will* be well in this city he is entering. He is not at all tired, even though he has driven so far. A restless excitement stirs in him, a sense of being on the verge of deep and different things.

The expressway turns to cross water full of the redness of the sky, and there, floating on the horizon above the shining red water, are the clustered towers of the inner city, purple with distance, lights shining in a million windows – exactly as he has always known they would be. Now other freeways are converging upon his, passing above and beneath, wheeling and turning all round him. He follows the Downtown postings, up, round, through, and over; one of a thousand particles circling the orbits of a complex molecule.

When he emerges from this the towers are much closer. They rise straight up into the sky above him. He can see into some of the windows. In one room two people are dancing to music which only they can hear. In another a family is just sitting down to its evening meal. Faintly he can smell soup, and taste radishes and wine.

Now he is driving slowly along a straight street cut like a slot between the towers. It's hot. People stroll in their shirtsleeves, and sit at sidewalk cafés. One man is just taking another by the arm as he passes, and laughing in surprise. Yellow taxicabs race past, swerving in front of him, braking violently at stop lights.

He drives on until he comes to an open square with people eating at tables under the trees. High up on the other side of the square is a sign on which words pass rapidly from right to left across a bank of lights.

'Howard Baker?' say the words on the sign as Howard gets out of the car. He looks up, surprised, then glances round to see if anyone else has noticed.

'So here you are!' forms the sign smoothly. 'But don't feel any sense of anticlimax, because everyone here wants to meet you, and all sorts of parties are being arranged, and several people are going to be calling you in the morning.'

He grins, embarrassed and pleased. 'The silly buggers!' he says.

In your first few hours in a new place, while you're still dazed, before you can even really believe you've arrived, you see it more vividly and more clearly than you ever will again. Even after a few minutes – even while the porter is still showing him to his room – Howard feels that he has understood a great deal about this city. He could write a book about it.

'There's something in the air in this place!' he tells the porter. 'I really feel alive here!'

'Sure,' says the porter. 'You're really going to have yourself a good time.'

He's got brown eyes and a smiling face – the sort of man who knows his way around, and who'll fix anything for you. Howard takes to him. He feels he can talk seriously with him.

'What's happening here?' he asks him seriously. 'What's the political situation at the moment? When are the elections coming up? Are you free? What do you have to pay for a pair of men's shoes, for example? Have you been hit by inflation?'

'Don't worry,' says the porter. 'It's okay here. You don't have to worry.'

He leads Howard across little courtyards full of hibiscus, where you can hear fountains playing, and people laughing softly; along candlelit cloisters; straight across lawns with metal labels stuck in them saying 'Fellows only'.

Howard feels a great need to talk in Spanish.

'Quale sono le questione politiche le piu importante in questo momento?' he asked effortlessly. 'But this is fantastic! I've never been able to speak Spanish before, apart from a few odd phrases like *spaghetti bolognese* and *virtuosi di Roma*! And here I am just doing it, like that!'

'You can do anything here,' says the porter. 'You want to sing? Then sing! You want to dance? So dance! This is the golden land of opportunity. If I wanted to be a doctor or a lawyer, I could be one tomorrow. Just like that. Just by snapping my fingers. I could have one of the finest practices in the city. Sometimes I've thought of going into business. I could do that. No trouble. I could buy up this hotel tomorrow. I could buy up the whole block. Ride up and down in a chauffer-driven limousine, smoking big cigars. Only one thing stops me.'

'What's that?' asks Howard.

'I don't want to. I'm happy the way I am. Why fool around with money, or taking teeth out, when I might not enjoy it as much? This is what I'm used to – carrying gentlemen's bags up, turning on the lights and the air-conditioner, taking a look round to make sure everything's just so. This is the way I am, and I figure why be different? But you, you could do anything. You've got ambition, you've got drive, you're open to new experience. Have you ever thought of becoming a hotel porter, for instance?'

'No?' says Howard, astonished.

'Because remember – in this place anything's possible. Look, make a little experiment.'

He stops, and puts down Howard's bags. They are in a lobby surrounded by staircases and landings.

'Bend your knees slightly,' he tells Howard.

'What?'

'Look, like this. Now, up on tiptoe. Then – push off.'

Howard pushes off. He drifts slowly up into the air.

'This is fantastic!' he says.

He drifts back towards the floor.

'I *knew* it was possible!' he calls back to the porter.

'But before I could never do it! I knew it was just a matter of getting the knack!'

'Push off from the banisters. Do frog-kicks. Force the air away underneath you with your hands.'

Howard is enchanted by the slowness with which he can move, and the smallness of the gestures which are needed to change course and height. He steers himself into the current of warm air rising above the chandelier, and is carried effortlessly upwards, past floors where people are sitting at little tables and eating ice-cream out of metal goblets. Some of them smile at him, and wave.

'This is fantastic!' he shouts back at the porter, now several floors below him. 'This is staggering! It's amazing! It's ... well, it's fantastic!'

'Mind your head on the ceiling,' shouts the porter.

'Why don't you take off and come up here, too?'

The porter shrugs.

'Why should I?' he says. 'I'm happy where I am.'

'But it's fantastic up here!'

'It's fantastic down here.'

Howard laughs. A ridiculous thought has just occurred to him. He glides downwards, vertiginously, holding his breath at the emptiness beneath him.

'I'm sorry,' he says, as he sets foot to floor. 'That wasn't Spanish I was talking to you in. That was Italian.'

'Italian – Spanish,' shrugs the porter. 'Who cares?' Here you speak any language you please, and they'll all come running.'

Michael Frayn, *Sweet Dreams*,
Fontana, London 1973, pp. 5–11.

Vocabulary

protuberant swelling or curving outward – *Hornsey Lane, Highgate Hill* major roads in the north of London – *internal trim* contrasting strip along doors, windows, etc. – *marina* area near the sea where small boats can come into harbour – *sardonic* scornful, cynical – *to cluster* to gather or grow in a large number – *to converge* to come together towards a common point – *to take to s.o.* to like s.o. – *fellow* high-ranking member of an Oxford or Cambridge college – *knack* (infml) special skill or ability – *chandelier* branched ornamental holder for electric lights or candles – *goblet* drinking glass with foot and stem and without handles – *vertiginous* (fml) causing unsteadiness as if one's head were spinning round, esp. when looking down from a great height

Assignments

1. To what extent does the passage refer to reality, to what extent is it unreal? How must this irreality be explained?
2. Retell in some detail Howard Baker's perceptions and thoughts.
3. What impression of the metropolis is evoked and how is it developed?
4. Retell the scene at the hotel and try to explain it.
5. How is Howard Baker characterized both through description and through his thoughts?
6. Comment on the use of point of view in this passage.
7. Characterize the tone of each of the three sections. Find some stylistic features by which it is brought about.

Sweet Dreams

This is a fantasy presented with disarming lightness of touch and tone which is profounder than it looks. Howard Baker, driving to Highgate, finds himself suddenly in a strange but most attractive megalopolis which is the capital city of Heaven. It is run by Cambridge men and women: God is Freddie Vigars, a distinguished but decent scholar of good family, whose wife Caroline is "a kindly-looking girl with thick white legs and her slip showing". She says that Freddie, or God, is a terrific radical. The food eaten at heavenly parties begins with *taramasalata*, continues with *gigot aux haricots* and ends with apple crumble. Howard is set to work, with a team of awfully decent mountain-designers, on designing the Alps. The world is being made, but the world we know (which is being made) already exists. Selections from *Fiddler on the Roof* are played at receptions to meet God. Other Cambridge men are engaged on putting inspiration into the heads of great poets like Donne and Milton; one is even designing man. Howard ends as a planning assistant to God. "This is our task," he says, as he carves the *gigot*; "to provide the harsh materials on which men's imaginations can be exercised, and to offer, through the cultured and civilized life that we ourselves lead here in the metropolis, some intimations of the world they might envisage." ("Meanwhile," murmurs Miriam Bernstein, "here we all sit waiting for second helpings.")
It is an impossible liberal vision, all too Cambridge. But Frayn, who refrains from comment, who is altogether too charming – like his characters – with his easy-going colloquial prose, is fundamentally grim and sardonic. Cambridge cannot redesign the universe. The dream ends. Still, it might be very pleasant if these awfully nice and intelligent Cantabrians of good family could replace blind chance or grumbling bloody bearded Jehovah. There is no sin here, only liberal errors. Frayn was trained as a philosopher. This is a philosophical novel. It is deceptively tough.

Anthony Burgess, *Ninety-Nine Novels,* Alison & Busby, London 1984, p. 108.

Assignments

1. How does A. Burgess judge M. Frayn's book?
2. What does this evaluation/presentation of the novel contribute to your understanding of the extract from *Sweet Dreams*?

6 The Family Novel

Dinner at the Homesick Restaurant

ANNE TYLER

In her mid-forties Pearl Tull is deserted by her husband, Beck, her junior by six years, and is thus forced to raise her children Cody, Ezra and Jenny single-handedly. In her frustration she turns out to be a formidable mother. Domineering, selfish, possessive, cruel, apt to fly into a rage at the slightest provocation, she does not even shrink from physical violence. The children suffer from the situation, their emotional lives stunted forever. Cody becomes completely success-oriented as an efficiency expert, but remains unsettled after his marriage to Ruth, whom he has turned away from his brother Ezra in a compulsive act of jealousy. Ezra, gentle and with a touch of the artist, takes over Mrs Scarlatti's restaurant, calling it the Homesick Restaurant. His desperate attempts to keep the family together fail: family dinners at his restaurant are forever disrupted by quarrels. Jenny successfully studies pediatrics, but has difficulty relating to people.

At Pearl's funeral Cody finally confronts his father and, as he begins to understand him, suddenly feels strongly drawn towards his family.

Monday morning, he looked for Edith on the way to school but he didn't see her. As it turned out, she was tardy. She arrived in homeroom just after the bell. He tried to catch her eye but she didn't glance his way; only gazed fixedly at the teacher all during announcements. And when the first bell rang she walked to class with Sue Meeks and Harriet Smith. Evidently, she was no longer friendless.

By third period, it was clear she was avoiding him. He couldn't even get near her; she had a constant bodyguard. But what had he done wrong? He cornered Barbara Pace – a plump, cheerful redhead who served as a kind of central switchboard for ninth-grade couples.

"What's the matter with Edith?" he asked.

"Who?"

"Edith Taber. We were getting along just fine and now she won't speak."

"Oh," she said. She shifted her books. She was wearing a man-sized shirt with the tails out. Come to think of it, so were half the other girls. "Well," she said, "I guess she likes somebody else now."

"Is it my brother?" Cody asked.

"Who's your brother?"

"Ezra. My brother, Ezra."

"*I* didn't know you had a brother," she said, peering at him.

"Well, she liked me well enough last week. What happened?"

"See," she told him patiently, "now she's been to a couple of parties and naturally she's developed new interests. She's got a sort of ... broader view, and also she didn't realize about your reputation."

"What reputation?"

"Well, you do drink, Cody. And you hung around with that cheap Lorena Schmidt all summer; you smell like a walking cigarette; and you almost got arrested over Halloween."

"Did my brother tell her that?"

"What's this about your brother? Everybody told her. It's not exactly a secret."

"Well, I never claimed to be a saint," Cody said.

"She says you're real good-looking and all but she wants a boy she can respect," said Barbara. "She thinks she might like Francis Elburn now."

"Francis Elburn! That fairy."

"He's really more her type," said Barbara.

"His hair is curly."

"So?"

"Francis Elburn; Jesus Christ."

"There's no need to use profanity," Barbara told him.

Cody walked home alone, long after the others had left, choosing streets where he'd be certain not to run into Edith or her friends. Once he turned down the wrong alley and it struck him that he was still an outsider, unfamiliar with the neighborhood. His classmates had been born and raised here, most of them, and were more comfortable with each other than he could ever hope to be. Look at his two best friends: their parents went to the movies together; their mothers talked on the telephone. *His* mother ... He kicked a signpost. What he wouldn't give to have a mother who acted like other mothers! He longed to see her gossiping with a little gang of women in the kitchen, letting them roll her hair up in pincurls, trading beauty secrets, playing cards, losing track of time – "Oh, goodness, look at the clock! And supper not even started; my husband will kill me. Run along, girls." He wished she had some outside connection, something beyond that suffocating house.

And his father: he had uprooted the family continually, tearing them away as soon as they were settled and plunking them someplace new. But where was he now that Cody *wanted* to be uprooted, now that he was saddled with a reputation and desperate to leave and start over? His father had ruined their lives, Cody thought – first in one way and then in another. He thought of tracking him down and arriving on his doorstep: "I'm in trouble; it's all your fault. I've got a bad name, I need to leave town, you'll have to take me in." But that would only be another unknown city, another new school to walk into alone. And there too, probably, his grades would begin to slip and the neighbors would complain and the teachers would start to suspect him first when any little thing went wrong; and then Ezra would follow shortly in his dogged, earnest, devoted way and everybody would say to Cody, "Why can't you be more like your brother?"

He let himself into the house, which smelled of last night's cabbage. It was almost dark and the air seemed thick; he felt he had to labor to move through it. He climbed the stairs wearily. He passed Jenny's room, where she sat doing her homework in a tiny dull circle of yellow from the lamp. Her face was thin and shadowed and she didn't bother greeting him. He climbed on up to his own room and flicked on the light switch. He had set his books on the bureau before he realized Ezra was there. Asleep, as usual – curled on his bed with a sheaf of homework papers. Oh, Ezra was so slow and dazed; he could sleep anytime. His lips were parted. His cat, Alicia, lay in the crook of his arm, purring and looking self-satisfied.

Cody knelt beside his bed and pulled from beneath it a half-filled bottle of bourbon, an empty gin bottle, five empty beer bottles, a crumpled pack of Camels, and a box of pretzels. He strewed them around Ezra, arranging them just right. He went to the hall storage closet and took out his father's Six-20 Brownie camera. In the doorway of his room he aimed and paused and clicked the shutter. Ezra didn't wake, amazingly enough. (The light from the flashgun was so powerful, you'd see swimming blue globes for minutes after being photographed.) But the cat seemed mildly disturbed. She got to her feet and yawned. What a yawn! – huge and disdainful. It would have made a wonderful picture: dead-beat Ezra and his no-account cat, both with gaping mouths. Cody wondered if she'd do it again. "Yawn," he told her, and he advanced the film for another photo. "Alicia? Yawn." She only smirked and settled down again. He yawned himself, demonstrating, but apparently cats didn't find such things contagious. He lowered the camera and came closer to pat her head, scratch beneath her chin, stroke her throat. Nothing worked. "Yawn, dammit," he said, and he tried to pry her teeth apart by force. She drew up sharply, eyes wide and glaring. Ezra woke.

"Your cat is *retarded*," Cody told him.

"Huh?"

"I can't get her to yawn."

Ezra reached over, matter-of-factly, and circled the cat with his arm. She gave a luxurious yawn and nestled down against him, and Ezra went back to sleep. Cody didn't try for another picture, though. He'd never seen anyone take the fun out of things the way Ezra could.

Cody and Ezra and Jenny went shopping for a Christmas present for their mother. Each of them had saved four weeks' allowance, which meant forty cents apiece, and Cody had a dollar extra that he'd taken from Miss Saunders's center desk drawer. That made two dollars and twenty cents – enough for some winter gloves, Cody suggested. Jenny said gloves were boring and she wanted to buy a diamond ring. "That's really stupid," Cody told her. "Even you ought to know you can't buy a diamond ring for two-twenty."

"I don't mean a real one, I mean glass. Or anything, just so it's pretty and not useful."

They were forced to shop in the stores near home, since they didn't want to spend money on carfare. It was mid-December and crowds of other people were shopping too – plowing past with their arms full of packages, breathing white clouds in the frosty air. Further downtown the department store windows would be as rich and bright as the insides of jewel boxes, and there'd be carols and clanging brass bells and festoons of tinsel on the traffic lights, but in this neighborhood the shops were smaller, darker, decorated with a single wreath on the door or a cardboard Santa Claus carrying a carton of Chesterfield cigarettes. Soldiers on leave straggled by in clumps, looking lost. The shoppers had something grim and determined about them – even those with the gaudiest packages. They seemed likely to mow down anyone in their path. Cody took a pinch of Jenny's coat sleeve so as not to lose her.

"I'm serious," she was saying. "I don't want to get her anything warm. Anything necessary. Anything –"

"Serviceable," Ezra said.

They all grimaced.

"If we bought her a ring, though," Ezra said, "she might feel bad about the wastefulness. She might not really enjoy it."

Cody hated the radiant, grave expression that Ezra wore sometimes; it showed that he realized full well how considerate he was being. "What do *you* want for Christmas?" Cody asked him roughly. "World peace?"

"World what? I'd like a recorder," Ezra said.

They crossed an intersection with a swarm of sailors. "Well," said Cody, "you're not getting one."

"I know that."

"You're getting a cap with turn-down earflaps and a pair of corduroy pants."

"Cody!" said Jenny. "You weren't supposed to tell."

"It doesn't matter," Ezra said.

They separated for a woman who had stopped to fit her child's mittens on. "It used to be," Jenny said, "that we got toys for Christmas, and candy. Remember how nice last Christmas was?"

"This one's going to be nice too," Ezra told her.

"Remember down in Virginia, when Daddy bought us a sled, and Mother said it was silly because it hardly ever snowed but December twenty-sixth we woke up and there was snow all over everything?"

"That was fun," Ezra said.

"We had the only sled in town," Jenny said. "Cody started charging for rides. Daddy showed us how to wax the runners and we pulled it to the top of that hill ... What was the name of that hill? It had such a funny –"

Then she stopped short on the sidewalk. Pedestrians jostled all around her. "Why," she said.

Cody and Ezra looked at her.

"He's really not ever coming home again. Is he," she said.

No one answered. After a minute they resumed walking, three abreast, and Cody took a pinch of Ezra's sleeve, too, so they wouldn't drift apart in the crowd.

Cody sorted the mail, setting aside for his mother a couple of envelopes that looked like Christmas cards. He threw away a department store flyer and a letter from his school. He pocketed an envelope with a Cleveland postmark.

He went upstairs to his room and switched on the goose-necked lamp beside his bed. While the lightbulb warmed, he whistled and stared out the window. Then he tested the bulb with his fingers and, finding it hot enough, wrapped the envelope around it and counted slowly to thirty. After that he pried open the flap with ease and pulled out a single sheet of paper and a check.

... says they should be producing to capacity by June of '45 ... his father wrote. *Sorry the enclosed is a little smaller than expected as I have incurred some ...* It was his usual letter, nothing different. Cody folded it again and slid it back in the envelope, though it hardly seemed worth the effort. Then he heard the front door slam. "Ezra Tull?" Pearl called. Her cloppy high heels started rapidly up the stairs. Cody tucked the envelope into his bureau and shut the drawer. "Ezra!"

"He's not here," Cody said.

She came to stand in the doorway. "Where is he?" she asked. She was out of breath, untidy-looking. Her hat was on crooked and she still wore her coat.

"He went to get the laundry, like you told him to."

"What do you know about this?"

She bore down on him, holding out a stack of snapshots. The one on top was so blurred and gray that Cody had trouble deciphering it. He took the whole collection from her hand. Ah, yes: Ezra lay in a stupor, surrounded by liquor bottles. Cody grinned. He'd forgotten that picture completely.

"What could it mean?" his mother asked. "I take a roll of film to the drugstore and I come back with the shock of my life. I just wanted to get the camera ready for Christmas. I was expecting maybe some scenes from last summer, or Jenny's birthday cake ... and here I find Ezra like a derelict! A common drunk! Could this be what it looks like? Answer me!"

"He's not as perfect as you think he is," Cody told her.

"But he's never given me a moment's worry."

"He's done a lot that might surprise you."

Pearl sat down on his bed. She was shaking her head, looking stunned. "Oh, Cody, it's such a battle, raising children," she said. "I know you must think I'm difficult. I lose my temper, I carry on like a shrew sometimes, but if you could just realize how ... helpless I feel! How scary it is to know that everyone I love depends on me! I'm afraid I'll do something wrong."

She reached up – for the photos, he thought, and he held them out to her; but no, what she wanted was his hand. She took it and pulled him down beside her. Her skin felt hot and dry. "I've probably been too hard on you," she said. "But I look to you for support now, Cody. You're the only person I can turn to; it may be you and I are more alike than you think. Cody, what am I going to do?"

She leaned closer, and Cody drew back. Even her eyes seemed to give off heat. "Uh, well ..." he said.

"Who took that picture, anyhow? Was it you?"

"Look," he said. "It was a joke."

"Joke?"

"Ezra didn't drink that stuff. I just set some bottles around him."

Her gaze flicked back and forth across his face.

"He's never touched a drop," Cody told her.

"I see," she said. She freed his hand. She said, "Well, all I can say is, that's some joke, young man." Then she stood up and took several steps away from him. "That's some sense of humor you've got," she said.

Cody shrugged.

"Oh, I suppose it must seem very funny, scaring your mother half out of her wits. Letting her babble on like a fool. Slandering your little brother. It must seem hilarious, to someone like you."

"I'm just naturally mean, I guess," Cody said.

"You've been mean since the day you were born," she told him.

After she had walked out, he went to work resealing his father's letter.

Anne Tyler, *Dinner at the Homesick Restaurant,* Viking Penguin, New York 1982, pp. 57–64.

Vocabulary

homeroom a schoolroom where pupils of the same class or grade but often with different academic programs report at the opening of school and meet informally for class business under a teacher's guidance – *fairy* (infml) a man (esp. a homosexual) who behaves like a woman – *profanity* [prə'fænətɪ] socially shocking or impolite language (esp. with improper use of religious words or the name of God) – *saddled with* burdened with – *dogged* ['dɒgɪd] refusing to give up in the face of difficulty or opposition – *disdainful* showing lack of respect, disrespectful, contemptuous – *dead-beat* (infml) exhausted, tired out – *no-account* (AE infml) worthless, unable to do anything good – *retarded* (of a child) slower in development than others – *Miss Saunders* Cody's teacher – *festoon* a chain of flowers, leaves, ribbons etc. used for decoration – *recorder* (= Blockflöte) – *to bear down on* to approach quickly and threateningly

Assignments

1. Subdivide the passage. Briefly sum up each section and explain how the sections are related to each other.
2. Describe Cody's character as developed in the passage and discuss how it is psychologically motivated. Comment on the author's skill of presentation.
3. Judging from this passage, try to state why Anne Tyler's *Dinner at the Homesick Restaurant* has found such a wide readership in the USA.
4. Considering Cody's problems, what is the general theme of the passage? How relevant is it to modern society?

Family Happiness

In Anne Tyler's fiction, family is destiny, and (nowadays, at least) destiny clamps down on one in Baltimore. For an archeologist of manners with Tyler's skills, the city is a veritable Troy, and she has been patiently excavating since the early 1970s, when she skipped off the lawn of southern fiction and first sank her spade in the soil which has nourished such varied talents as Edgar Allan Poe, iconoclastic journalist H.L. Mencken, jazz singer Billie Holiday and underground filmmaker John Waters.

It is without question some of the fustiest soil in America; in the more settled classes, social styles developed in the 19th century withstand, with spore-like tenacity, all that the present century can throw at them. From this rich dust of custom, Tyler is steadily raising a body of fiction of major dimensions. One of the persistent concerns of this work is the ambiguity of family happiness and unhappiness. Since coming to Baltimore, Tyler has probed this ambiguity in seven novels of increasing depth and power, working numerous changes on a consistent set of themes.

The Accidental Tourist is one of Anne Tyler's best books, as good as *Morgan's Passing, Searching for Caleb* and *Dinner at the Homesick Restaurant.* The various domestic worlds we enter are delineated with easy skill; now they are poignant, now funny. Tyler shows, with a fine clarity, the mingling of misery and contentment in the daily lives of her families, reminding us how alike – and yet distinct – happy and unhappy families can be. Muriel Pritchett is as appealing a woman as Tyler has created; and upon the quiet Macon she lavishes the kind of intelligent consideration that he only intermittently gets from his own womenfolk.

At the level of metaphor, Tyler has never been stronger. The concept of an accidental tourist captures in a phrase something she has been saying all along, if not about life, at least about men: they are frequently accidental tourists in their own lives. Macon Leary sums up a long line of her males. Jake Simmes in

Earthly Possessions (1977) is an accidental kidnapper. The lovable Morgan Gower of *Morgan's Passing* (1980), an accidental obstetrician in the first scenes, is an accidental husband or lover in the rest of the book. Her men slump around like tired tourists – friendly, likable, but not all that engaged. Their characters, like their professions, seem accidental even though they come equipped with genealogies of Balzacian thoroughness. All of them have to be propelled through life by sharp, purposeful women – it usually takes not only a wife and a girlfriend but an indignant mother and one or more devoted sisters to keep these sluggish fellows moving. They poke around haphazardly, ever mild and perennially puzzled, in the foreign country called Life. If they see anything worth seeing, it is usually because a determined woman on the order of Muriel Pritchett thrusts it under their noses and demands that they pay some attention. The fates of these families hinge on long struggles between semiattentive males and semiobsessed females. In her patient investigation of such struggles, Tyler has produced a very satisfying body of fiction.

New York Times Book Review,
reprinted in: *Dialogue* 2, 1986.

Assignments

1. According to this review, what is the significance of Baltimore as the background to Anne Tyler's novels?
2. To what extent does this particular book review generalize on Anne Tyler's work?

7 The Ethnic Novel

Linden Hills

GLORIA NAYLOR

In 1820 the black Luther Nedeed, moving north to Wayne county from Tupela, Mississippi, acquires a patch of worthless hillside land known as Linden Hills, where he founds an undertaker's business. Financially successful, he soon begins to build wooden shacks, which he rents out to poor Negroes, while he himself resides in a large white clapboard house at the bottom of the hill.

Five generations later the Nedeeds have become the wealthiest people in Wayne County, which has changed a great deal in the meantime. Through housing developments Linden Hills is gaining more and more value, but the Nedeeds, resisting the white community's attempt to appropriate it, are bent on spitting white America in the eye by turning it into a showcase community, with the finest and richest homes in the county entirely reserved for blacks. "There were other black communities with showcase houses, but somehow making it into Linden Hills meant 'making it'". A Linden Hills address means success, and moving down the hill towards Tupelo Drive and the Nedeeds becomes tantamount to climbing up the social ladder. However, Luther Nedeed finally has to recognize the futility of his "black American dream", the nothingness and emptiness of success. Not only does success not advance his people, it also makes them indistinguishable from the whites, i.e. it makes them lose their true identity.

This is also what two young black street poets, Willie and Lester, experience while they work their way down the hill, doing odd jobs in the last days before Christmas. What they observe is essentially a repulsive world of hypocrisy, vain ambition, social snobbery, opportunism, blackmail, broken relationships, solitude and suicide.

Luther Nedeed has rejected his young son, whose light skincolour made him suspect his wife Willa of treachery. He has banished both from his sight, locking them in the morgue in his basement, where the son has died. On Christmas Eve Willa manages to escape and, in a scuffle with her husband, accidentally sets the house on fire. They both die in the flames while Willie and Lester are looking on, shocked that nobody in Linden Hills is willing to rescue the Nedeeds.

Xavier heard the first set of chimes and decided to let the bell ring again before he answered. But Maxwell had no intention of ringing twice. After one depression of exactly two seconds, he stood there calmly waiting for the door to be opened. He knew he was expected, made sure he had been heard, and so the only logical sequence would now be admittance into the house. Xavier sat nervously in the lenghtening silence, finally realizing that Maxwell wasn't going to ring again. If he opened it now, he needed some excuse for not answering immediately, but if he waited much longer he gambled on Maxwell's leaving. It was a play of wills on each side of the oak door, and Maxwell won out.

"Hey, sorry I took so long. I was upstairs when you first rang and I was waiting for the second ring to be sure that it was the bell."

"No sweat, mon ami." Maxwell's scarf glided off and was held out to Xavier. "What's shakin'?"

His greeting told Xavier that he considered this a very intimate visit because he was willing to engage in French and ghetto dialect, the two pet passions he reserved for close friends. He walked toward the couch, intently surveying the room. The few times Maxwell had been there before he had glanced around, seeming to sniff the air in case some new addition or omission might call for him to realign his opinion of Xavier.

"Can I fix you a drink?"

"If you have Chardonnay – with just a *kiss* of a chill."

Xavier shrugged his shoulders. "Well, it's cold."

He poured himself a double shot of bourbon and Maxwell allowed him to talk about the weather, car repairs, and the company's annual meeting for what he deemed an appropriate amount of time, and then choosing a place in the conversation where he knew Xavier would least expect it – "So what really brings me here, mon copain? I know about the cold; I've just driven through it with my rebuilt carburetor after interrupting the outline for my brilliant presentation for the spring convention, but what I still don't know is *why*?" He leaned back on the velvet cushions and smiled, enjoying the flicker of consternation in Xavier's eyes. He had heard the suppressed panic in his voice over the phone and a true curiosity had brought him out of his house to see what could be so important that Xavier had to try so hard to make it sound trivial.

"Well, I thought it might be nice to have you over. Except for a few hurried lunches at work, we never really get a chance to relax and just be friends."

Maxwell knew that Xavier fully understood that sparing the time to lunch with a subordinate at work was an act of friendship, so he remained silent and waited for a real answer to his question.

Xavier took a deep swallow of his bourbon. "And, uh, I wanted a little feedback on some longer-range plans. The thought had occurred to me that I might want to start to think about thinking about marrying Roxanne Tilson."

"Sacré Dieu, blood. Why?"

Xavier panicked; that wasn't what he had really meant to say and now he didn't have a ready answer that would retain Maxwell's respect. How many times had he heard him say that love was for teenagers and fools? He sought desperately for a reply, wishing that he smoked. "I know this may sound bizarre" – he took another swallow of his drink – "but there are times when she reminds me of Eleanor Roosevelt."

Maxwell frowned and thought a moment. "Well, my cleaning lady bears a striking resemblance to Indira Gandhi, but that's no reason for me to drag her down to City Hall. Are you sure that's the only reason?"

"There's nothing to be sure or unsure about." Xavier got up and went over to the bar. "It was just an idea I thought about playing with, that's all. And she was just one of the many women who came to mind. To be honest, she's not even a serious contender. I mean, the real issue is whether or not this is the time for me to settle down. But I'm not too sure that I should rush into anything, you know?"

"Oh, I know perfectly well what you mean. A decision like that is loaded with disaster – even if you could find 'a serious contender,' as you put it. And I don't hold out much hope for your doing that."

"Really?"

Maxwell shook his head and sighed, turning his wineglass gently between his fingers. "Now, let's be reasonable. I know that, for whatever reasons, you're only into black women. I'm not knocking it, mind you. But you're going to have to face some hard, cold facts: there just aren't enough decent ones to choose from. They're either out there on welfare and waiting to bring you a string of somebody else's kids to support, or they've become so prominent that they're brainwashed into thinking that you aren't good enough for them. The few who just might be up to your standards, who've distinguished themselves in the world, are into white men. Name me one black woman who's making a name for herself in the arts or entertainment and I'll name you two who have white husbands. Don't we see it every day in the magazines and newspapers, or right downtown? The best and the brightest are going that way, so what's left for you? The Roxanne Tilsons of this world."

Xavier winced. "I don't really see anything wrong with her," he mumbled.

"Well now, of course she's been to the right schools – Wellesley, wasn't it? And you're from the same neighborhood – even though she's up there on the border, it's still Linden Hills."

"Of course." Xavier's voice was slightly impatient. "How could I have even looked at her if that wasn't the case?"

"And she's pretty enough, although there's a bit too much avoirdupois."

"I wouldn't call her fat." Xavier narrowed his eyes. "She's full."

"Yes, she's full *now*, but you know that most black women have a tendency to let themselves go. Look in any spa or gym and they're outnumbered ten to one. And believe me, it's not Roxanne's fault. It's an old throwback to the jungle days when they had to store up food like camels because the women did most of the hauling. So what they do now is starve themselves until they get you and then gain ten pounds before the reception's over. And from then on in ..." Maxwell shook his head slowly and shuddered. "But the real question is not whether you can find one who'll fit into your Porsche, but who'll fit, period."

Xavier stared off into space and thought. But we read the same books, like the same music. We both want to travel. He found himself wishing that

Maxwell would shut up and go home. He hadn't called him here to listen to all this. He had done nothing but cause him to think of all the reasons why he should run out tomorrow and buy an engagement ring, but somehow he didn't want that. And what he needed desperately to know was why.

"Look, Maxwell, I find that just a little hard to buy. They're out there in all shapes and sizes once I'm ready. But maybe I'm just not ready now, you know?"

"Oh, you're ready. Ready and raring to go. But the sad thing is that there isn't a mother's daughter out there ready for you. And you want to know why?" Maxwell sat on the edge of the sofa. "Because Roxanne Tilson is only the clone of a whole mass that are coming out of these colleges with their hot little fists clenched around those diplomas and they aren't ready to hear nothing from nobody, least of all you. When they've done that four-or six-year stint at the Yales, Stanfords, or Brandeises, they no longer think they're women, but walking miracles. They're ready to ask a hell of a lot from the world then and a hell of a lot from you. They're hungry and they're climbers, Xavier, with an advanced degree in expectations. Hook up with one of them and whatever you're doing isn't good enough, and you're doing damned good as it is."

Maxwell's knuckles tightened around the stem of his glass. "I'm going to make a confession." He leaned toward Xavier. "I once thought about marrying a woman like Roxanne and she wasn't half so attractive, but she had a Ph.D. from Princeton and I was much younger then and could have forced myself to overlook a lot of other things. But when it came right down to the line, I realized that she just didn't understand me. She just didn't appreciate the problems I was going through. And if a woman can't do that, at least she should be quiet and stay out of your way. Remember, a man only lives two places – at work and at home. You and I both know the sacrifices we made and are still making to walk that tightrope out there; it takes every ounce of strength we've got. So, can you afford to be drained when you come in here?" He stabbed his finger toward the ground. "Can you afford to be reminded – in five-syllable vocabularies no less – that the rope's a lot thinner than you think and it's a lot farther to the ground?" Maxwell's voice had risen a quarter of an octave, which was his equivalent of hysteria, and it stunned Xavier.

"But if you feel that way about it," Xavier almost whispered, "I don't understand why you were willing to weather all that flack when you promoted Mabel Thompson."

"Of course I promoted her." Maxwell leaned back and smiled, taking a split second to regulate his breathing. "Any fool could see from her résumé that she was overqualified for that lousy job in the bookkeeping department. I brought her into my office and now I have one of the most efficient cost analysts in the eastern division. While all those other clowns were busy looking at her color and sex, I looked at her personnel file. And I knew that any woman who managed to support herself and two younger brothers while getting through accounting school with straight A's would have to be a tiger. But you know what happens when you try to bed down with one? You get your balls clawed off. And that's the bottom line, isn't it?"

Yes, that was the bottom line. Xavier could never see himself with any woman who wasn't determined to go somewhere with her life. But he knew that the road was a lot more cluttered for a black woman and a successful journey meant sharpening her spirits to grind away all the garbage that stood in her way. And just maybe when that switch was turned on, it couldn't tell the difference between his living flesh and anything else. If he needed anything more than Roxanne, he needed those constant reminders hung on him healthy and intact that he could still hang on.

"Mabel probably needed those claws to survive." Xavier frowned into his bourbon.

"I'm sure she did. And I thank her, and my twenty percent reduction in marketing costs thanks her. But let somebody else marry her."

Xavier sighed and watched his ice cubes melt away into the amber fluid. He knew that if he watched them long enough, the frozen crystals would lose their shape and edges, become indistinguishable from the mahogany sea that was keeping them afloat. We read the same books, like the same … Just concentrate on the brown liquid that's dissolving the ice. He didn't have to get up and find a stirrer, or even rotate the glass. Just sit there and soon, very soon, there would be nothing but a mouthful of watery bourbon that could be gotten rid of in a single swallow with no harm to his throat or stomach, and definitely no chance of heartburn.

"I understand what you're saying, Maxwell. But that doesn't leave much for me, and I've no intention of spending the rest of my life alone."

"You don't have to – and it leaves quite a bit for you. And I'm hardly talking about only white women; this whole planet is full of women to choose from if you're willing to branch out."

"Well, I guess I could ask to be transferred to one of the offices overseas – there's no telling who I might meet on the plane."

"Laugh if you want to, but it won't be a laughing matter when –"

They were startled by a sharp rap on the back door. Oh God, he'd forgotten all about Lester being out in the garage. Xavier opened the kitchen door on two sweaty and grimy faces.

"Your aunt said you'd pay us when we were through," Lester greeted him curtly. "Well, we're through."

"That was pretty quick." Xavier started to smile at Lester but was stopped with, "Well, there was two of us, so what's the problem?"

"No, no problem. I'm just amazed at how efficient you were, because I know how cluttered that garage was."

"You can go out there and check if you don't believe me. The newspapers are bundled and stacked beside the garbage bags and the boxes she left for all that other crap. And it's all on the side of the house for the trash collectors."

"I believe you, Lester." He turned to the darker boy. "I'm sure you fellas did a great job. I hope the car didn't get in your way. Please, come in and I'll go upstairs and get my wallet." At that moment, Xavier's conscience called for a great deal of generosity toward anything associated with Roxanne, even her arrogant kid brother.

"We'd rather wait out here."

"Well, I could stand to use your bathroom." Willie put his foot up on the back step.

"Sure, come on in."

"You know the cold has a way of working on your bladder."

"Yes, I know what you mean." Xavier held out his hand to Willie. "Xavier Donnell."

"Willie Mason, but I don't think we should shake." Willie turned his palms over. "My hands are pretty grubby."

"That's okay, a little honest dirt won't hurt me."

Lester stuck his hands in his pockets and rolled his eyes.

Willie was amazed at the softness of Xavier's skin. It felt like a woman's hand against his rough knuckles and calloused palm. This guy probably never lifted anything heavier than a ballpoint pen.

Maxwell, feeling that he had been left alone for more than an appropriate time, appeared in the kitchen door. "Xavier, I'll have to be going."

Xavier turned toward him quickly. "Yes, let me get your scarf." He didn't really want to introduce the boys, but felt it would be rude not to. "This is Lester Tilson, Roxanne's brother, and his friend, Willie – Maxwell Smyth."

"Hiya." Willie smiled.

Maxwell nodded silently as he looked directly at Xavier. "It seems that this is your day for company."

"They're not company," he said a bit too quickly, and then turned back to them apologetically. "They're doing some work for my aunt outside."

"That's industrious." Maxwell's eyes swept over them.

"No, that's poverty." Lester leaned against the sink.

Maxwell seemed surprised – as if a parrot had been trained to answer him back. "Well, I suppose that poverty leads to industry," intending his remark to be the final word in a useless exchange.

Willie watched Maxwell's face and had the strange feeling that this man's words weren't really meant to reach across the kitchen toward them. His eyes seemed to stop at the green tiles on the floor in front of their feet. Why, it was the same feeling that you got talking to some white people. He suddenly felt very invisible to this tall, impeccable man and needed to hear his own voice to prove that he was in the kitchen.

"No, poverty just seems to lead to more poverty if you're black," Willie said loudly, and stared directly at Maxwell.

Xavier looked nervously from Willie to Maxwell. "I'll get your scarf. You can use the bathroom in the basement," he said over his shoulder to Willie and started for the door.

"No, wait." Maxwell held up his finger. Willie saw his linty pea jacket, frayed jeans, and cheap shoes materialize in Maxwell's eyes as they made their way slowly down his body. "You know, it's that sort of an attitude that will keep some people cleaning out garages for the rest of their lives. Being black has nothing to do with being poor. And being poor doesn't mean that you have to stay that way."

"Then I guess it's just a coincidence" – Willie felt his heart pounding – "that the majority of black folks in this country are poor, have been poor, and will be poor for a long time to come."

"Well, I see that you can conjugate verbs." Maxwell brushed an invisible speck off his jacket sleeve. "And a difficult verb at that. So it's probably not too much for you to understand that the only reason so many black people are still nothing is because they keep their eyes turned backward toward the times when they could be little else, and are still crying about what they could never do while what they can do is swiftly passing them by. And so, in that case, you're absolutely right – that type will always be nothing."

"First of all, I didn't say that poor black people were nothing. And second –"

"You might as well have," Maxwell cut him off. "Because that's just what it amounts to. It amounts to a blind, senseless existence due to an inability to take advantage of the progress that's continually going on."

"Bullshit!" Lester's voice startled everyone in the kitchen. "Man, you're the one who has blinders on. You wanna know why most black people aren't gonna move anywhere? Because this man's government is ruled by the few for the few. And I don't know how they taught you to spell progress in the school you went to, but on the streets you spell it W-H-I-T-E."

"I'm the living proof that that's a lie," Maxwell said softly. "And Xavier proves it too. And there are thousands just like us."

"Yeah, there are thousands," Lester said, "in a community of tens of millions which is surrounded by a white community of hundreds of millions. And you know what your thousands boil down to? A handful of raisins in the sun, a coupla jigaboos by the door – and that's it."

"But Lester, don't you understand?" Xavier frowned. "Those doors are opening – slowly, it's true – but they *are* opening. And we have to be ready to take advantage of it."

Gloria Naylor, *Linden Hills*,
Viking Penguin, New York 1986,
pp. 106–114.

Vocabulary

no sweat (sl) don't worry – *What's shakin'* (sl) What's happening? – *to survey* [sə'veɪ] to look at s.th. as a whole – *to realign* [riːə'laɪn] to form a new – *chardonnay* dry white table wine of Chablis type – *to deem* (fml) to consider – *mon copain* [mõ kopɛ̃] (French infml) my friend – *flicker* short unsteady shine or light – *consternation* great surprise and fear – *Sacré Dieu* (French) Holy God – *blood* here: (sl) man (used by one black person to another) – *to hold out* to offer – *to be into* (sl) to be keen on, interested in – *I'm not knocking it* (sl) I'm not criticizing you – avoirdupois [ˌævədə'pɔɪz] here: weight – *period* (esp. AE infml) = BE full stop (used at the end of a statement to express finality and strong feeling) – *raring to go* eager to start

– *clone* non-sexually-produced descendants of a single plant or animal – *stint* a limited or fixed amount of work – *to hook up with* (sl) to marry – *tightrope* (= gespanntes Seil für Seiltänzer) – *to weather* to pass safely through a storm or difficulty – *flack* usually *flak* anti-aircraft gun or gunfire; here: severe criticism – *straight A's* the best possible marks – *balls* (taboo sl) testicals – *to claw off* to tear off (with a claw) – *crap* (taboo sl) here: nonsense – *bladder* (med. = Blase) – *grubby* dirty – *calloused* = *callous* [ˈkæləs] (of the skin) hard and thick from rough work – *industrious* [ɪnˈdʌstrɪəs] hard-working – *industry* [ˈɪndəstrɪ] continual hard work – *impeccable* faultless – *linty* fuzzy, fluffy, thin (like lint) – *pea-jacket* short double-breasted overcoat of wool cloth – *a coupla jigaboos* (derogatory sl) a couple of Negroes

Assignments

1. Analyse the conversation between Xavier and Maxwell:
   a. Under what circumstances does it take place? b. What is it about? c. What is revealed about the relationship between the two characters?
2. To what extent is the passage structured by character contrast? How do the characters differ in their backgrounds and attitudes?
3. What does language contribute to characterization?
4. What relevant problems are dealt with in the passage?
5. Describe the techniques used by the author to present the problems. What other techniques could you think of?

8 The Novel of Awareness

Zuckerman Unbound

PHILIP ROTH

After the publication of **Carnovsky**, *a novel of sexual liberation, Jewish author Nathan Zuckerman finds himself rocketed into notoriety and wealth, which completely upsets the relatively unremarkable life he has led hitherto. People, mistaking him for this fictional hero or recognizing him as the successful author he is, address him in public to express their admiration or their disgust. The media spread rumours about him; he receives anonymous letters and phone calls; someone threatens to kidnap his mother if he should refuse to fork out fifty thousand dollars. In a shabby restaurant he is approached by Alvin Pepler, a psychopath and one-time quiz-show celebrity with a grudge against television producers, whom he holds responsible for ruining his life. Zuckerman is haunted by Pepler, who tries to cadge his advice, first, for the publication of a novel and, later, for some literary criticism of* **Carnovsky**, *while his real intention is to accuse Zuckerman of stealing his life. His agent, André Schevitz, disappointed to see that Zuckerman is reluctant to adjust his life-style to his newly acquired fame and wealth, persuades him to buy expensive suits and spend an evening out with movie-actress and sex-symbol Caesara O'Shea, which promptly causes a stir in the media. Meanwhile, with his creativity flagging, Zuckerman reflects on the nature of fiction and reality, on his relation to women (he has divorced three wives) and his Jewish family. His dying father calls him a bastard, and so does his brother, reproaching him with lack of responsibility, self-denial and morality. When, finally, he goes to Newark to visit the neighbourhood where he grew up, he realizes that everything has changed and that all his ties with the past have been severed.*

He wrote steadily for over an hour, every irate word of Pepler's deposition, and then, suddenly, broke into a sweat and telephoned André at his office to recount to him the details of the phone calls, right down to the haw, haw, haws.
"To resist all the temptations I strew in your path, this I understand. To fight the way your life is going," said André, capitalizing, for the sake of the satire, on the Mitteleuropa inflections, "to be unable to accept what has happened to you, this I also understand. Even if it is you yourself who has kicked over your traces, what happens when you kick over your traces can take anybody by surprise. Especially a boy with your background. What with Papa telling you to be good, and Mama telling you to be nice, and the University of Chicago training you four years in Advanced Humanistic

Decisions, well, what chance did you ever have to lead a decent life? To take you away to that place at sixteen! It's like stealing a wild little baby baboon from the branches of the trees, feeding him in the kitchen, letting him sleep in your bed and play with the light switch and wear little shirts and pants with pockets, and then, when he is big and hairy and full of himself, giving him his degree in Western Civilization and sending him back to the bush. I can just imagine what an enchanting little baboon you were at the University of Chicago. Pounding the seminar table, writing English on the blackboard, screaming at the class that they had it all wrong – you must have been all over the place. Rather like in this abrasive little book."

"What's your point, André? Someone is threatening to kidnap my mother."

"My point is that to turn a jungle baboon into a seminar babbon is a cruel, irreversible process. I understand why you won't ever be happy around the waterhole again. But paranoia is something else. And my point for you, my question to you, is how far are you going to let paranoia take you before it takes you where it goes?"

"The question is how far the abrasive little book is going to take *them*."

"Nathan, who are 'they'? Nathan, you must do me a favor and stop going nuts."

"I had three phone calls last night from some madman threatening to kidnap my mother. Nuts it sounds, *but it happened*. What I am now trying to figure out is what to do in response that isn't nuts. I thought a worldly fellow with your admirable cynicism might have had some experience with this sort of thing."

"I can only tell you that I haven't. Among my clients are the richest and best-known stars in the world, but as far as I know, nothing like this has ever 'happened' to any of them."

"Nothing like this ever happened to me, either. That may account for why I sound the way I do."

"I understand that. But you have been sounding this way for some time. You have been sounding this way from the day it began. In all my years of experience with high-strung prima donnas, I have never seen anyone make such a fiasco of fame and fortune. I have seen all sorts of crazy indulgence, but never before indulgence in anything like this. To be chagrined by such good fortune. Why?"

"Because of the madmen who call me on the phone, for one."

"Then don't answer the phone. Don't sit there waiting by the phone, and that takes care of the phone. To take care of the bus, don't ride the bus. And while you're at it, stop eating in those filthy delicatessens. You are a rich man."

"Who says I eat in filthy delicatessens? The *News* or the *Post*?"

"I say so. And isn't it true? You buy greasy takeout chickens at these foul little barbecue holes and you eat them with your hands in that barren apartment. You hide out in Shloimie's Pastrami Haven, pretending to be harmless Mr Nobody from Nowhere. And by now it is all beginning to lose its eccentric charm, Nathan, and is taking on a decidedly paranoiac aroma. What are you up to, anyway? Are you out to appease the gods? Are you trying to show them up in heaven and over at *Commentary* that you are only a humble, self-effacing yeshiva *bucher* and not the obstreperous author of such an indecent book? I know about all those index cards you carry around in your wallet: fortifying quotations from the great literary snobs about fame giving satisfaction only to mediocre vanities. Well, don't you believe it. There's a lot to be had out of life by a writer in your position, and not at Shloimie's, either. Those buses. To begin with, you should have a car with a driver, Nathan. Thomas Mann had a car with a driver."

"Where'd you hear that?"

"I didn't. I rode in it with him. You should have a girl to answer your mail and run your errands for you. You should have somebody to carry your dirty things down Madison Avenue in a pillowcase – somebody instead of yourself. At least treat yourself to a laundry that picks up sackcloth and delivers."

"They lean on the bell when they pick up – it interrupts my concentration."

"A housekeeper should answer the bell. You should have someone to cook your meals and to shop for your groceries and to deal with the tradesmen at the door. You don't have to push a cart around Gristede's ever again."

"I do if I want to know what a pound of butter costs."

"Why would you want to know that?"

"André, Gristede's is where we poor writers go to lead a real life – don't take Gristede's away from me too. It's how I keep my finger on the pulse of the nation."

"You want to succeed at that, get to know what I know: the price of a pound of flesh. I am being serious. You should have a driver, a housekeeper, a cook, a secretary –"

"And where do I hide in that crowd? Where do I type?"

"Get a bigger place."

"I just got a bigger place. André that is *more* ridiculousness, not less. I just moved in here. It's quiet, it's plenty big for me, and on East Eighty-first at five hundred a month, it's no slum."

"You should have a duplex at the United Nations Plaza."

"I don't *want* one."

"Nathan, you are no longer the egghead kid I plucked out of the pages of *Esquire*. You have achieved a success as only a handful of writers ever do – so stop acting like those who don't. First you lock yourself away in order to stir up your imagination, now you lock yourself away because you've stirred up theirs. Meanwhile, everybody in the world is dying to meet you. Trudeau was here and he wanted to meet you. Abba Eban was here and mentioned your name to me. Yves Saint Laurent is giving a big party and his office called for your number. But do I dare to give it? And would you even go?"

"Look, I already met Caesara. That should hold me for a while. By the way, tell Mary I received my Dear Juan letter from Havana. She can phone in the news to *Women's Wear Daily*. I'll send them a Xerox by messenger."

"At least Caesara got you out of that cell for one night. I wish I had another lovely lure like her. My dear boy, you live in that apartment, as far as I can tell, thinking about nothing but yourself from one day to the next. And when you even dare to go out into the street, you're worse. Everybody looks at you, everybody sidles up to you, everybody wants either to tie you to a bed or to spit in your eye. Everybody has you pegged for Gilbert Carnovsky, when what anybody with an ounce of brains should know is that you are really you. But if you recall, Nathan dear, being really you was what was driving you crazy only a few short years ago. You told me so yourself. You felt stultified writing 'proper, responsible' novels. You felt stultified living behind your 'drearily virtuous face'. You felt stultified sitting in your chair every night making notes for your files on another Great Book. 'How much more life can I spend preparing for my final exam? I'm too old to be writing term papers.' You felt stultified calling Florida every Sunday like the good son, you felt stultified signing stop-the-war petitions like the good citizen, you felt stultified most of all living with a do-gooder like your wife. The whole country was going haywire and you were still in your chair doing your homework. Well, you have successfully conducted your novelistic experiment and now you are famous all over the haywire country for being highly haywire yourself, and you're even more stultified than before. What is more, you are outraged that everybody doesn't know how proper, responsible, and drearily virtuous you really are, and what a great achievement it is for mankind that such a model of Mature Adult Behavior could have given the reading public a Gilbert Carnovsky. You set out to sabotage your own moralizing nature, you set out to humiliate all your dignified, high-minded gravity, and now that you've done it, and done it with the relish of a real saboteur, now you're humiliated, you idiot, because nobody aside from you seems to see it as a profoundly moral and high-minded act! 'They' misunderstand you. And as for those who do understand you, people who've known you for five and ten and fifteen years, you'll have nothing to do with them, either. As far as I can tell, you don't see a single one of your friends. People call me to ask what's happened to you. Your closest friends think you're out of town. Somebody called me up the other day to ask if it was true that you were in Payne Whitney."

"Oh, am I supposed to be in the bin now too?"

"Nathan, you are the decade's latest celebrity – people are going to say everything. The question I am asking is why you won't at least see old friends."

Simple. Because he couldn't sit complaining to them about becoming the decade's latest celebrity. Because being a poor misunderstood millionaire is not really a topic that intelligent people can discuss for very long. Not even friends. Least of all friends, and especially when they're writers. He didn't want them talking about him talking about his morning with the investment counselor and his night with Caesara O'Shea and how she jilted him for the Revolution. And that was all he could talk about, at least to himself. He was not fit company for anyone he considered a friend. He would get started on all the places where he no longer could show his face without causing a sensation, and soon enough he would make them into enemies. He would get started on the Rollmops King and the gossip columns and the dozen crazy letters a day, and who *could* listen? He would start talking to them about those suits. Six suits. Three thousand dollars' worth of suits to sit at home and write in. When he could write naked, if need be; when he could sit there as he always had, in work shirt and chinos, perfectly content. With three thousand dollars he could have bought one hundred pairs of chinos and four hundred work shirts (he'd worked it out). He could buy sixty pairs of Brooks Brothers suede walking shoes of the kind he'd been wearing since he went off to Chicago. He could buy twelve hundred pairs of Interwoven socks (four hundred blue, four hundred brown, four hundred gray). With three thousand dollars he could have clothed himself for life. But instead there were now fittings with Mr White twice a week, discussions with Mr White about padding the shoulders and nipping the waist, and who could possibly listen to Zuckerman carrying on about such stuff? He could hardly listen – but, alas, alone with himself, he couldn't shut up. Better they should think he was in Payne Whitney. Maybe he ought to be. Because there was also the television – couldn't stop watching. Downtown on Bank Street, all they saw regularly was the news. At seven and again at eleven he and Laura used to sit together in the living room to watch the fires in Vietnam: villages on fire, jungles on fire, Vietnamese on fire. Then they went back to their work on the night shift, she to her draft dodgers, he to his Great Books. During his weeks alone, however, Zuckerman had probably spent more hours by the TV set than in all the years since they had begun to broadcast test patterns back when he was finishing high school. There was little else he could concentrate on, and then there was the strangeness of sitting in your bathrobe on your Oriental rug eating a takeout barbecued chicken and hearing someone suddenly talking about *you*. He couldn't get over it. One night a pretty rock singer whom he'd never seen before told Johnny Carson about her one and 'Thank God' only date with Nathan Zuckerman. She brought the house down describing the 'gear' Zuckerman advised her to wear to dinner if she wanted 'to turn him on'. And just the previous Sunday he had watched three therapists sitting in lounge chairs on Channel 5 analyzing his castration complex with the program host. They all agreed that Zuckerman had a lulu. The following morning André's lawyer had gently to tell him that he couldn't sue for slander. "Your nuts, Nathan, are now in the public domain."

They were right in their way – he *was* in the bin.

"The threats, the threats, the *threats*. André", cried Zuckerman, "what about those threats? That is the subject here."

"Delivered as you described them the threats don't seem to me very serious, frankly. But then I am not you, with this sense you have that everything suddenly is beyond your control. If you are feeling the way you sound, then telephone the police and see what they say."

"But you think it's all a joke."

"I wouldn't be surprised."

"And if it isn't? If my mother winds up in the trunk of a car in the Everglades?"

"If this and if that. Do as I say. You want advice, I'm advising you. Phone the police."

"And what can they do? That's the next question."
"I have no idea what they can do when nothing actually has happened to anyone. My concern is defusing the persecution mania, Nathan. That is the job of a literary agent. I should like to restore in you some peace of mind."
"Which calling the police isn't likely to do. Call the police and it's as good as calling the city desk. Call the police and it'll be in Leonard Lyons by tomorrow, if not headlined on page one. PUG THREATENS PORN MOM. The kidnapping of Mrs Carnovsky – that would really top off the sixties for them. Susskind will have to have three specialists in to think it through with him. 'Who in Our Sick Society Is Responsible?' Sevareid will tell us what it means to the Future of the Free World. Reston will write a column on the Breakdown of Values. If this thing happens, the torment to my mother will be nothing next to what the rest of the country is going to have to put up with."
"Ah, and this is a little more like your old amused self."
"Is it? My old amused self? Wouldn't recognize him. Who is Sleepy Lagoon, while we're at it? What is this in *Variety* about a million dollars for the sequel?"
"Bob Lagoon. I would wait before spending his million."
"But he exists."
"Off and on."
"And Marty Paté? Who is he?"
"Don't know."
"Never heard of a producer on East Sixty-second Street named Marty Paté?"
"As in *'de foie gras'*? Not yet. Why do you ask?"
No, best not to go into that. "What about Gayle Gibraltar?"
André laughed. "Sounds like you're writing a sequel right now. Sounds like some figment of Carnovsky's imagination."
"No, not Carnovsky's. What I ought to do is get a bodyguard. For my mother. Don't you think?"
"Well, if that's what's necessary for your sense of security –"
"Only it's not going to give her much of one, is it? I hate to think of her sitting across from him when he takes off his coat to eat his lunch and she sees the shoulder holster."
"Then why not restrain yourself, Nathan? Why not wait to see if this character phones again? If there is, in fact, no call to make arrangements about extortion money, so much for that. It was somebody's idea of a good time. If there is such a call –"
"Then I notify the police, the F.B.I., and whatever the papers print –"
"Exactly."
"If and when it turns out to be nothing, she'll have been protected just the same."
"And you'll feel that you did the right thing by her."
"Only there it'll be in the papers. Then the bright idea will dawn on some maniac to take a crack at it himself."
"You worry too much about maniacs."

"But they live. The maniacs live better than we do. They flourish. It's their world, André. You should read my mail."

"Nathan, you take everything too seriously, starting with your mail and ending with yourself. Maybe it's starting with yourself and ending with the mail. Maybe that's all the kidnapper is trying to tell you."

"Doing it for my education, is he? You make it sound as though it might even be you."

"I'd like to say that it was. I wish I were clever enough to have thought of it."

"I wish you were too. I wish somebody were, other than whoever it is."

"Or isn't."

Philip Roth, *Zuckerman Unbound,* Penguin, Harmondsworth 1983, pp. 86–94.

Vocabulary

irate (fml) showing (strong) anger – *deposition* solemn statement (made in a court of law) – *to kick over the traces* to free o.s. from control – *abrasive [ə'breɪsɪv]* harsh, rough – *chagrined ['ʃægrɪnd]* suffering from a feeling of sorrow, annoyance or disappointment – *self-effacing* [ˌself-ɪ'feɪsɪŋ] avoiding the attention of others – *yeshiva bucher* [je'ʃi:və 'bukə] (Hebrew) a scholarly, shy, naive person – *obstreperous* [əb'strepərəs] noisy and uncontrollable – *Abba Eban* born 1915, foreign minister of Israel (1966–1974), noted for his eloquence – *Pierre Trudeau* born 1919, Canadian Prime Minister (1968–1984) – *Yves Saint Laurent* born 1936, French fashion designer – *Gilbert Carnovsky* the main character of Zuckerman's bestseller – *stultified* made foolish, stupid or useless – *to go haywire* (sl) to become disorganized and confused – *relish* pleaseur, enjoyment – *Payne Whitney* (1872–1930) financier and sportsman, married Gertrude Vanderbilt, a sculptor and art promoter – *to jilt* to refuse to see (a lover) again – *the Rollmops King* (he wanted Zuckerman to advertize his appetizer snacks in television commercials) – *chinos* style of trousers made of cotton – *suede* [sweɪd] soft leather with a rough surface – *to nip the waist* (of clothes) to make narrow – *Laura* Zuckerman's third wife, whom he divorced – *draft dodger* s.o. who dodges, i.e. avoids, military service by trickery or cunning – *gear* a set of things used for a particular purpose, here: clothes – *to turn on* to excite, to arouse sexual desire – *lulu* anything outstanding or remarkable – *to sue for* to bring a legal claim against s.o., to claim damages – *nuts* (taboo sl) testicles – *to defuse* to make less dangerous – *Sleepy Lagoon/Variety* The newspaper "Variety" had published the false news that Bob "Sleepy" Lagoon had paid about a million dollars for Zuckerman's unfinished sequel to Carnovsky – *sequel* story or film continuing an earlier one – *Marty Paté/Gayle Gibralter* Broadway producer and filmstar invented by Alvin Pepler – *extortion money* money obtained by violence or threats – *to make a crack at* (infml) to try, to make an attempt

Assignments

1. What is the situation presented? How does it arise? Who are the characters involved and what is their relationship?
2. What is André's criticism and what is his advice? How does Zuckerman react?
3. Discuss techniques of presentation, e.g. structure and point of view.
4. What are André's methods of persuasion? Analyse his arguments and his use of language.
5. Discuss to what extent the passage is representative of the successful artist's dilemma in today's society.

The Pleasure and Pain of Writing Novels

This degree of authorial self-consciousness may explain why the same, or similar, characters seem always to be turning up in Roth's fiction, and always with the same, or related, problems. What's really happening, as he said, is that 'you're talking to yourself and you're talking to the book, and in doing both of those things you may become intelligent about what you're doing, and you may be instructive in some way, or professorial in your approach, or analytic about the very thing you're writing.'

Yes, maybe, but how tedious for all except the most 'professorial' of readers if that's all you're doing. Of course, self-description of this kind need not be taken as definitive; it tends to come out in documentaries earnestly inquiring into an author's method. And fortunately, despite all the superficial evidence of plot synopsis and authorial account of himself, Roth is anything but boring in print.

Why? Well, to start with the most obvious but least analysable fact of his prose, it's very funny. The joke has something to do with accurate impersonation and sudden shifts in tone and diction. Here is Zuckerman's persistent admirer in *Zuckerman Unbound* constructing a picture of almost unimaginable luxury:

Then upstairs, where Marty actually lives, resides, completely done up in modern design. Red leather, recessed lights, pitch-black walls. Plants in like an oasis ... The floral bill is a thousand a month. Toilets like dolphins and the handles on everything gold-plate. And the food is all send-out, down to salt and pepper ... He's got a million-dollar kitchen in there and I don't think anybody's ever used it except to get water for an aspirin. A line on the phone direct to the restaurant next door. The old man calls down and the next thing, shish kebab. In flames.

This extract alone should be enough to show that, whatever his claims to the contrary, Roth is a realist for whom the narrative surface is not an object of interest in itself but, almost classically, a transparency through which characters are seen to have a life of their own.

The accuracy of Roth's vignettes does

more than establish comic local colour, however. These powerful voices get inside Zuckerman's head, and are too authentic to be shaken off.

One of the things these voices tell the typical Roth protagonist is that he is becoming obsessed with a particular enthusiasm or antipathy. Characteristically, the central consciousness will acknowledge the debilitating effect of this obsession, but carry on with renewed aggression and ever more outrageous flights of verbal invention. Again, utility and rhetorical 'class' conflict. In a way very hard to explain, this device is both exhilarating and wildly comic.

Zuckerman goes through the same process in *The Anatomy Lesson*, first fulminating against his austere Jewish critic – for the most part behind his back – and then assuming his name and introducing himself all around Chicago as a porn merchant. The comic invention is breathtaking, but the elaborate plot sidetracks Zuckerman from his original object and leads him finally to the point of breakdown.

This is the serious side of the comedy: that it can't be escaped. What Roth's characters fail to do, in Ralph Ellison's words, is 'change the joke, and slip the yoke'. Irving Howe, who may be the model for Zuckerman's accuser in *The Anatomy Lesson*, once criticised Roth for reworking the old chlichés of Jewish stand-up comedy. Portnoy's mother, he wrote, has little reality even within the fiction, 'because the conventional lampoon of the Jewish mother is by now so well established in our folklore it has almost become an object of realistic portraiture in its own right.' Reading this, anyone would think that Portnoy himself was not aware that he was reliving all the jokes of American Jewis vaudeville:

Listen, come to my aid, will you – and quick! Spring me from this role I play of the smothered son of the Jewish joke! Because it's beginning to pall a little, at 33! And it *hoits*, you know, there is *pain* involved ... . 'Help, help, my son the doctor is drowning!' ha ha *ha*, ha ha *ha*, only what about the *pain*, Myron Cohen! What about the guy who is actually drowning?

The exaggerated expression and the shift in tone from whine to aggressive attack, are funny, but the device of the relived cliché has a serious side, too. In noisy environments, such as Roth has perceived the American fictional market to be, a message needs to be repeated or rephrased in case part of it has been lost the first time round. That's why announcements in railway stations often come out in triplicate. Roth's own audience has reacted with a bewildering variety to his precise details of local colour, his jokes, his exaggerations; some thinking them hilarious, some anti-Semitic, some taking his fantasies as fact, and others the other way round. The revitalised clichés or old jokes are a signpost in an environment of unpredictable reception. But they also produce an almost apocalyptic sense of old prophecies coming at last to fulfilment. As Hamlet said in a mood not unlike Portnoy's: 'This was sometime a paradox, but now the time gives it proof.' The serious side to Roth's comedy is that it hides the snares of paranoid tragedy.

Stephen Fender in: *The Listener*, 19/12/1985.

Assignments

1. Why does Stephen Fender find Philip Roth's novels remarkable?
2. What positive and negative reactions to Roth's novels are referred to in this review?

9 Suggestions for Project Work

1. Study the novel *I'm the King of the Castle* carefully. Then write a report on it, using Linda Taylor's book review of D. Wheldon's *The Viaduct* as a model.

2. Read the complete text of *The Viaduct* and compare your own views with those of Linda Taylor.

3. Study D. Wheldon's next novel *The Course of Instruction* and compare it with *The Viaduct*.

4. Study the complete text of *Sweet Dreams* and explain why some of the scenes in the book may be regarded as particularly dramatic.

5. Read the complete text of *Dinner at the Homesick Restaurant* and discuss it in terms of a) major themes b) writing techniques/point of view c) relevance to contemporary life in the US.

6. Study the full text of *Linden Hills*. Then give short talks on the following subjects: a) the time structure of the novel b) the relationship between Luther Nedeed and his wife and the techniques used for its presentation c) the role of women d) interpersonal relationships e) the "black" American dream f) the function of Willie and Lester.

7. Study Gloria Naylor's first novel, *The Women of Brewster Place* and compare it with *Linden Hills*.

8. Study Alice Walker's *The Color Purple* and compare it with *Linden Hills* as to setting/background, plot, structure, major theme, and language.

9. Read the complete text of *Zuckerman Unbound*. Then analyse the main character. What techniques of characterization are used? How is the reader to judge the main character? What is the main idea of the novel and how is it developed? Discuss the social criticism implied.

10. Study the setting in *The Viaduct* or *Linden Hills* and comment on its relative importance. To what extent is it symbolical, to what extent does it contribute to the creation of a particular atmosphere?

11. Study a novel of your choice and report on it in class in terms of the criteria used in the introduction (p. 109).
Then present a personal appreciation of the book, for which the book reviews in this collection may serve as models.

12. Study a novel of your choice and present it by chosing a passage of approximately 2–3 pages and analysing it with reference to the novel as a whole. Explain in detail why you think the passage may be considered pivotal.

Albert-Reiner Glaap

Drama

Contents

1 Approaching Drama

What is a Play?

We all think we know what a play is, but no one has ever succeeded in defining it. A novel or a poem is neither more nor less than the words it consists of, but a script is obviously less than a play, while a production is obviously more. So how do we locate its limits? Is it like a chemical substance which can never be isolated, existing only in combination with other substances?
Reading a script can be all the more enjoyable if we remember that it wasn't intended for reading. We see words; we imagine sounds and pictures. When we go to the theatre, we hear words and sounds, but we see people and backgrounds; when we read, we use our eyes on the element that is invisible in performance. During Shakespeare's lifetime, it was natural to talk of *hearing* a play. "We'll hear a play tomorrow," promises Hamlet. "Will the King hear this piece of work?" Today, we always talk of *seeing* a play, putting the emphasis on the action that is visible.
When we read a play or a novel, we cannot take in more than one impression at a time. As our eyes move laterally across the printed lines, our brain receives each impact separately. The information comes in a single jet, like water passing through a narrow hole. In performance, several taps can be turned on at the same time. Words, silences, sound effects, background music, facial expressions, gestures, movements across the stage, lighting, groupings, shadows, shapes and colours in the costume and décor – all these may be telling us something. At the same time we are emotionally involved by the appearance, the voice, the personality of the actors. We may feel in sympathy with one, hostile to another. The words are all filtered to us through a mesh.
Our awareness of what they mean is inseparable from our awareness of vocal timbre, tone, timing, inflexion and atmosphere. In poetry and fiction, the basic currency is words; in drama it is the physical presence of the actors.

Ronald Hayman, *How to Read a Play,* Eyre Methuen, London 1977, pp. 11–12.

Seeing the Actors

When I was a lad and regularly took my place in the queue or the early door of the gallery in the old Theatre Royal, Bradford, the actors on their way to the stage door had to walk past us. I observed them with delight. In those days, actors looked like actors and like nothing else on earth. There was no mistaking them for wool merchants, shipping clerks, and deacons of Baptist chapels, all those familiar figures of my boyhood. They wore suits of startling check pattern, outrageous ties, and preposterous overcoats reaching down to their ankles. They never seemed to remove all their make-up as actors do now, and always had a rim of blue-black round their eyelids. They did not belong to our world and never for a moment pretended to belong to it. They swept past us, fantastically overcoated, with trilbies perched raffishly on brilliantined curls, talking of incredible matters in high tones, merely casting a few sparkling glances – all the more sparkling because of that blue-black – in our direction; and then vanished through the stage door, to reappear, but out of all recognition, in the wigs and knee-breeches of "David Garrick", or "The Only Way". And my young heart, as innocent as an egg, went out to these romantic beings; and, perhaps it was then, although I have no recollection of it, that the desire was born in me to write one day for the Theatre. Now, after working on so many stages, I know all about actors, and I doubt if the very least of their innumerable maddening tricks and absurd egoisms has escaped my observation; but, quite apart from the work we do together and without reference to the needs of my profession, I have a soft spot for actors, and probably it is because of that old delight I used to feel as they went swaggering past us on their way to the stage door. And indeed I sometimes wish they would swagger more now, buy bigger overcoats and wilder hats, and retain those traces of make-up that put them outside respectability and kept them rogues and vagabonds, which is what at heart – bless'em! – they are.

J.B. Priestley in: W.E. Williams, *A Book of English Essays,* Penguin, Harmondsworth 1967, pp. 347–348.

The Critic

"Where were *you* last night?"
"Out."
"Where'd you go?"
"Theatre."
"What'd you see?"
"A play."
"Amazing. Enjoy it?"
"Yes."
"Why?"
"It was good."
"What was so good about it?"
"Well ... it was funny."
"Tell us a joke from it then."
"Well, there weren't any ... not what you'd call real jokes."
"No jokes. Sounds a funny sort of comedy."
"It was the way they did things."
"What things?"
"And said things."
"*What* things?"
"Go and see for yourself."
"Not likely. I went to see a play once. It was boring."
"Why was it so boring then? Go on, tell me, I'm interested."

"I wasn't. I was bored rigid by it. Can't remember much about it, it was so boring."

"Why? Was it the way the actors spoke the lines? Or was it a bad script?"

"Search me."

"Was the director treating the script to a suitable style of production?"

"Never asked him. I kept falling asleep."

"That's really useful. Falls asleep, then says the play was boring."

"I fell asleep *because* the play was boring."

"Why was it boring?"

"I don't know, do I? How come you know so much all of a sudden? Why was this play you saw so good?"

"Well ..."

We can usually tell whether we have enjoyed a play or not. It can be far more difficult to understand *why* we have reacted as we have. Like the two tongue-tied talkers above, we tend to lapse into vague words such as "good" or "bad", or words like "boring" or "interesting". The trouble with such words as these is that they tend to tell only about our reactions and nothing about the aspects of the play that caused us to react in such a way.

The process of examining how a play and its production work is called criticism. To criticise often means to find fault with something. The word is used in this book more widely. Its purpose is to help increase our understanding and, through that, our enjoyment. To have a critical mind may mean that we come to dislike some of the things we find fault with. On the other hand, it should help to give us experiences we would otherwise have missed.

Timothy Ramsden/Pauline Courtice, *Stagecraft,* Harrap, London 1984 ([1]1982), p. 45.

Drama and the Dramatic

It will be useful [...] to examine the way in which the words 'drama' and 'dramatic' are used in common speech outside the context of literature or the theatre. We may speak, for instance, of 'a dramatic moment'. Imagine yourself one of a roomful of people, at a party for instance, standing and talking in groups. Suddenly the door opens and a woman stands in the doorway. She looks round the room, and her gaze settles on a man standing at the far end of the room. He looks at her as she closes the door behind her and moves slowly across the room. This is in itself a thoroughly commonplace happening, and might well attract no attention whatsoever; it is not, in itself, dramatic. Yet let us imagine further that the man and woman are known to you, and that the man has already told you of a quarrel they have had on the way to the party, after which she has insisted on his continuing alone. Add to this your knowledge of the grounds of the quarrel, her jealousy of another woman who is also in the room. Given that her entrance has attracted your attention, her survey of the room and her approach to the man, arousing in you certain expectations or forebodings, will give rise in you to a certain tension; it will be, for you, a dramatic moment; you will be an audience of one to a scene in which everyone else is an actor, and this basic scene is capable of taking on an increasing complexity and depth. You may, for instance, know something about the attitude of the second woman which neither of the two main actors is aware of. And so on ...

Here is another example – the newspaper headline 'Minister's dramatic intervention in wage dispute'. The implications of this are (1) the intervention was unexpected; thus our attention is seized. (2) It has created a new and interesting situation. (3) The situation takes its meaning and interest from a certain context; it is part of an 'action' that has a beginning (which we know) and must lead to some end (which we do not know). The journalist's aim is to seize and hold our attention, beginning with a single unexpected and startling act, and going on to make us aware of certain possibilities inherent in the situation created by that act. But, if he is a good journalist, he knows that our interest will not be long held by one set of possibilities – tomorrow's story must give us another situation, with a slightly different set of possibilities, lest we quickly become bored by it all. To keep his readers' expectations aroused over a number of days, and to bring the story to a satisfactory conclusion, the journalist makes it into an 'action'; a satisfactory conclusion here is one which will not cause us to be disappointed when, on opening our newspaper next day, we do not find the story continued. A newspaper story has more in common with drama than has an ordinary story, since the writer is concerned with immediacy, a sense of its happening *now*, not in the past. (Headlines are usually in the present tense.) This immediacy is integral to drama, since what is happening on the stage is happening now, for the first time, and not in what Suszanne Langer calls the 'virtual past' of narrative literature.

S.W. Dawson, *Drama and the Dramatic. The Critical Idiom,* Methuen, Norfolk 1970, pp. 12–13.

2 The Well-Made Play

Absent Friends

ALAN AYCKBOURN

Colin's friends arrange a tea-party for Colin to comfort him in his grief over the death to his fiancée. They feel uneasy, because they do not know what to say to him; they never met the girl. But when he arrives he is happy and relaxed, and the others, due to emotional involvements and cross-marital ties, are nervous and uncomfortable. The scene reprinted here is just before the end of Act One.

MARGE Give us a chance.

(*A silence*)

(COLIN *suddenly slaps his knees and springs to his feet. Everyone jolts*)

What's the matter?

COLIN Wait there, wait there.

(COLIN *rushes out to the front door*)

DIANA (*in a shocked whisper*) Where's he gone?

PAUL I don't know.

MARGE Is he all right?

DIANA I didn't upset him, did I, saying that?

MARGE No. Lovely.

JOHN I'll have a look, shall I?

DIANA Would you, John.

PAUL What did you want to get on to that for?

DIANA What?

PAUL All that going on about grief and so on.

DIANA I only said ...

PAUL We're supposed to be cheering him up. He didn't want to listen to that.

DIANA It had to be said.

MARGE You have to say it.

PAUL He obviously didn't want to be reminded of it, did he? There was no need to, no need at all. We were all getting along perfectly happily.

DIANA You can't sit here and not say anything about it.

(JOHN *returns*)

JOHN He's gone out the front door.

DIANA Where to?

JOHN His car, I think. He's getting something out of the boot.

PAUL Probably going to hang himself with his tow rope. After what she said.

DIANA He seemed perfectly recovered. Very cheerful. I thought someone should say something.

PAUL Cheerful? You can see that was only skin deep.

DIANA I couldn't.

PAUL I was talking to him in here. You could tell. He's living on his nerves. On a knife edge. You could tell, couldn't you, John?

JOHN He seemed quite cheerful.

PAUL He could snap like that. Any minute. Same with anyone in this situation. Up one minute …

JOHN I've never seen him quite so cheerful.

PAUL Exactly. All the signs are there. The last thing he wanted to do was to talk about this fiancée of his. It's a known fact, people never …

MARGE Oh yes, they do. My Aunt Angela …

PAUL It is a known fact …

(*Slight pause*)

(*Door bangs*)

JOHN He's coming back.

PAUL Now, not another word about her. Keep it cheerful. For God's sake, Evelyn, try and smile, just for once.

(COLIN *returns. He carries a photo album and an envelope of loose snapshots, all contained, at present, in a large chocolate box*)

ALL Ah …

COLIN (*breathless*) Sorry. I forgot to bring these in. It's some photos. You can see what she looked like.

DIANA Of her?

COLIN Yes, I thought you'd like to.

MARGE Oh.

COLIN Yes. There's one or two quite good ones. Thought you might like to see some. Of course, if you'd rather …

PAUL No, no …

COLIN She was very photogenic. Shall I sit here next to you, Di? Then I can … (*He sits next to* DIANA) Now then. (*Taking snaps from the envelope*) Ah yes, these are some loose ones I haven't stuck in yet. They're the most recent. Can I give those to you, Marge? I think they're mostly on holiday, those. (*He hands loose snapshots to* MARGE)

MARGE Thank you.

COLIN (*with the album*) These are mostly at home in the garden at her house.

MARGE Oh, is this her? Oh, she is lovely, Colin. Wasn't she?

DIANA (*as* COLIN *opens the first page*) Oh.

COLIN There she is again. That's with her Mum.

DIANA She's a fine looking woman too.

COLIN Wonderful. She's been really wonderful. She's got this terrible leg.

DIANA Ah.

MARGE Oh, that's nice one ... Do you want to pass them round, John?

JOHN Oh yes, sure.

(MARGE *passes them to* JOHN *who in due course passes them to* PAUL *who passes them to* EVELYN)

DIANA That's nice. Was that her house?

COLIN No. That's the back of the Natural History Museum, I think.

DIANA I was going to say ...

COLIN Went there at Easter.

MARGE (*at photo*) Oh.

PAUL (*at photo*) Ah.

DIANA (*at album*) Oh.

MARGE Oh look, John, with her little dog, see?

JOHN Oh yes.

COLIN That was her mother's.

MARGE Oh. Sweet little dog.

EVELYN I like that handbag.

COLIN That's her again. Bit of a saucy one. It's not very good though, the sun's the wrong way.

DIANA I wish I had a figure like that. It's so nice you brought them, Colin.

MARGE Oh yes.

DIANA It's nice, too, that you can look at them without – you know ...

COLIN Oh no, it doesn't upset me. Not now.

MARGE That's wonderful.

COLIN I was upset at the time, you know.

DIANA Naturally.

COLIN But – after that – well, it's a funny thing about somebody dying – you never know, till it actually happens, how it's going to affect you, I mean, we all think about death at some time, I suppose, all of us. Either our death, somebody else's death. After all, it's one of the few things we have all got in common ...

(JOHN *has risen and is jiggling about*)

DIANA Sit down, John.

(JOHN *sits reluctantly*)

COLIN And I suppose when I first met Carol, it must have passed through my mind what would I feel like if I did lose her. And I just couldn't think. I couldn't imagine it. I couldn't imagine my life going on without her. And then it happened. All of a sudden. One afternoon. All over. She was caught in this under-current, there was nothing anybody could do. I wasn't even around. They came and told me. And for about three weeks after that, I couldn't do anything at all. Nothing. I just lay about thinking, remembering and then, all of a sudden, it came to me that if my life ended there and then, by God, I'd have a lot to be grateful for. I mean, first of all, I'd been lucky enough to have known her. I don't know if you've ever met a perfect person. But that's what she was. The only way to describe her. And I, me, I'd had the love of a perfect person. And that's something I can always be grateful for. Even if for nothing else. And then I thought, what the hell am I talking about, my whole life's been like that. All through my childhood, the time I was growing up, all the time I lived here, I've had what a lot of people would probably give their right arm for – friends. Real friends, like John and Paul and Gordon and Di. So, one of the things I just wanted to say, Di – Paul – Marge – John – Evelyn and to Gordon if he was here, is that I'm not bitter about what happened. Because I've been denied my own happiness, I don't envy or begrudge you yours. I just want you to know that, despite everything that happened, in a funny sort of way, I too am very happy.

(*He smiles round at them serenely. A silence. A strange whooping noise. It is* DIANA *starting to weep hysterically. Unable to contain herself, she rushes out. After a moment,* MARGE *fumbles for her handkerchief and blows her nose loudly.* JOHN, *looking sickly, gives* COLIN *a ghastly smile.* PAUL *opens his mouth as if to say something, gives up.* COLIN *stands looking slightly bemused. He looks at* EVELYN. *She looks back at him, expressionless, chewing*)

COLIN Did I say the wrong thing?

(EVELYN *shrugs and resumes her reading*)

Curtain

Alan Ayckbourn, *Three Plays,* Chatto & Windus, London 1977, pp. 130–134.

Vocabulary

boot place for luggage at the back of a car – *to begrudge* to show or feel envy

Assignments

1. An underlying tension between the characters creates the atmosphere in this scene. How is this tension brought about?
2. How does Ayckbourn succeed in handling a delicate theme with great care?
3. How do the different characters react to Colin's showing the photographs?
4. The scene contains moments of meaningless conversation. What is left unsaid? What might have been said?
5. The characters in Ayckbourn's plays are ordinary people in recognizable domestic situations and all come from the middle classes. What are typical features of the middle-class people in *Absent Friends*?
6. To what extent is "a fiction of consistent and continuous reality" maintained in the scene from *Absent Friends*? Study the following extract:

Master of the Well-Made Play

The most assured master of the well-made play is Alan Ayckbourn. He manipulates his characters through a gamut of actions and reactions with great deftness, always providing neat preparation for future surprises so that the unexpected resolutions are not merely ingenious. In the hands of Ayckbourn, coincidences, U-turns, mistakes, transformations – all managed within one set and two and a half brief hours – heighten and refine an audience's awareness, and release laughter. Recognition of the skill needed to maintain a fiction of consistent and continuous reality adds to the pleasures of the evening's entertainment.

Some critics have dismissed Ayckbourn as a writer who can offer no more than 'light comedy'; but he seems always to be intent on making an audience look and listen very closely; he is so deft and makes so little fuss that one can even fear that the best laugh may pass unnoticed.

John Russell Brown, *A Short Guide to Modern British Drama,* Heinemann Educational Books, London 1982, pp. 35–36.

3 Comedy and Tragedy

Albert

RICHARD HARRIS

Albert is a short play of only sixteen pages. The actors play a Finn, an Italian and an Englishman – none of whom speak a word of the others' languages. In the following scene, Karin, a Finnish au pair, who has been employed by Mr and Mrs Garbold, has only just arrived, when Nico from Sicily, a little man with a big moustache, bursts in.

A summer evening. A sitting room in middle class suburbia. C. a sofa and low table. L. of the sofa, a low easy chair in inflated plastic. R., a table holding drinks, a telephone and a vase of flowers. U.R. paintings on the wall. D.R. a second easy chair. U.L. an archway leading into the hallway.

(KARIN *sits on the sofa checking through a letter she has written, pen to hand. She is a severe young woman wearing dressing gown over nightclothes. Her hair is pulled back in two bunches.*)

KARIN (*reading*) Dearest Mother. Mr and Mrs Garbold have gone to the cinema, so I'm having a quiet evening alone. It shows that they like – (*Now she inserts with her pen.*) and trust – me, don't you think, to leave me with the baby on my first night here? From what I understand, the last au pair was a French girl who couldn't be trusted to do anything. So like the French. I feel a little cut off of course – not speaking a word of English – but I'm sure I shall soon learn. Incidentally, Mrs Garbold is Italian, so I hope to learn something of both languages. I miss you all, of course – but in the main, I'm very happy – (*She stops reading, looks miserably ahead.*) I'm so miserable – (*The doorbell rings.*) Who's that? Go away! (*Another ring.*) Oh God – you'll wake the baby – I've only just got her off – (*She gets up, puts down the letter and pen, and turns.*)

(NICO *bursts in through the archway. He is a little man with a big moustache. He is hidden behind a huge toy teddy bear and a bunch of flowers.*)

NICO Surprise, surprise! (*He lowers the flowers, beams, but realises.*) Oh. I'm terribly sorry. I thought you were my sister.

(KARIN *backs away, pulling her dressing gown tighter. She points.*)

KARIN Who are you?

(NICO *looks round, points to the archway, nods.*)

NICO Yes, it was – you must have left it off the latch.

KARIN I don't understand – I don't speak English.

NICO I'm sorry – I don't speak English.

KARIN (*realising*) You're not English.

NICO (*dubiously*) Are you English?

(*They stare at each other for a moment.*)

KARIN Do you speak Finnish – I'm Finnish.

NICO I'm Italian – do you speak Italian?

(*Still they stare at each other.*)

I speak a little French. 'French'. (*Mimes.*) Me.

KARIN Ah – 'French'.

NICO (*nods*) Yes.

KARIN (*shakes head*) No. I know a little German. 'German'.

NICO Ah – 'German'.

KARIN (*nods*) Yes.

NICO (*shakes head*) No.

(*They smile emptily at each other.*)

(*holding smile*) I suppose I've come to the right house. (*He moves a little towards her, she jumps away.*) This is the house of Mr and Mrs Garbold.

KARIN (*seizing on the name*) Garbold (*Nods.*) – yes.

NICO (*thumbs chest*) I'm Mrs Garbold's brother.

KARIN Ah! You've come to see Mr Garbold.

NICO Yes – she is my sister.

KARIN Ah!

(*They smile, more relaxed now. He remembers the flowers he holds.*)

NICO For my sister.

KARIN For me?

NICO Yes.

KARIN How very nice.

(*She takes them, sniffs them, puts them down. He indicates the bear, puts it down on the chair R., pats its head.*)

NICO For the baby. (*He mimes a babe in arms.*)

KARIN What a ridiculous thing to give a three months old baby.

NICO (*beaming*) Yes, I thought so.

(*They are smiling at each other.* NICO *moves away and peers through the archway.*)

KARIN There's nobody in.

NICO Ah. Is anyone in?

KARIN (*pointing to self*) I'm the new au pair.

NICO What?

KARIN Au pair.

NICO Ah! (*Moves towards her, hand extended. Points to self.*) Me – Nico.

(*They shake hands.*)

KARIN I only came this morning.

(NICO *shrugs, doesn't understand.*)

I help Mrs Garbold in the house. (*She thinks – mimes a bit of dusting – goes to wall – mimes dusting the paintings.*)

NICO (*studying this*) You're a painter.

(KARIN *nods, mimes holding baby.*)

A painter of children. (*Gets it.*) You're a children's portrait painter!

(*They are delighted at having made contact.*)

KARIN Au pair – yes.

NICO 'Au pair' means painter. I must remember that.

KARIN (*pointing*) You?

NICO Me – au pair? No. Mind you, I've done a bit of pottery. (*He mimes doing some pottery-making.*)

KARIN (*miming*) Could you speak more slowly, please?

NICO No, thank you, I had something on the plane.

(*A moment.*)

I haven't seen my sister for nearly two

years. (*He holds up two fingers at her. Attempting mimes.*) Since she came to England. When she wrote and told us about the baby, I just had to come. We are Sicilians. Our family is very strong, you understand.

Karin No.

Nico Yes.

Together Ah!

(*Pause.*)

Karin Mr and Mrs Garbold –

Nico Garbold, yes –

Karin – have gone out – (*Goes to archway, waves goodbye.*) – to the pictures – err – (*She rotates her wrist, camera-fashion.*)

Nico Ah! They've gone for a ride on their bicycles!

Karin Yes.

Nico Yes.

Karin I think they – (*Cranks wrist.*) about twice a week – (*Holds up two fingers.*)

Nico Francesca always was a very athletic girl. (*Pause.*) I tried to telephone.

Karin Telephone.

Nico (*nodding*) Yes.

Karin Ah! (*She fetches him the telephone.*)

Nico But I couldn't understand the instructions, you see.

Karin Telephone. (*She thrusts the telephone at him.*)

Nico Yes. I tried to telephone – from the airport.

Karin Telephone.

(*He keeps trying to explain, she keeps thrusting the receiver at him. Finally he sighs, takes the telephone, vaguely dials and puts his ear to the receiver.*)

Nico Hello, mother? This is Nico. I'm at Francesca's. I'm having a charming conversation with a psychotic painter who doesn't understand a word I'm saying. Goodbye.

(*He puts down the receiver, smiles at* Karin. *She takes the telephone away. He mops his brow wearily.*)

Thank you.

Richard Harris, *Albert. A Comedy,*
Samuel French, London 1972, pp. 1–5.

Vocabulary

suburbia the suburbs; the life and ways of people who live there – *psychosis* [saɪ'kəʊsɪs]: disorder of the mind; *psychotic* [saɪ'kɒtɪk] (adj)

Assignments

1. Which aspects of this scene are calculated to make the audience laugh?
2. Is the scene "realistic"? Would you react like the characters if you were placed in a similar predicament?
3. Is the scene as amusing for the two people involved as it is for the audience?
4. How do you account for the fact that a total lack of communication can produce such hilarity?

5. How would you stage this play? Should the characters speak English with different accents or should they speak different foreign languages?
6. What part does mime play in the introductory scene of *Albert*? To what extent is the way in which we express ourselves through gesture, facial and body movements an indicator of our feelings and attitudes?

Educating Rita

WILLY RUSSELL

Educating Rita is a two-hander about Rita, a 26-old hairdresser, who is an uneducated, yet an alert product of the working class in northern England. She registers for a Humanities course at the Open University, completely against the will of her husband. Frank is her tutor. "The play is about giving people the confidence and the skills to make decisions about what to value and what to do with their lives," says Russell. The following scene is from Act I. Rita has come to Frank to tell him that she went to "a proper one, a professional theatre".

ACT I

Scene 6

The Lights come up

Frank enters carrying a briefcase and a pile of essays. He goes to the filing cabinet, takes his lecture notes from the briefcase and puts them in a drawer. He takes the sandwiches and apple from his briefcase and puts them on his desk and then goes to the window-desk and dumps the essays and briefcase. He switches on the radio and then sits in the swivel chair. He opens the packet of sandwiches, takes a bite and then picks up a book and starts reading.

Rita bursts through the door out of breath

FRANK What are you doing here? (*He looks at his watch*) It's Thursday, you ...

RITA (*moving over to the desk, quickly*) I know I shouldn't be here, it's me dinner hour, but listen, I've gorra tell someone, have y' got a few minutes, can y' spare ...?

FRANK (*alarmed*) My God, what is it?

RITA I had to come an' tell y', Frank, last night, I went to the theatre! A proper one, a professional theatre.

Frank gets up and switches off the radio and then returns to the swivel chair

FRANK (*sighing*) For God's sake, you had me worried, I thought it was something serious.

RITA No, listen, it was. I went out an' got me ticket, it was Shakespeare, I thought it was gonna be dead borin' ...

FRANK Then why did you go in the first place?

Rita I wanted to find out. But listen, it wasn't borin', it was bleedin' great, honest, ogh, it done me in, it was fantastic. I'm gonna do an essay on it.

Frank (*smiling*) Come on, which one was it?

Rita moves URC

Rita "... Out, out, brief candle!
Life's but a walking shadow, a poor player
That struts and frets his hour upon the stage
And then is heard no more. It is a tale
Told by an idiot, full of sound and fury
Signifying nothing."

Frank (*deliberately*) Ah, *Romeo and Juliet.*

Rita (*moving towards Frank*) Tch. Frank! Be serious. I learnt that today from the book. (*She produces a copy of "Macbeth"*) Look, I went out an' bought the book. Isn't it great? What I couldn't get over is how excitin' it was.

Frank puts his feet up on the desk

Wasn't his wife a cow, eh? An' that fantastic bit where he meets Macduff an' he thinks he's all invincible. I was on the edge of me seat at that bit. I wanted to shout out an' tell Macbeth, warn him.

Frank You didn't, did you?

Rita Nah. Y' can't do that in a theatre, can y'? It was dead good. It was like a thriller.

Frank Yes. You'll have to go and see more.

Rita I'm goin' to. *Macbeth*'s a tragedy, isn't it?

Frank nods

Right.

Rita smiles at Frank and he smiles back at her

Well I just – I just had to tell someone who'd understand.

Frank I'm honoured that you chose me.

Rita (*moving towards the door*) Well, I better get back. I've left a customer with a perm lotion. If I don't get a move on there'll be another tragedy.

Frank No. There won't be a tragedy.

Rita There will, y' know. I know this woman; she's dead fussy. If her perm doesn't come out right there'll be blood an' guts everywhere.

Frank Which might be quite tragic –

He throws her the apple from his desk which she catches

–but it won't be a tragedy.

Rita What?

Frank Well – erm – look; the tragedy of the drama has nothing to do with the sort of tragic event you're talking about. Macbeth is flawed by his ambition – yes?

Rita (*going and sitting in the chair by the desk*) Yeh. Go on. (*She starts to eat the apple*)

Frank Erm – it's that flaw which forces him to take the inevitable steps towards his own doom. You see?

Rita offers him the can of soft drink. He takes it and looks at it

(*Putting the can down on the desk*) No thanks. Whereas, Rita, a woman's hair being reduced to an inch of stubble, or – or the sort of thing you read in the paper that's reported as being tragic, "Man Killed By Falling Tree", is not a tragedy.

Rita It is for the poor sod under the tree.

Frank Yes, it's tragic, absolutely tragic. But it's not a tragedy in the way that *Macbeth* is a tragedy. Tragedy in dramatic terms is inevitable, pre-ordained. Look, now, even without ever having heard the story of *Macbeth* you wanted to shout out, to warn him and prevent him going on, didn't you? But you wouldn't have been able to stop him, would you?

Rita No.

Frank Why?

Rita They would have thrown me out the theatre.

Frank But what I mean is that your warning would have been ignored. He's warned in the play. But he can't go back. He still treads the path to doom. But the poor old fellow under the tree hasn't arrived there by following any inevitable steps, has he?

Rita No.

Frank There's no particular flaw in his character that has dictated his end. If he'd been warned of the consequences of standing beneath that particular tree he wouldn't have done it, would he? Understand.

Rita So – so Macbeth brings it on himself?

Frank Yes. You see he goes blindly on and on and with every step he's spinning one more piece of thread which will eventually make up the network of his own tragedy. Do you see?

Rita I think so. I'm not used to thinkin' like this.

Frank It's quite easy, Rita.

Rita It is for you. I just thought it was a dead excitin' story. But the way you tell it you make me see all sorts of things in it. (*After a pause*) It's fun, tragedy, isn't it? (*She goes over to the window*) All them out there, they know all about that sort of thing, don't they?

Frank Look, how about a proper lunch?

Rita Lunch? (*She leaps up, grabs the copy of "Macbeth", the can of drink and the apple and goes to the door*) Christ – me customer. She only wanted a demi-wave – she'll come out looking like a friggin' golliwog! (*She comes back to the table*) Ey' Frank, listen – I was thinkin' of goin' to the art gallery tomorrow. It's me half-day off. D' y' wanna come with me?

Frank (*smiling*) All right.

Willy Russell, *Educating Rita. A Comedy,* Samuel French, London 1981, pp. 27–29.

Vocabulary

I've gorra I have got to – *it done me in* it killed me; I am overwhelmed – *blood an' guts* an unpleasant scene – *poor sod* (= armes Luder) – *friggin'* (= verdammt) – *golliwog* black-faced doll with thick stiff hair

Assignments

1. How can Rita's attitude towards the theatre be described?
2. What does the scene tell us about the social backgrounds the two characters come from and belong to?
3. Frank and Rita speak in two completely different language registers. What effects does the playwright achieve by using these for his characters?
4. What is the relationship between Frank and Rita? Do you think the playwright is being objective in his portrayal of these two characters?
5. If you were producing this scene, which elements would you expect to raise laughter in the audience and why?
6. Both *Albert* by Richard Harris and *Educating Rita* by Willy Russell are comedies. What makes them comedies?
7. "Comedy is a play for the theatre, dealing with life and character in a humorous way, usually with a happy ending" *(Oxford Advanced Learner's Dictionary).*
   "After all, comedy is really only tragedy interrupted at the right point" *(Alan Ayckbourn).*
   Which of these definitions apply to *Albert* and/or *Educating Rita*?
8. In "Tragedy, Comedy, Tragicomedy" Martin Esslin tries to account for the differences between tragedy, comedy and farce from the director's point of view. With reference to this article, list terms and expressions which denote the different genres.

Tragedy, Comedy, Tragicomedy

As a critic I am, of course, fascinated by the difficult problems of the definition of the genres and their aesthetic and philosophical implications. But as a practitioner of drama, a working director, I look at them from a completely different angle. This is not to say that, even from this practical point of view, I think the definition of the genres is unimportant. Quite the contrary. But that importance is practical rather than theoretical. As a director one has to make a decision about the genre to which the play one tackles should belong. Not from some abstract principle, but simply from the point of view of how it is to be acted. Indeed, it is quite possible to act a play as either comedy or tragedy …

Whether the director sees (…) a play as

tragedy, comedy or even farce will have an immediate and very practical effect on his handling of the production: it will influence his casting, the design of the set and costumes, the tone, rhythm and pacing of the performance. And, above all, the style in which it is to be acted.

Let me illustrate this by a simple example. Here is a brief dialogue which, in itself, might be part of a tragedy, a comedy or a farce. In the text itself there is nothing to indicate which of the three it is:

SHE What has happened? Are you hurt, my darling?
HE Oh, it's nothing. I slipped ...
SHE But you are bleeding there is blood on your ... nose –
HE I slipped ... I must have broken my leg ...
SHE It looks worse than that ... I'm afraid

Imagine how this text would be acted if it formed part of a tragedy, if, for example, the wound was really a serious one and this dialogue preceded a scene in which the man died. Read it aloud in that manner. The actors – in this case you – would have to bring out real anxiety, fear, the gradual dawning of the seriousness of the situation. The man would have to try and play down the seriousness of the wound and make a brave effort to laugh it off, yet underneath that there would be his own anxiety and fear of death, and so on. The actors would have to develop a very high degree of empathy, of identification with the characters; they would have to make an immense effort to reach the highest possible pitch of emotion. As a result the timing of the scene would be slow, the pauses indicated by dots would be long and pregnant.

Now imagine the same five lines in the context of a light character comedy, a gently amusing play in which perhaps a scene like this, by revealing the girl's deeper interest in the young man, might set off a romance between them. It would soon turn out that the wound was not serious, but the girl's anxiety would have shown how fond she is of the young man. The way the actors would have to attack the scene would then be quite different; far more playful, more detached, with more emphasis on elegance of expression, lightness of touch, urbane manners. Even the way the actors use their voices would be different. Instead of heavy, emotional chest-tones, the lines could now come from a higher register. The pauses would probably be less pregnant and therefore shorter. There would still have to be genuine feeling and compassion in the delivery, but compassion in a far lighter, more playful vein.

And now try to read the same five lines as they would be acted in a farce, let us say during the pursuit of the lover by the husband: the lover has jumped from the bedroom window and is found by his mistress. The delivery of the lines will be very fast, breathless, in a falsetto voice; they will sound caricatured, mechanical, grotesque. Instead of coming out of real anxiety, a line like "there is blood ... on your ... nose" will appear as a grotesquely hysterical shriek. This is the cruel laughter that greets the man who has slipped on a banana skin. The French philosopher

Henri Bergson identified the source of laughter as the experience of seeing a human being treated or acting as a mechanism. Farce does just that: in farce events develop with the relentless mechanical precision of a machine and the characters appear as mere cogs. Charlie Chaplin being fed on the conveyor belt by a feeding machine in *Modern Times* and Buster Keaton on an ocean liner trying to cook an egg in the vast cauldron designed to cook for thousands are classical embodiments of this concept.

Martin Esslin, *An Anatomy of Drama,* Abacus, London 1978, pp. 68–71.

4 *Addressing the Audience*

Breaking the Code

HUGH WHITEMORE

Breaking the Code *is based on the book "Alan Turing, The Enigma" by Andrew Hodges. Turing, a mathematician and computer pioneer, and his colleagues developed machines that could crack the German Enigma code during World War II. The play, however, is not about a wartime achievement; it tackles the question of the relationship between science and morality. Turing also broke his time's moral code; he was a homosexual and died in 1954 by suicide.*
In the following scene, Turing addresses the audience.

ACT TWO
Scene One

TURING *enters and addresses the audience.*

Mr Headmaster, members of the staff, boys. I want you to imagine a bowl of porridge. A bowl of cold porridge. When I was a boy at Sherborne – some twenty-five years ago – we always had porridge for breakfast – every day, winter and summer – or so it seems. And for some unaccountable reason, by the time the porridge reached me it was cold. My friend, Christopher Morcom, was more fortunate; he enjoyed his porridge and ate it heartily. But I always sat there at breakfast, staring into a bowl of cold porridge: grey and soft and wrinkled on top. You must be wondering why I'm telling you this. The Headmaster asked me here to talk about my work with computers, and here I am describing bowls of cold porridge. Well, there's a good reason for it and I'll come to that in a moment. I dare say the word computer is unfamiliar to many of you. It is to a lot of people. But if I said electronic brain – ahh – that's much more interesting. And if I were to ask – can a machine think? – I'm sure you'd all be intrigued to know the answer. But before we can consider that properly I must explain something about computers and how they work. First of all, let me compare a computer with the human brain – which brings us back to our bowl of cold porridge, because that's what a human brain looks like: the same colour, the same texture. A computer is very different. It's big – the size of several large wardrobes all joined together; it's hard and metallic on the outside and terribly complicated on the inside, with lots of valves and condensers – not a bit like cold porridge, but that doesn't matter. It's the logical pattern of the brain that counts, not the grey stuff it's made of. The same with a computer. What matters is its logic. And the logic of a computer is really very simple. All it does is to read a list of instructions – we call this a program – and then it carries it out methodically. The only thing you have to do is to write down exactly what you want done in the language the computer understands. I know this may sound like a fanciful theory, but I assure you that it's not. The computer at Manchester University has been working for over four years, since 1949, and it has successfully tackled a wide variety of tasks. Many people think that computers are glorified c-c-calculating machines. Not so. It's true that computers are often used to do calculating because they calculate very quickly – but computer programs don't have to have anything to do with numbers. A colleague of mine has got our computer to hum tunes – it once sang "Jingle Bells". We've even got it to write love letters! Doing calculations, humming a tune, writing love letters. These are very d-d-different tasks, but they're all done by one machine – and that's an extremely important fact about computers. A computer is a universal machine and I have *proved* how it can perform any task that can be described in symbols. I would go further. It is my view that a computer can perform any task that the human brain can carry out. Any task. Now you might think from what I've said that a computer can only do what it's told to do. Well, it's true that we may start off like that – but it's only the start. A computer can be made to learn. Suppose, for example, that it were set to play chess. It could find out for itself, in the light of its own experience, which are winning and which are losing strategies, and then drop the losing ones. After a while we wouldn't know what instructions it was actually using. So it would hardly be fair to say that we had instructed it what to do. That would be like crediting the master with any originality shown by the pupil. The question thus arises as to whether or not we would credit such a machine with intelligence. I would say that we must. What I would very much like to do is to educate a computer, partly by direct training and partly by letting it find out things for itself. We don't know how to do this yet, but I believe that it will be achieved in the near future. And I feel sure that by the year 2000 it will be considered perfectly correct to speak of an intelligent machine, or to say that a computer is thinking. Of course, not everyone agrees with this view; far from it. Some people say that thinking is a function of man's immortal soul and since a machine has no soul, it cannot think. Surely this is blasphemous. Who are we to deny the possibility that God may wish to grant a soul to a machine? Then there is what I call the "Heads in the Sand" objection. "The consequences of machines thinking are too dreadful to contemplate," people say. "Such a thing could never happen." This point of view is usually expressed by intellectuals. They have the most to lose. Another objection – this is one I hear very frequently – is that a machine cannot be said to think until it can write a sonnet or compose a concerto, feel grief when its valves fuse, be warmed by flattery, by angry or depressed when it can't get what it wants. Well, of course, one might reply that there are precious few human beings who can write a sonnet or compose a concerto – and I can see no reason at all why a thinking machine should not be kind, resourceful, and beautiful, and friendly, have a sense of humour, tell right from wrong, make mistakes, fall in love, or enjoy strawberries and cream. At the moment these considerations should not concern us – but it might be rather nice, don't you think, if, one day, we could find out what a machine can feel?

(*Lighting change: autumn evening*)

Hugh Whitemore, *Breaking the Code,* Amber Lane Press, Oxford 1987, pp. 47–49.

Vocabulary

valve (= Röhre)

Assignments

1. Looking at the introductory lines of Turing's speech, why does he speak about porridge first?
2. What stage in the development of computers is this speech referring to? Which sentences in the text give the best clues about this?
3. Although we do not see Mr Turing's audience, what reactions do you think the schoolboys would have to what he has to say? Which parts of his speech would they be interested in or bored by? Go through the speech and try to list their reactions in sequence.
4. How would you sum up your reaction to this speaker? How do you account for this?
5. Do we learn anything about Mr Turing from his speech? How would you describe him to someone who had not been present?
6. A soliloquy is a speech made by a character who is alone on the stage. He reveals his feelings, his thoughts and intentions to the audience. Brian Clark, the English dramatist, when asked about the functions of the many soliloquies in one of his plays, said:

   "Part of the technique of the play was to find ways of dealing with the soliloquy problem in modern drama. The soliloquy in Shakespeare is a wonderful device which his convention allowed him to use. I don't really understand why, but we can't just do soliloquies these days."

   Do you share Brian Clark's opinion? Can you think of other means that Turing could have used to convey his "message"?

5 *Play and Film*

True West

SAM SHEPARD

True West *by Sam Shepard focuses on the relationship of two brothers who represent different lifestyles in the American West. Austin is an example of success; Lee has no home, no career. Austin is the thinker, the "civilized man"; Lee is the man of instinct and impulse. The catalyst who reveals the character of both men is Saul Kimmer, a film producer who has arrived to look over Austin's new screenplay. But he chooses Lee's cowboy story, with its clichés and stereotyped patterns of the "true" West.*

Scene Six

Afternoon, LEE *and* SAUL *in kitchen,* AUSTIN *in alcove.*

LEE Now you tell him. You tell him, Mr Kipper.

SAUL Kimmer.

LEE Kimmer. You tell him what you told me. He don't believe me.

AUSTIN I don't want to hear it.

SAUL It's really not a big issue. Austin. I was simply amazed by your brother's story and –

AUSTIN Amazed? You lost a bet! You gambled with my material!

SAUL That's really beside the point, Austin. I'm ready to go all the way with your brother's story. I think it has a great deal of merit.

AUSTIN I don't want to hear about it, okay? Go tell it to the executives! Tell it to somebody who's going to turn it into a package deal or something. A TV series. Don't tell it to me.

SAUL But I want to continue with your project too, Austin. It's not as though we can't do both. We're big enough for that aren't we?

AUSTIN 'We'? *I* can't do both! I don't know about 'we'.

LEE (*To* SAUL) See, what'd I tell ya'. He's totally unsympathetic.

SAUL Austin, there's no point in our going to another screenwriter for this. It just doesn't make sense. You're brothers. You know each other. There's a familiarity with material that just wouldn't be possible otherwise.

AUSTIN There's no familiarity with the material! None! I don't know what 'Tornado Country' is. I don't know what a 'gooseneck' is. And I don't want to know! (*Pointing to* LEE.) He's a hustler! He's a bigger hustler than you are! If you can't see that, then –

LEE (*To Austin*) Hey, now hold on. I didn't have to bring this bone back to you, boy. I persuaded Saul here that you were the right man for the job. You don't have to go throwin' up favors in my face.

AUSTIN Favors! I'm the one who wrote the fuckin' outline! You can't even spell.

SAUL (To AUSTIN) Your brother told me about the situation with your father. (*Pause*)

AUSTIN What? (*Looks at* LEE.)

SAUL That's right. Now we have a clear cut deal here, Austin. We have big studio money standing behind this thing. Just on the basis of your outline.

AUSTIN (*To* SAUL) What'd he tell you about my father?

SAUL Well – that he's destitute. He needs money.

LEE That's right. He does.

(AUSTIN *shakes his head, stares at them both.*)

AUSTIN (*To* LEE) And this little assignment is supposed to go toward the old man? A charity project? Is that what this is? Did you cook this up on the ninth green too?

SAUL It's a big slice, Austin.

AUSTIN (*To* LEE)I gave him money! I already gave him money. You know that. He drank it all up!

LEE This is a different deal here.

SAUL We can set up a trust for your father. A large sum of money. It can be doled out to him in parcels so he can't misuse it.

AUSTIN Yeah, and who's doing the doling?

SAUL Your brother volunteered.

(AUSTIN *laughs.*)

LEE That's right. I'll make sure he uses it for groceries.

AUSTIN (*To* SAUL) I'm not doing this script! I'm not writing this crap for you or anybody else. You can't blackmail me into it. You can't threaten me into it. There's no way I'm doing it. So just give it up. Both of you.

(*Long pause.*)

SAUL Well, that's it then. I mean this is an easy three hundred grand. Just for a first draft. It's incredible, Austin. We've got three different studios all trying to cut each other's throats to get this material. In one morning. That's how hot it is.

AUSTIN Yeah, well you can afford to give me a percentage on the outline then. And you better get the genius here an agent before he gets burned.

LEE Saul's gonna' be my agent. Isn't that right, Saul?

SAUL That's right. (*To* AUSTIN.) Your brother has really got something, Austin. I've been around too long not to recognize it. Raw talent.

AUSTIN He's got a lota' balls is what he's got. He's taking you right down the river.

SAUL Three hundred thousand, Austin. Just for a first draft. Now you've never been offered that kind of money before.

AUSTIN I'm not writing it.

(*Pause*)

SAUL I see. Well –

LEE We'll just go to another writer then. Right, Saul? Just hire us somebody with some enthusiasm. Somebody who can recognize the value of a good story.

SAUL I'm sorry about this, Austin.

AUSTIN Yeah.

SAUL I mean I was hoping we could continue both things but now I don't see how it's possible.

AUSTIN So you're dropping my idea altogether. Is that it? Just trade horses in mid-stream? After all these months of meetings.

SAUL I wish there was another way.

AUSTIN I've got everything riding on this, Saul. You know that. It's my only shot. If this falls through –

SAUL I have to go with what my instincts tell me –

AUSTIN Your instincts!

SAUL My gut reaction.

AUSTIN You lost! That's your gut reaction. You lost a gamble. Now you're trying to tell me you like his story? How could you possibly fall for that story? It's as phony as Hopalong Cassidy. What do you see in it? I'm curious.

SAUL It has the ring of truth, Austin.

AUSTIN (*Laughs*) Truth?

LEE It is true.

SAUL Something about the real West.

AUSTIN Why? Because it's got horses? Because it's got grown men acting like little boys?

SAUL Something about the land. Your brother is speaking from experience.

AUSTIN So am I!

SAUL But nobody's interested in love these days, Austin. Let's face it.

LEE That's right.

AUSTIN (*To* SAUL) He's been camped out on the desert for three months. Talking to cactus. What's he know about what people wanna' see on the screen! I drive on the freeway every day. I swallow the smog. I watch the news in color. I shop in the Safeway. I'm the one who's in touch! Not him!

SAUL I have to go now, Austin. (*He starts to leave.*)

AUSTIN There's no such thing as the West anymore! It's a dead issue! It's dried up, Saul, and so are you.

(SAUL *stops and turns to* AUSTIN.)

SAUL Maybe you're right. But I have to take the gamble, don't I?

AUSTIN You're fool to do this, Saul.

SAUL I've always gone on my hunches. Always. And I've never been wrong. (*To* LEE.) I'll talk to you tomorrow, Lee.

LEE All right, Mr Kimmer.

SAUL Maybe we could have some lunch.

LEE Fine with me. (*Smiles at* AUSTIN.)

SAUL I'll give you a ring.

(SAUL *exits, lights to black as brothers look at each other from a distance.*)

Sam Shepard, *True West,* Faber & Faber, London/Boston 1981, pp. 36–40.

Vocabulary

gooseneck cattle trailer; constructed lower to the ground, needs a high look to be attached to the truck that pulls it – *a grand* (AE) a thousand dollar – *he's got a lota' balls* he is being very aggressive – *to trade horses in mid-stream* to change one's mind halfway through a project – *I've got everything riding on this* I have risked everything I have on this – *Hopalong Cassidy* a cowboy in the old West, who was not a real person – *Safeway* big chain of supermarkets

Assignments

1. What does the scene tell us about the relationship between the two brothers, Lee and Austin?
2. What has just happened to sour this relationship?
3. Why does Austin call his brother a "hustler"?
4. Which details indicate that the scene takes place in the United States and more particularly in California? What does the "West" stand for?
5. From the evidence in this excerpt, can you work out what Austin's film script was going to be about and what sort of film Lee envisages?
6. In the scene, the film producer prefers Lee's cowboy story to Austin's screenplay, because Lee "is speaking from experience" and his script has "the ring of truth". With reference to the following article, discuss the difference between film and stage.

Talks About THEATRE and FILMS

DOUGLAS FAIRBANKS, Jr.

I've been virtually retired for the past 12 years. I've done five plays and no films at all. I like working on a new play like this, because you never know what's going to happen. There's some slight change in every performance – in running order, lyrics, placement, staging. Film and stage are quite different, really. It's sort of like asking "What's different between sculpting or painting, or between water colors or pen and ink?" They are so completely different. They're both reproductions of a design, but they're done in different ways. One has a certain consistency in the sense that when you're onstage, you have the continuity of action and the actor is a little more in control. And in films, you are only in control if you happen to be your own producer. Even then you have to make so many compromises with directors, with other stars, and primarily with the distributors who tell you who you can have and who you can't have from the box office point of view. But on the other hand, in film, the finished product is there forever. Whereas the minute it's completed, a play is over; it's gone. It remains only in your memory. If I told you that I saw the last performance ever given by Sarah Bernhardt and I told you what it was like, you'd only have my impression. I can't prove it. In film, however, even though they may have cut a whole sequence out or though some things may be different from the way they were intended, still it is there and it's permanent.

From the acting point of view, I suppose the stage is the most gratifying in terms of interpretation. But in terms of the finished product, I think films are.

It's largely an illusion that film is a director's medium, though it's become fashionable to think so in recent years. To a certain extent, yes, it has been. Much depends upon the director, and the force of personality of that person. But much also depends upon the force of personality of the producer or the star. Perhaps in the last five years or so, directors have become more important than ever was the case before. In the old days, someone would get credit as director, but often he would have nothing to say about the production at all. Some producer who's name didn't even appear on the screen had told the director what to do. In other cases, the director might define the contract so that his name went up on the screen while someone else would do the directing. And in still other instances, the star would be so powerful and would say, "This is the way I want it." You never really knew who was responsible unless you were close to the production. Consequently, a lot of very fine directors have not been given the credit they deserve; and a lot of very poor directors have been given credit they didn't deserve.

I've been at my job for 54 years, and in 54 years, there's nothing left to do that you haven't done at least five or six times. That doesn't mean that you've always done them well, but you've done them. Most of the roles I like to do I'm too old for now. I suppose I can still do King Lear. The show I'm doing now is a musical. But do I sing? I did the first really big revival of MY FAIR LADY, but then that was something that was designed for a minimum of singing. And I've done records with Andre Kostelanetz. But that's one of those things that if you don't get it right the first time, you go back and do it twenty times until you get it. Singing? I suppose in a court of law, they'd call it singing. But I don't think anyone from the Metropolitan is going to scream, "We must have him!"

Shepard's "True West": A Comic Treat From a Prize-Winning Dramatist

"True West" is a true treat, although, as usual, Shepard has not given us any strong female characters.

In the past, Shepard's rather sardonic wit has emerged only in brief flashes that are in contrast to the overall heavy context. "True West" is his first true comedy.

Thus, even though "True West" is the most naturalistic play Shepard has written, it has the excitement of an experimental work because the playwright is striking out in unfamiliar directions.

There is a new geniality, a willingness to present characters as they are without making them bear the burden of metaphysical significance.

At times in Shepard's previous work it seems although the drama stops to call attention to a particularly poetic speech. In this play, his use of language is as fine as ever, but springs more naturally from the action and characterizations.

Like Shepard's earlier plays, such as "Tooth of Crime," "True West" dramatizes the shifting balance of power in a crucial one-on-one confrontation. And like more recent plays, such as "Buried Child," it explores the love-hate relationship between close relatives.

Austin – an elegantly casual, well educated screenwriter – is trying to finish a script while housesitting for his mother. He is interrupted by the arrival of his ne'er-do-well brother Lee, an obnoxious loudmouth and small time thief.

Lee manages to sell a story idea to Austin's producer, and by the second act the brothers' roles have been reversed. Austin is getting drunk and stealing toasters while Lee is trying to write a screenplay.

The brothers represent the two sides of every writer's dilemma: should you stay at the typewriter, polishing your craft by writing about life, or should you be out in the world actually living it?

Lee has experience worth writing about, but does not have the ability to express himself. Austin has the skill but has lost touch with the vitality of real life.

Ellin Stein in: *San Francisco Chronicle,* 14/7/1980 (excerpt).

6 Character Portrayal

Golden Girls

LOUISE PAGE

This is a play about a 4 × 100 metres women's relay team competing in the Olympics for Britain. At the centre of the play are three black and two white women. The clash between individual ambitions and cooperative demands in **Golden Girls** *encapsulates the concept of athletics in Louise Page's play, which is different from the image created by the film* **Chariots of Fire***. This scene is the last but one in the play.*

ACT II
Scene Five

The race.

The runners come down the stage passing the baton sideways between them.

Announcement of the race and the start in Greek etc.

They take their tracksuits off. For the first time we see them all in The Golden Girls running stripe.

The race: as they run each girl has one chant in the rhythm of her race.

SUE Go! Go! (*She repeats until the baton is passed to* MURIEL.)

MURIEL For me! For me! (*She repeats until the baton is passed to* JANET.)

JANET Want to win! Want to win! (*She repeats until the baton is passed to* DORCAS.)

DORCAS Go for it! Go for it! (*She repeats until she goes through the tape and the clock stops.*)

Jubilation; the sound of the stadium; flash bulbs and a moment while they look at their time.

Enter PAULINE.

PAULINE You were fucking wonderful.

The official time goes up on the scoreboard: 39.99 seconds.

DORCAS Yes!

JANET History!

MURIEL *starts to cry.*

MURIEL I'm just so happy.

SUE This year's men's record!

Enter MIKE *and* NOËL.

DORCAS We did it!

MIKE You were like the wind. Ten second legs!

SUE You see that Dad? You see that time?

NOËL *takes a photo of her.*

MURIEL If only George was here.

MIKE I didn't know you could run like that. I never dreamed.

JANET I've got a gold medal. Me.

Enter LACES.

SUE (*bugging* LACES). We did it!

LACES Well done.

NOËL Is that all you can say?

LACES gives DORCAS the dope testing card.

LACES Short straw I'm afraid. Ableman, Farr, Kinder, Morris –

JANET (*to* DORCAS). I told you you'd get tested in the end!

Enter HILARY. *She carries a bust crowned with laurel leaves.*

HILARY I was so excited, Athena, the Goddess of Victory. We wanted to mark the occasion.

SUE I must have done ten seconds.

LACES Now!

LACES and MIKE chair DORCAS. As they carry her off, she seizes the bust from HILARY.

HILARY The traditional victor's crown. Everybody'll be wanting pictures, stories – Dorcas! (HILARY *goes*.)

SUE Take that for me, Dad. Take that!

NOËL *tries to find an angle to get the shot.*

NOËL You did it for me. The time of my life. (*He goes in order to get the picture.*)

JANET Fancy having to piss into a jar at a time like this!

PAULINE Yes, but it's one in the eye for Tom Billbow.

MURIEL What?

PAULINE He just never gives up. He says he can prove we're taking Hydromel.

JANET Nothing showed yesterday.

SUE Where's he got this from?

PAULINE If nothing shows up there is no proof.

SUE Of course there's no proof. We've been taking it and being tested for months.

Enter VIVIEN.

VIVIEN Did I tell you all? (*She hugs them.*) You must be thrilled.

JANET I'm getting a gold medal!

Re-enter HILARY *with the wreath back on the bust.*

HILARY (*to Vivien*). Congratulations.

VIVIEN Couldn't have done it without Ortolan.

HILARY (*gathering them to her*). Our Golden Girls.

TANNOY The medals ceremony of the 4 × 100 meters relay has been suspended pending an official enquiry.

Pause.

HILARY What?

VIVIEN Some technical hitch. That equipment is very sensitive.

SUE That stuff you gave us?

VIVIEN Pardon?

PAULINE Dorcas has got caught. Hasn't she?

VIVIEN No.

SUE I've got to go and be tested.

VIVIEN Nothing illegal.

MURIEL Hydromel's not legal. If it was, you wouldn't have told us to keep quiet.

HILARY You were giving them drugs?

VIVIEN Nothing that could possibly disqualify them.

SUE She's been caught.

JANET I don't know what I'll do if I'm disqualified.

HILARY Who gave you permission?

VIVIEN Look at their results.

HILARY I thought we had made it quite clear. Play by the rules.

VIVIEN I did.

MURIEL You doped us.

VIVIEN No. Never.

SUE All those pills?

VIVIEN There was nothing in them.

MURIEL You told us it was Hydromel.

Pause.

VIVIEN What I gave you was something called Similexon. A placebo. Flour and sugar in a gelatine shell.

JANET What's going to happen to me in there?

PAULINE Just one of us Tom Billbow said.

VIVIEN Did he say what?

PAULINE Hydromel! What you told us it was.

MURIEL Dorcas?

VIVIEN If Dorcas is taking something, it's nothing to do with me. It's something she's done on her own. She's always wanted to be brightest and best.

JANET When I was thirteen she used to be my God.

Enter TOM.

TOM I thought there'd be a surfeit of smiles. I did try and warn you.

HILARY One out of five?

TOM I always suspected Ableman was half crazy.

HILARY How did you get on to it?

TOM Women rivalling men. There had to be an explanation.

HILARY There's still Sue's run. Janet's. Muriel's.

JANET I did run that fast?

VIVIEN Yes.

Enter DORCAS.

DORCAS Why?

HILARY I knew you were a liability.

JANET You're a cheat.

VIVIEN Why Dorcas? Why?

DORCAS Safe you said. Safe.

VIVIEN I was pretending.

DORCAS It isn't a game. It isn't a game.

VIVIEN What I gave you was safe.

HILARY Do you know how much money you've just poured down a very dirty drain?

DORCAS Do you know where I got the money.

TOM Ortolan?

HILARY This is nothing to do with us.

DORCAS What about our accounts? I got all sorts of things. I swapped. Couldn't have got it without your money.

SUE If you wanted to run faster why didn't you just ask her.

DORCAS If she'd given me two she could have given you two.
(*To* VIVIEN). We had a deal. It was safe. Nothing was supposed to show.

VIVIEN That's because there was nothing there. Anything else you got is due to your own stupidity.

DORCAS I'm not stupid.

VIVIEN You went and got more of what I gave you.

SUE You did give it to us?

VIVIEN Of what you thought I gave you.

DORCAS You gave us stuff. I got more. What's the difference? How was I supposed to know it wasn't real?

VIVIEN Did it never cross your mind?

DORCAS No, because I'm stupid. All I wanted was to win.

HILARY How can you possibly call that winning?

TOM Feet of clay.

DORCAS You pathetic little man.

PAULINE Dorcas!

DORCAS Sniff, sniff, sniff.

TOM Nothing to do with me. You were dope tested.

DORCAS Not for months and months. Why today?

TOM You can't let the flag go up for someone who doesn't play by the rules.

DORCAS What fucking rules? No one else has any rules. (*She goes at him.*)

MURIEL Dorcas, don't.

DORCAS *struggles with* TOM.

MURIEL Leave him.

DORCAS I'm going to kill him.

MURIEL Get him out.

VIVIEN *and* HILARY *rescue* TOM. JANET *starts to scream. The other women hold* DORCAS.

HILARY I can assure you Golden Girls has no part in any of this.

TOM I suppose I should be thankful it wasn't steroids.

They take him off.

PAULINE (*to* VIVIEN *as they go*). I could have run. If there was something I could have had to calm me down.

Enter LACES. *He has the others' dope testing cards.*

LACES They're waiting. It's the rules.

Louise Page, *Golden Girls,* Methuen, London/New York 1985, pp. 101–106.

Vocabulary

baton ['bætən] (= Staffelstab) – *in the eye* (= ein Denkzettel) – *Hydromel, Ortolan* unallowed anabolica – *steroids* artificial hormones used to build up muscles

Assignments

1. This short scene touches on sport as a struggle against one's own physical limitations which results in a feeling of personal achievement. What other kinds of competition are treated? Do you think that despite the multiplicity of topics the scene is tightly structured?
2. Twelve people take part in the scene. If you were producing it for the stage, how would you group them? What would you give them to do so that they are not just standing around while other characters are speaking?
3. Would you have chosen a different point in the action to start presenting hotly debated topics of sporting ethics to the audience? What are the advantages of the playwright's choice?
4. How is the idea of personal versus collective responsibility handled in the scene? Do you get the feeling that you are listening to an academic debate or is it interwoven into the plot and character presentation?
5. To what extent do the following excerpts from an interview with Louise Page contribute to an understanding of this scene from *Golden Girls*?

Interview with Louis Page (excerpt)

GLAAP As far as *Golden Girls* is concerned, is that in your eyes primarily a play about the exploitation of athletes or is it about the pressures of ambition, or is it about racism, or is it about maybe rivalry between Eastern and Western nations in sports?

PAGE I think it's about all those things. I think I would say it was about all the things sport is not supposed to be about. If you know *Chariots of Fire*[1], that movie which was all the things sport is supposed to be about, it's the flip side to that … I think whatever form of socialist ideology you have people are still ambitious and people are not necessarily ambitious in career terms; they're ambitious that they grow the biggest cucumber, or their children are the cleverest at school or what ever. People need those things, they need those moments of hope and I think that's one of the things about ambition, the good side of ambition is that it gives people a moment of hope. But "drive" makes it sound too hard, rather than in the future there is something that one could grow a beautiful flower or what ever. Women weren't supposed to be personally ambitious, at the beginning of the feminist festival there was an emphasis on sisterhood and I kept meeting people who said "Oh, Louise, you're so ambitious." … We all know people who pretend they're not ambitious, who are the worst sort of people because they're so busy pretending they're not ambitious, but behind the scenes they are manipulating people all the time. I wanted to write about that sort of ambition, it's summed up in Dr. Vivien Blackwood in *Golden Girls*, ambition which leads to corruption.

[1] The story of two very different athletes, who at the Olympic Games 1924 (in Paris) won gold medals. The film praises victory and does not touch the problems of unreflected demands for achievement.

7 Language and Dialogue

Whose Life is it Anyway?

BRIAN CLARK

Ken, in Brian Clark's play, is paralysed from the neck down as a result of a car accident which severed his spinal cord. He is discontent and cannot accept his present "inhuman" state. The problem is seen from different angles. We are confronted with various opinions and arguments – those of the patient, the doctors, the nurses and the lawyers.

The following extract is from the first act of the play. Mrs Gillian Boyle, a medical social worker, is seeing the patient.

(SISTER *and* NURSE SADLER *come in with the trolley.*)

SISTER Good morning, Mr Harrison. How are you this morning?

KEN Marvellous.

SISTER Night Sister said you slept well.

KEN I did. I had a lot of help, remember.

SISTER Your eyes are bright this morning.

KEN I've been thinking.

SISTER You do too much of that.

KEN What other activity would you suggest? ... Football? I tell you what, Sister, just leave me alone with Nurse Sadler here. Let's see what the old Adam can do for me.

SISTER I'm a Sister, not a Madame.

KEN Sister – you dark horse you! All this time you've been kidding me. I've been wondering for months how on earth a woman could become a State Registered Nurse and a Sister and still think you found babies under a gooseberry bush – and you've known all along.

SISTER Of course I've known. When I qualified as a midwife I learnt that when they pick up babies from under the gooseberry bushes they wrap them up in women to keep them warm. I know because it was our job to unwrap them again.

KEN The miracle of modern science! Anyway, Sister, as I said, I've been thinking, if I'm going to be around for a long time, money will help.

SISTER It always does.

KEN Do you remember that solicitor chap representing my insurance company a few months ago? Mr Hill. I think he said his name was. He said he'd come back when I felt better. Do you think you could get him back as soon as possible? I'd feel more settled if we could get the compensation sorted out.

SISTER Sounds a good idea.

KEN You'll ring him up?

SISTER Of course.

KEN He left a card: it's in my drawer.

SISTER Right. (*She goes to the locker and takes out the card.*) Mr Philip Hill, Solicitor. Right, I'll ring him.

KEN Thanks.

SISTER That's enough. (*They cover him up again and straighten the bed.*)

SISTER Mrs Boyle is waiting to see you, Mr Harrison.

KEN Mrs Boyle? Who's she?

SISTER A very nice woman.

KEN Oh God, must I see her?

SISTER Dr Emerson asked her to come along.

KEN Then I'd better see her. If I refuse, he'll probably dissolve her in water and inject her into me. (SISTER *has to choke back a giggle.*)

SISTER Mr Harrison! Come on, Nurse; this man will be the death of me.

KEN (*cheerfully*) Doubt it, Sister. I'm not even able to be the death of myself. (SISTER *goes out with* NURSE SADLER. MRS GILLIAN BOYLE *enters. She is thirty-five, attractive, and very professional in her manner. She is a medical social worker.*)

MRS BOYLE Good morning.

KEN Morning.

MRS BOYLE Mr Harrison?

KEN (*cheerfully*) It used to be.

MRS BOYLE My name is Mrs Boyle.

KEN And you've come to cheer me up.

MRS BOYLE I wouldn't put it like that.

KEN How would you put it?

MRS BOYLE I've come to see if I can help.

KEN Good. You can.

MRS BOYLE How?

KEN Go and convince Dr Frankenstein that he has successfully made his monster and he can now let it go.

MRS BOYLE Dr Emerson is a first-rate physician. My goodness, they have improved this room.

KEN Have they?

MRS BOYLE It used to be really dismal. All dark green and cream. It's surprising what pastel colours will do, isn't it? Really cheerful.

KEN Yes; perhaps they should try painting me. I'd hate to be the thing that ruins the decor.

MRS BOYLE What on earth makes you say that? You don't ruin anything.

KEN I'm sorry. That was a bit … whining. Well don't let me stop you.

MRS BOYLE Doing what?

KEN What you came for I suppose. What do you do? Conjuring tricks? Funny stories? Or a belly dance? If I have any choice, I'd prefer the belly dance.

MRS BOYLE I'm afraid I've left my bikini at home.

KEN Who said anything about a bikini?

MRS BOYLE Dr Emerson tells me that you don't want any more treatment.

KEN Good.

MRS BOYLE Why good?

KEN I didn't think he'd heard what I'd said.

MRS BOYLE Why not?

KEN He didn't take any notice.

MRS BOYLE Well as you can see, he did.

KEN He sent you?

MRS BOYLE Yes.

KEN And you are my new treatment; get in.

MRS BOYLE Why don't you want any more treatment?

KEN I'd rather not go on living like this.

MRS BOYLE Why not?

KEN Isn't it obvious?

MRS BOYLE Not to me. I've seen many patients like you.

KEN And they all want to live?

MRS BOYLE Usually.

KEN Why?

MRS BOYLE They find a new way of life.

KEN How?

MRS BOYLE You'll be surprised how many things you will be able to do with training and a little patience.

KEN Such as?

MRS BOYLE We can't be sure yet. But I should think that you will be able to operate reading machines and perhaps an adapted typewriter.

KEN Reading and writing. What about arithmetic?

MRS BOYLE (*smiling*) I dare say we could fit you up with a comptometer if you really wanted one.

KEN Mrs Boyle, even educationalists have realised that the three r's do not make a full life.

MRS BOYLE What did you do before the accident?

KEN I taught in an art school. I was a sculptor.

MRS BOYLE I see.

KEN Difficult, isn't it? How about an electrically operated hammer and chisel? No, well. Or a cybernetic lump of clay?

MRS BOYLE I wouldn't laugh if I were you. It's amazing what can be done. Our scientists are wonderful.

KEN They are. But it's not good enough you see, Mrs Boyle. I really have absolutely no desire at all to be the object of scientific virtuosity. I have thought things over very carefully. I do have plenty of time for thinking and I have decided that I do not want to go on living with so much effort for so little result.

MRS BOYLE Yes, well, we shall have to see about that.

KEN What is there to see?

MRS BOYLE We can't just stop treatment, just like that.

KEN Why not?

MRS BOYLE It's the job of the hospital to save life, not to lose it.

KEN The hospital's done all it can, but it wasn't enough. It wasn't the hospital's fault; the original injury was too big.

MRS BOYLE We have to make the best of the situation.

KEN No. "We" don't have to do anything. I have to do what is to be done and that is to cash in the chips.

MRS BOYLE It's not unusual, you know, for people injured as you have been to suffer with this depression for a considerable time before they begin to see that a life is possible.

KEN How long?

MRS BOYLE It varies.

KEN Don't hedge.

MRS BOYLE It could be a year or so.

KEN And it could last for the rest of my life.

MRS BOYLE That would be most unlikely.

KEN I'm sorry, but I cannot settle for that.

MRS BOYLE Try not to dwell on it. I'll see what I can do to get you started on some occupational therapy. Perhaps we could make a start on the reading machines.

KEN Do you have many books for those machines?

MRS BOYLE Quite a few.

KEN Can I make a request for the first one?

MRS BOYLE If you like.

KEN How to be a sculptor with no hands.

MRS BOYLE I'll be back tomorrow with the machine.

KEN It's marvellous you know.

MRS BOYLE What is?

KEN All you people have the same technique. When I say something really awkward you just pretend I haven't said anything at all. You're all the bloody same ... Well, there's another outburst. That should be your cue to comment on the lightshade or the colour of the walls.

MRS BOYLE I'm sorry if I have upset you.

KEN Of course you have upset me. You and the doctors with your appalling so-called professionalism, which is nothing more than a series of verbal tricks to prevent you relating to your patients as human beings.

MRS BOYLE You must understand: we have to remain relatively detached in order to help ...

KEN That's alright with me. Detach yourself. Tear yourself off on the dotted line that divides the woman from the social worker and post yourself off to another patient.

MRS BOYLE You're very upset ...

KEN Christ Almighty, you're doing it again. Listen to yourself, woman. I say something offensive about you and you turn your professional cheek. If you were human, if you were treating me as human, you'd tell me to bugger off. Can't you see that this is why I've decided that life isn't worth living? I am not human and I'm even more convinced of that by your visit than I was before, so how does that grab you? The very exercise of your so-called professionalism makes me want to die.

MRS BOYLE I'm ... Please ...

KEN Go ... For God's sake get out ... Go on ... Get out ... Get out.

Repr. from: A.-R. Glaap (ed.), *Brian Clark: Whose Life is it Anyway?*, Cornelsen Verlag Hirschgraben, Frankfurt/M. 1985, pp. 21–26.

Vocabulary

Madame [mə'da:m] here: Puffmutter – *dark horse* a person with unexpected qualities – *State Registered Nurse* fully qualified nurse – *compensation* (= Schadenersatz) – *the three r's* reading, (w)riting and (a-)rithmetic – *to bugger off* to go away – *how does that grab you?* how do you like that?

Assignments

1. How does Mrs Boyle, the medical social worker, deal with Ken Harrison? How does the patient react?
2. Despite being injured, Ken jokes about his situation. Do you think that this will cause embarrassment on the part of the audience?
3. "I do not want to go on living with so much effort for so little result" (Ken Harrison). Do you get the impression that Ken is seriously thinking of putting an end to his life?
4. What difficulties in coming to a decision are the doctors faced with in Ken's case?
5. How does the style in which this scene is written set the general mood? Discuss with reference to the following excerpt from Esslin's book.

The Level of Language

Martin Esslin

The level of language, the style in which a play is written – and consequently acted – has something to do with the level at which the audience looks at the characters. The distinguished Canadian critic Northrop Frye has pointed out to four levels of discourse – and these apply to the novel as well as to drama: if the audience is to look at the characters as infinitely above them, as gods, we are in the realm of myth; if the audience is to look up to them as men high above them, we are in the realm of the heroic; if the audience is to look at the characters as being on the same level as themselves, we are in a realistic style; and if the audience looks down on the characters as contemptible, this is the ironic mode.
Myths – like Greek tragedy – will require the highest flights of poetic language. Heroic plays about kings and queens and almost superhuman men and women will still need an elevant language.
On the realistic level, when the author confronts us with people inhabiting the same social level as ourselves, prose is indicated. And if we look down on the characters, if we are meant to feel superior to them in intelligence – for example in farce or satire – the language can again be stylised, because we are looking at people removed from ourselves, even though that distance is a distance beneath us; the language there can be mechanically repetitive or exaggeratedly silly or indeed mock-verse, as in satires and parodies.

Martin Esslin, *An Anatomy of Drama. Style and Character*, Abacus, London 1987, pp. 38–39.

Children of a Lesser God

Mark Medoff

Children of a Lesser God *is a play by the American dramatist Mark Medoff. It takes place in the mind of James Leeds, a speech teacher at a State School for the Deaf. Characters step from his memory. Sarah Norman is in her mid-twenties, she is deaf from birth and does not lip read. When James is speaking to her, he signs what he says to her.*
In the following scene, Sarah's mother, who has not seen her daughter in eight years, appears on the scene.

(*Mrs Norman enters. She hasn't seen her daughter in eight years. She struggles to communicate with Sarah, more through gesture than sign*)

Mrs Norman Congratulations, Sarah. I'm very happy to see you. You're so grownup. You're … Eight years. My, a person can't digest that in …

(*Sarah does not understand Mrs Norman's sign*)

I don't know how to say that.

(*A beat. To James*)

She didn't want to come, did she? You made her.

JAMES You don't *make* Sarah do anything, Mrs Norman.

SARAH Tell me.

MRS NORMAN (*Managing to communicate, if haltingly*) I said, you didn't want to come. I don't know why you've come.

SARAH I don't either. To hurt you maybe.

MRS NORMAN (*To James*) I'm sorry, I'm rusty – what did she say?

(*Sarah insists on her mother's attention*)

SARAH (*Very slowly*) To h-u-r-t you. Maybe.

MRS NORMAN H.U.R. To hurt me. Maybe.

SARAH To show you I've done fine without you.

JAMES To show you she's done fine without you.

(*Silence: mother and daughter. Then Sarah breaks, begins to look around the "house"*)

MRS NORMAN Do your parents know?

JAMES No, my mother's dead and my father and I haven't spoken for several years.

SARAH Can we spend the night in my old room?

JAMES Sarah would like to know if we can spend the night in her old room.

(*A beat*)

MRS NORMAN If she'll promise to make conversation with me at breakfast in the morning.

JAMES [If you promise to make conversation with her at breakfast in the morning.]

(*A beat*)

SARAH Try.

JAMES She'll try.

MRS NORMAN Yes, I remember that sign. [Try.]

(MRS NORMAN *recedes as the scene shifts*)

SARAH My room.

JAMES Your old room? Bit spare.

SARAH I threw everything out the last time I came.

JAMES You threw everything out the last time you came. You can't destroy that time by throwing things away.

SARAH I did.

(*James picks her up and carries her into the room*)

JAMES Small bed.

SARAH That's why I want to sleep in it with you.

JAMES That's why you want to spend the night in it with me.

SARAH No man has been in this room since I was five. That was the night before they sent me to school.

JAMES No man has been in this room since you were five. That was the night before they sent you away to the school.

SARAH My father stayed with me that night. He cried. I never saw him again.

JAMES Your father stayed with you that night. He cried. You never saw him again.

SARAH After he left, my mother put a picture of the Virgin Mary on the wall; one weekend when I came to visit, I drew a hearing aid in her ear. My mother cried.

JAMES After he left, your mother put a picture of the Virgin Mary on the wall; one weekend when you came to visit, you drew a hearing aid in her ear. Your mother cried. Yes, I can imagine.

SARAH The next visit there was a picture of Ricky Nelson.

JAMES The next visit there was a picture of Ricky Nelson. Makes sense. Why Ricky Nelson?

SARAH I don't know. I never asked, she never explained.

JAMES You never asked, she never explained.

SARAH Nothing else on my walls.

JAMES Nothing else on the walls.

SARAH Just that picture: "To Sarah, Good Luck, From Ricky." In my mother's handwriting.

JAMES Just that picture : "To Sarah, Good Luck, From Ricky." In your mother's handwriting.

(*A beat*)

Your mother wanted very much to touch you tonight. But you … Maybe you wanted to touch her.

SARAH I can't give more than I gave.

JAMES You can't give more than you gave? I wonder. Maybe you could. You hardly ever get a second chance to …

(*James turns away*)

SARAH What are you talking about?

JAMES Nothing. Forget it. None of my business.

SARAH Tell me.

JAMES Just the way your mother was standing there, staring into space.

SARAH You're hiding.

JAMES I'm hiding? No, I'm not … Yes, I am. You remember I told you my mother died two years ago …

SARAH Yes.

JAMES She killed herself. My father had left her after twenty-eight years. Just strolled away. Left me to take care of her. She lived with me for almost three years. When I raised the rent, she …

(*A beat*)

Look, I really don't think we're gonna fit on that little bed, whudduya say?

SARAH Tell me the rest.

JAMES Tell you what rest?

(*She lifts his hands up, encouraging him to go on*)

JAMES All right. One night, instead of sitting on her bed pretending to listen to that day's outpouring of grievances against the world, I tried a little variation on the ritual. Nothing much, I just said to her, "I can't take care of you any more. The thought of living with you one more day makes me want to put a gun to one of our heads." She was very good. She picked a cracker crumb off her blanket. Helpfully, I took it from her, put it in my mouth. And she just sat there staring into the space, until finally she smiled – not at me, but at some absent third party – and she said, "James can't save me; he never could. Amen." And then she turned out the light. I swallowed the cracker; she swallowed [the pills]. Her note said, "Don't blame yourself. When I see you in heaven, I'll still give you a great big Jesus hug."

(*She takes him to her. He breaks.*)

I'm fine. I'm sorry.

SARAH We're not so different. We were both born to parents who would have been better off without us.

JAMES We're not so different, huh? We were both born to parents who would have been better off without us.

SARAH I love you.

JAMES Oh, Sarah, I love you too.

(*They cling to each other. He breaks gently, moves downstage*)

And the next day we were married by a Justice of the Peace, with Sarah's mother in attendance. The Justice didn't sign, of course, so I translated the ceremony for Sarah. When it was done, she said to me:

SARAH Let no one, living or dead, absent or present, ever come between us.

JAMES Let no one, living or dead, absent or present, ever come between us.

JAMES And I promised.

SARAH You and me. Joined.

(*James turns toward Sarah. He begins to move toward her as the lights fade to black*)

Mark Medoff, *Children of a Lesser God*, Amber Lane Press, Ambergate 1982 ([1]1980), pp. 41–45.

Vocabulary

beat sound of a regular repeated stroke – *whudduya say?* what do you say? – *Justice of the Peace* magistrate; civil officer acting as a judge

Assignments

1. What function do the "beats" have in structuring the scene?
2. Which parts of the text indicate that Mrs Norman and her daughter have difficulty in communicating. Why is this?
   Why do you think James repeats such a lot of what Sarah says?
3. Do you get the impression from the text that Sarah is suffering from some kind of disability? If so, which?
4. What does the scene tell us about the distant and recent past?
   How does what we learn influence our reaction to the scene?
   Does it become more poignant, grotesque, tender ...?
5. Is there anything that this scene has in common with the excerpt from *Whose Life is it Anyway*? What could be gained from a contrastive analysis of the two scenes?
6. In our times, voluntary euthanasia, problems of life and death and the treatment of handicapped people are some of the most important issues. What is the advantage of seeing plays to reading books about these problems?
7. The story of a play is told mostly through dialogue. What are the functions of dialogue?
   Discuss with reference to the following article. What is the special function of dialogue in Clark's and Medoff's plays?

Following the Story in Dialogue

The story of a play is told entirely through dialogue. [...]

First of all, the dialogue identifies the characters for you. The first few speeches made by a character – or by someone else speaking to him or about him – gives you clues to his nature.

Second, dialogue reveals the *relationship* of the characters to one another. It is this relationship that usually reveals the situation on which the play is based. The characters want something, or fear something, or in some other way conflict with one another. Whatever the exact nature of the situation is, you feel a certain tension: a problem exists and must be settled before the play can end.

A third function of dialogue is to carry the story along: it is the wheels on which the plot moves. Most often, you will have no difficulty in following the course of action, but if you do, pause a moment to ask yourself: who is trying to achieve a definite purpose? what is that purpose? what opposition is he meeting? what desires of other characters are in conflict with his desire? Answering these questions to yourself, you will be prepared for decisive moments, when one side or the other gains an advantage and pushes ahead. Most important of all, you will share the emotions of the characters as they achieve success or meet with defeat.

That brings up the fourth special function of dialogue – to stimulate the audience to emotions and ideas. The dialogue of a play helps to set its *tone*, whether it is humourous or gloomy, happy or tragic. Since a dramatist cannot address his audience directly, his characters must say for him whatever feelings or ideas he wishes to convey to the audience. Look, then, for speeches that establish the tone of the play and seem to express its main theme.

Understanding these four uses of dialogue (this is a good time to review them), you can take a second look at any line that puzzles you and discover just why it is in the play. For you can be sure that in the limited space of a play, every speech must serve one or more of these four purposes.

Inglis/Gehlmann/Bowman/Schramm (eds.): *Adventures in American Literature.* Book I and Book II. Mercury Edition. Harcourt, Brace and Co., New York/Chicago 1952, pp. 334–335.

8 Social Plays

The Road to Mecca

ATHOL FUGARD

Athol Fugard's play is set in the eccentric home of an Afrikaaner artist by the name of Miss Helen, who is based on Helen Martins, a sculptress Fugard heard about in the Karoo desert halfway between Capetown and Port Elizabeth. Helen is an outcast in her small African village. She has filled her garden with sculptures, which point towards Mecca in defiance of her Christian neighbourhood. The Road to Mecca is a play about loneliness, a metaphor for all who are simply different. Marius Byleveld, the local minister, tries to talk Helen into accepting the security of an old age home in place of her Mecca of dreams. Elsa, a 28-year-old schoolteacher from Capetown has driven 800 miles to spend a night with Helen.

ELSA What are you thinking?

HELEN So many things! About the way you *did* arrive. I wasn't joking. For a few seconds I did think I was seeing a ghost. I heard the front door open ... I thought it was little Katrina, she also never knocks ... but instead there you were. (*She wants to say more but stops herself.*)

ELSA Go on.

HELEN It was so strange. Almost as if you didn't really see me or anything else at first ... didn't want to. And so cross! I've never seen you like that before.

ELSA This isn't quite like the other times, Miss Helen.

HELEN That's a pity. They were all good times.
(*Pause*)
So what sort of time is this going to be? A bad one?

ELSA (*Evenly*) I hope not. Doesn't have to be. It depends on you.
(MISS HELEN *avoids* ELSA'S *eyes. The young woman looks around the room.*)
But you're right. I hadn't really arrived until now.

HELEN Where were you, Elsie?

ELSA (*She thinks about the question before answering*) Way back at the turn-off to the village from the National Road ... or maybe a few miles further along it now ... walking to Cradock.

HELEN I don't understand.

ELSA I gave a lift to a woman outside Graaff-Reinet. That's most probably where she is now. I dropped her at the turn-off to the village.

HELEN Who was she?

ELSA (*Shrugging with apparent indifference*) An African woman.

HELEN Cradock! That's a long walk.

ELSA I know.

HELEN It's about another eighty miles from the turn-off.

(*She waits for* ELSA *to say more.*)

ELSA I nearly didn't stop for her. She didn't signal that she wanted a lift or anything like that. Didn't even look up when I passed ... I was watching her in the rear-view mirror. Maybe that's what told me there was a long walk ahead of her ... the way she had her head down and just kept on walking. And then the baby on her back. It was hot out there, Miss Helen, hot and dry and a lot of empty space ... There wasn't a farmhouse in sight. She looked very small and unimportant in the middle of all that. Anyway, I stopped and reversed and offered her a lift. Not very graciously. I'd already been driving for ten hours and all I wanted was to get here as fast as I could. She got in and after a few miles we started talking. Her English wasn't very good, but when I finally got around to understanding what she was trying to tell me it added up to a good old South African story. Her husband, a farm labourer, had died recently, and no sooner had they buried him when the *Baas* told her to pack up and leave the farm. So there she was ... on her way to the Cradock district, where she hoped to find a few distant relatives and a place to live. (*Trying to remember the woman as clearly as possible.*) About my age. The baby couldn't have been more than a few months old. All she had with her was one of those plastic shopping bags they put your groceries in at supermarkets. I saw a pair of old slippers. She was barefoot.

HELEN Poor woman.

ELSA So I dropped her at the turn-off. Gave her what was left of my food and some money. She carried on walking and I drove here.

(*Pause.*)

HELEN Is there anything else?

ELSA No. That's all.

HELEN I'm sure somebody else will give her a lift.

ELSA (*Too easily*) Hope so. If not, she and her baby are in for a night beside the road. There's eighty miles of the Karoo ahead of her. Shadows were already stretching out across the veld when she got out of the car. The Great Karoo! And just when I thought I was getting used to it, beginning to like it, in fact. Down in Cape Town I've actually caught myself talking rubbish about its vast space and emptiness, its awesome stillness and silence! Just like old Getruida down the road. It's that all right, but only because everything else has been all but damned out of existence. It's so obvious where you Afrikaners get your ideas of God from. Beats me how you've put up with it so long, Miss Helen. Nearly seventy years? My God, you deserve a medal. I would have packed up and left it at the first opportunity ... and let's face it, you've had plenty of those.

HELEN I was born here, Elsa.

ELSA I sympathize, Miss Helen. Believe me, I truly sympathize.

HELEN It's not really as bad as you make it sound. The few times I've been away, I've always ended up missing it and longing to be back.

ELSA Because you wanted to get back to your work.

HELEN (*Shaking her head*) No. Even before all that started. It grows on you, Elsa.

ELSA Which is just about the only growing it seems to allow. For the rest, it's as merciless as the religion they preach around here. Looking out of the car window this afternoon I think I finally understood a few things about you Afrikaners … and it left me feeling just a little uneasy.

HELEN You include me in all you're saying.

ELSA Yes. You might not go to church any more, but you're still an Afrikaner, Miss Helen. You were in there with them, singing hymns every Sunday, for a long, long time. Bit of a renegade now, I admit, but you're still one at heart.

HELEN And that heart is merciless?

(*Pause.*)

ELSA No. That you aren't. A lot of other things maybe, but certainly not that. Sorry, sorry, sorry …

HELEN You're still very cross, aren't you? And something else as well. There's a new sound in your voice. One I haven't heard before.

ELSA What do you mean?

HELEN Like the way you talked about that woman on the road. Almost as if you didn't care, which I know isn't true.

ELSA Of course I cared. I cared enough to stop and pick her up, to give her money and food. But I also don't want to fool myself. That was a sop to my conscience and nothing more. It wasn't a real contribution to her life and what she is up against. Anyway, what's the point in talking about her? She's most probably curling up in a stormwater drain at this moment – that's where she said she'd sleep if she didn't get a lift – and I feel better for a good wash.

HELEN There it is again.

ELSA Well, it's the truth.

HELEN It was the way you said it.

ELSA You're imagining things, Miss Helen. Come on, let's talk about something else. It's too soon to get serious. We've got enough time, and reasons, for that later on. What's been happening in the village? Give me the news. Your last letter didn't have much of that in it.

(ELSA *gets into clean clothes.* MISS HELEN *starts to fold the discarded tracksuit.* ELSA *stops her.*)

I can do that.

HELEN I just wanted to help.

ELSA And you can do that by making a nice pot of tea and giving me the village gossip.

(MISS HELEN *goes into the lounge. She takes cups and saucers, etc., from a sideboard and places them on the table.*)

HELEN I haven't got any gossip. Little Katrina is the only one who really visits me any more, and all she wants to talk about these days is her baby. There's also Marius, of course, but he never gossips.

ELSA He still comes snooping around, does he?

HELEN Don't put it like that, Elsa. He's a very old friend.

ELSA Good luck to him. I hope the friendship continues. It's just that *I* wouldn't want him for one. Sorry, Miss Helen, but I don't trust your old friend, and I have a strong feeling that Pastor Marius Byleveld feels the same way about me. So let's change the subject. Tell me about Katrina. What has she been up to?

HELEN She's fine. And so is the baby. As prettily dressed these days as any white baby, thanks to the clothes you sent her. She's been very good to me, Elsa. Never passes my front door without dropping in for a little chat. Is always asking about you. I don't know what I would do without her. But I'm afraid Koos has started drinking again. And making all sorts of terrible threats about her and the baby. He still doesn't believe it's his child.

ELSA Is he beating her?

HELEN No. The warning you gave him last time seems to have put a stop to that.

ELSA God, it makes me sick! Why doesn't she leave him?

HELEN And then do what?

ELSA Find somebody else! Somebody who will value her as a human being and take care of her and the child.

HELEN She can't do that, Elsie. They're married.

ELSA Oh, for God's sake, Helen. There's the Afrikaner in you speaking. There is nothing sacred about a marriage that abuses the woman! I'll have a talk to her tomorrow. Let's make sure we get a message to her to come around.

HELEN Don't make things more difficult for her, Elsa.

ELSA How much more difficult can "things" be than being married to a drunken bully? She *has* got a few rights, Miss Helen, and I just want to make sure she knows what they are. How old is she now?

HELEN Seventeen, I think.

ELSA At that age I was still at school dreaming about my future, and here she is with a baby and bruises. Quick, tell me something else.

HELEN Let me see ... Good gracious me! Of course, yes! I have got important news. Old Getruida has got the whole village up in arms. Brace yourself, Elsa. She's applied for a licence to open a liquor store.

ELSA A what?

HELEN A liquor store. Alcoholic beverages.

ELSA Booze in New Bethesda?

HELEN If you want to put it that bluntly ... yes.

ELSA Now that *is* headline material. Good for old Gerty. I always knew she liked her sundowner, but I never thought she'd have the spunk to go that far.

HELEN Don't joke about it, Elsie. It's a very serious matter. The village is very upset.

ELSA Headed, no doubt, by your old friend Pastor Marius Byleveld.

HELEN That's right. I understand that his last sermon was all about the evils of alcohol and how it's ruining the health and lives of our Coloured folk. Getruida says he's taking unfair advantage of the pulpit and that the Coloureds get it anyway from Graaff-Reinet.

ELSA Then tell her to demand a turn.

HELEN At what?

ELSA The pulpit. Tell her to demand her right to get up there and put her case ... and remind her before she does that the first miracle was water into wine.

HELEN (*Trying not to laugh*) You're terrible, Elsie! Old Getruida in the pulpit!

ELSA And you're an old hypocrite, Miss Helen. You love it when I make fun of the Church.

HELEN No, I don't. I was laughing at Gerty, not the Church. And you have no right to make me laugh. It's a very serious matter.

ELSA Of course it is! Which is why I want to know who you think is worse: the Dominee deciding what is right and wrong for the Coloured folk or old Getruida exploiting their misery?

HELEN I'm afraid it's even more complicated than that, Elsa. Marius *is* only thinking about what's best for them, but on the other hand Getruida has offered to donate part of her profits to their school building fund. And what about Koos? Wouldn't it make things even worse for Katrina if he had a local supply?

ELSA They are two separate issues, Miss Helen. You don't punish a whole community because one man can't control his drinking. Which raises yet another point: has anybody bothered to ask the Coloured people what they think about it all?

HELEN Are we going to have that argument again?

ELSA I'm not trying to start an argument. But it does seem to me right and proper that if you're going to make decisions which affect other people, you should find out what those people think.

HELEN It is the same argument. You know they don't do that here.

ELSA Well, it's about time they started. I don't make decisions affecting the pupils at school without giving them a chance to say something. And they're children! We're talking about adult men and women in the year 1974.

HELEN Those attitudes might be all right in Cape Town, Elsa, but you should know by now that the Valley has got its own way of doing things.

ELSA Well, it can't cut itself off from the twentieth century for ever. Honestly, coming here is like stepping into the middle of a Chekhov play. While the rest of the world is hoping the bomb won't drop today, you people are arguing about who owns the Cherry Orchard. Your little world is not as safe as you would like to believe, Helen. If you think it's going to be left alone to stagnate in the nineteenth century while the rest of us hold our breath hoping we'll reach the end of the twentieth, you're in for one hell of a surprise. And it will start with your Coloured folk. They're not fools. They also read newspapers, you know. And if you don't believe me, try talking about something other than the weather and her baby next time Katrina comes around. You'll be surprised at what's going on inside that little head. As for you Helen! Sometimes the contradictions in you make me want to scream. Why do you always stand up and defend this bunch of bigots?

Athol Fugard, *The Road to Mecca,* Faber & Faber, London 1985, pp. 19–26.

Vocabulary

Cradock South African district – *Baas* boss – *veld* flat, treeless grassland of the South African plateau – *renegade* a person who changes his religious belief; traitor – *sop* s.th. offered to give temporary satisfaction – *sundowner* alcoholic drink – *spunk* courage – *Chekhov* a Russian author (1860–1904) – *The Cherry Orchard* a play by Chekhov

Assignments

1. At what point in the action do you realize that the play does not take place in Europe? Which details and topics does the playwright use to build up the scenario?
2. The playwright uses Elsa's reactions to events, the way she expresses herself and her actions, to paint a portrait of her character. From this excerpt, what impression do you get of Elsa? Which adjective(s) would you use to describe her?
3. Does your attitude towards Elsa change by the end of the scene? Is the portrayal of her character tailored to the particular difficulties of the South African situation or handled in a more general way?
4. In this scene Elsa is the dominant character. From what you have read so far, do you think the development of the plot will depend on her character or on the specifically South African issues mentioned?
5. "The living moment in a Fugard play tends to emerge as the climax of a shifting pattern of emotions of gradually increasing strength, a moment of revelation, expressed as an image" (Dennis Walder). With reference to the scene, discuss the validity of this statement.
6. With reference to the following excerpt, discuss Fugard's *The Road to Mecca.*

On Social Plays

The man that is driven to question the moral chaos in which we live ends up in our estimate as a possibly commendable but definitely odd fellow, and probably as a compulsively driven neurotic. In place of a social aim which called an all-around excellence – physical, intellectual, and moral – the ultimate good, we have set up a goal which can best be characterized as "happiness" – namely, staying out of trouble. This concept is the end result of the truce which all of us have made with society. And a truce implies two enemies. When the truce is broken it means either that the individual has broken out of his ordained place as an integer, or that the society has broken the law by harming him unjustly – that is, it has not left him alone to be a peaceful integer. In the heroic and tragic time the act of questioning the-way-things-are implied that a quest was being carried on to discover an ultimate law or way of life which would yield excellence; in the present time the quest is that of a man made unhappy by rootlessness and, in every important modern play, by a man who is essentially a victim.

Arthur Miller, *On Social Plays* in: R. Hogan/ S.E. Molin: *DRAMA: The Major Genres. An Introductory Critical Anthology,* Doss, Mead & Company, New York/ Toronto 1962, pp. 20–21.

9 The Short Play

Politics and Terror

WILLY RUSSELL

Politics and Terror *is a short play by Willy Russell, the author of* **Educating Rita**. *What follows is an unabridged version of this play.*

A young kid, in short trousers, is sitting on a low wall. He is chewing and staring into the distance, beyond the heat haze. He suddenly crouches low, produces his imaginary "pistol" and picks off three baddies. He returns the gun to his belt. He sits and continues his chewing. Behind him we see another kid (GEORGE) appear. He creeps up, and as he does so he unpins an equally imaginary "grenade" and lobs it at CHRIS. He waits a moment before making the sound of the explosion.

GEORGE (*As* CHRIS *looks round*) You're dead.

CHRIS No I'm not.

GEORGE Yis y'are. I got y' with a grenade, at point blank range.

CHRIS Well –

GEORGE Well what?

CHRIS Well, that means you're dead as well, cos you didn't move out of range.

GEORGE I don't have to. A grenade wouldn't injure me. I've got super powers.

CHRIS Which ones?

GEORGE All of them. I'm indestructible.

CHRIS No, y'not. None of the Super Heroes is indestructible.

GEORGE The Hulk is.

CHRIS No, he's not. Even Superman's not indestructible an' he's the most indestructible Super Hero there is. But even Superman can't face Kryptonite.

GEORGE (*Shrugging*) D'you live round here?

CHRIS (*Indicating*) Down there.

GEORGE What y' doin' round here?

CHRIS I've been the shops.

GEORGE What for?

CHRIS (*Immediately defensive*) Nothin'.

GEORGE (*Goes into the sound of a police wah-wah siren. Suddenly stops*) Gis a sweet.

CHRIS I haven't got any. (GEORGE *looks at him.* CHRIS *turns away and begins to make the sound of a bleep phone*)

GEORGE Which shop did y' go to?

CHRIS Supermarket.

GEORGE What for?

CHRIS What?

GEORGE What did y' go the supermarket for?

CHRIS For me mam. I was on a message.

GEORGE What did y' get?

CHRIS Nott'n. It was closed.

CHRIS (*Sceptical, but not to be put off*) It's dead lucky for you it was closed.

CHRIS Why?

GEORGE There's rats in that supermarket. An' y' know if y' bought somethin' from there, somethin' to eat, like sweets, an' y' ate them, y'd get the fever.

CHRIS The fever?

GEORGE Yeh. Y' die if y' catch the fever. There's three kids died from our street, y' know.

CHRIS (Pause) Y' wouldn't die if y' just ate one sweet from there, though. Would y'?

GEORGE Y' would. Y' don't even have to eat them. Just havin' them in y' pocket – that's enough. The germs travel up t' y' mouth. They fly. It's best if y' throw them away.

CHRIS (*Looking at him*) Listen, y' know somethin' eh?

GEORGE What?

CHRIS Isn't it lucky for me the supermarket was closed.

GEORGE (*Disgusted*) I seen you chewin'.

CHRIS Y' never, cos I wasn't chewin'.

GEORGE Y' were. I seen y' goin' like that .(*Exaggerated chew*)

CHRIS I wasn't chewin' nott'n though. I was tryin' t' bite off a piece of loose skin in me gum. Like that. (*Shows him the chewing action*)

GEORGE (*Pause*) I get that sometimes, inside me mouth.

CHRIS Yeh, well so do I.

GEORGE Look. (*Opens his mouth.* CHRIS *peers in*)

CHRIS Oh yeh ... I can see it. That's just like mine was.

GEORGE Let's have a look. (CHRIS *opens his mouth.* GEORGE *peers in.* GEORGE *suddenly pointing, accusing*) See ... I told y' you had sweets, there's all yellow over y' tongue ... You've got sweets.

CHRIS I haven't got sweets. I had some, but that was the last one. An' I didn't get it from the supermarket, I got it from the paper shop. (*He gets up to go*) I'm goin'. (*Making police wah-wah sound before zooming off*)

GEORGE Where?

CHRIS Home.

GEORGE Down there?

CHRIS Yeh.

GEORGE Y' know who's down there?

CHRIS (*Coming back a step*) Who?

GEORGE Tommo!

CHRIS Tommo? (GEORGE *nods*) Tommo isn't down there. Tommo got sent away. Tommo's in a home cos of bullyin' little kids an' murderin' dogs.

GEORGE Look. (*Points*)

CHRIS Is that Tommo?

GEORGE (*Nods*) Tommo's back now. (*He walks away leaving* CHRIS *worried and anxious, gawping down the road*) With an air pistol as well. (GEORGE *suddenly makes the Tarzan call.* CHRIS *moves across to him*)

CHRIS Tarzan's on telly tonight, y' know.

GEORGE The Lord of the Jungle, I know.

CHRIS Y' know Tarzan, all livin' things are his friends.

GEORGE I'll bet Tarzan wouldn't be Tommo's friend.

CHRIS He would. Tarzan says all livin' things are his friends.

GEORGE But what about Tommo? All livin' things are Tommo's enemies. Especially when they've got sweets. (*Pause*) I thought you were goin' home.

CHRIS (*Looking anxiously down the street*) Erm. ... I forgot, me mam won't be home yet.

GEORGE Y' know if I've got some sweets, I share them, with everyone.

CHRIS Do y'?

GEORGE Yeh. Cos that's what Jesus says y' should do. When I've got sweets I share them.

CHRIS (*Unimpressed*) An' another thing Jesus said was if y' tell lies y' go to hell when y' die.

GEORGE What's that bulge in your pocket?

CHRIS What? That? It's me hankie. I've got a cold. (Sniffs) I don't believe in Jesus and God, me dad says. (*Sniffs. Wheeling*) I'm goin' now. Tarar.

GEORGE (*Standing and pointing down the street*) There's Tommo, look.

CHRIS (*Stopping*) Where?

GEORGE There.

CHRIS That's not Tommo.

GEORGE (*Holding up pretend binoculars*). It is. An' there's three little kids there as well. They're cryin'. Tommo's got them. (CHRIS *begins to sniffle.* GEORGE *begins to laugh*) What's up?

CHRIS I've gorra get home. Me mam said I've gorra get in before dinner time, cos she's goin' out with our Maureen. But I can't go home ... not with Tommo there.

GEORGE Take the short cut.

CHRIS (*Stops crying. Hopeful*) Which short cut?

GEORGE It's a secret.

CHRIS What? Go on ... tell us.

GEORGE I can't. You've gorra be in the Indian Trackin' Gang if y' wanna know all the short cuts.

CHRIS Well I'll join.

GEORGE Y' can't. You've got no sweets.

CHRIS What?

GEORGE Y' have to pay a load of sweets when y' join the Indian Trackin' Gang.

CHRIS Well ... well ... well ... let me join now an' I'll give y' some sweets the next time I see y'.

GEORGE But I might never see y' again.

CHRIS Y' will.

GEORGE (*Shaking his head*) Not if you have to go down there, past Tommo. No one'll ever see you again. (*Craning to see down the road*) Ugh... Look what Tommo's doin to that little kid ...

CHRIS (*Sneaking his hand into his pocket and then bending as if to pick something up*) Look what I've just found, on the floor. Look, I can join with these. (*He shows a few sweets*)

GEORGE (*Taking them*) Nah. ... Y' could if you'd found more. But this isn't enough. ...

CHRIS But that's all I found ... that's all there were, on the floor.

GEORGE Have another look. There might be some more there.

CHRIS There won't be.

GEORGE (*Looking*) Ugh ... Tommo's gettin' dead mad with them kids.

CHRIS (*Quickly bending to "discover" more sweets*) Look ... look. I found some more. ... (*Giving them to* GEORGE) Where is it ... tell me where the short cut is.

GEORGE (*Shaking his head*) Not enough.

CHRIS (*Nearly in tears*) But I haven't got any more. I mean, I mean I can't find any more. ...

GEORGE I'd tell y' if I could. But it's in the rules of the gang. It says y' have to give "A load of sweets".

CHRIS You ... you ... y' just want all my sweets.

GEORGE You haven't got any sweets, have y'?

CHRIS The sweets I'm findin'.

GEORGE I don't want sweets. What do I want sweets for. It's you. Y' wanna know the short cut, don't y'?

CHRIS I've gorra get home ... I've got to.

GEORGE (*Looking at the sweets in his hand*) Well this is nearly loads. Maybe if y' had another look y' could find some more.

CHRIS (*Crying, frustrated. He turns and fishes the last of his sweets out of his pocket. Turns*) I found these. But I won't be able to find any more, I know I won't. You better tell me where that short cut is now ... Y' better had ...

GEORGE (*Taking the sweets*) Come here. Y' see down by there, by the church, well if y' bunk over the wall y'll see an alley ... If you run down there it brings y' out dead quick by your flats ...

CHRIS Over that wall ... There's no alley there.

GEORGE Have you ever been over that wall?

CHRIS No.

GEORGE Well don't argue ... I have. An' y' better hurry up 'cos if Tommo moves further down this way you'll be seen, even takin' the short cut.

CHRIS (About to go) I'm goin'. Listen ... before I go ... gis a sweet?

GEORGE No way.

CHRIS (*Laughing and pointing*) Well well ... you're gonna die ... You're gonna get the fever ... cos I bought them sweets in that supermarket! (*Laughing*)

GEORGE Well ... there's no alley behind that wall either. (*Laughs*)

(CHRIS*'s laugh fades. He turns suddenly and runs.* GEORGE *is beaming. Then a Webley air pistol appears, followed by* TOMMO, *a girl.* GEORGE *suddenly sobers*)

GEORGE Er, hiya, Tommo. (TOMMO *glares at him*) What y' doin'? Y' watchin' Tarzan on the telly tonight?

TOMMO Tarzan isn't on tonight.

GEORGE He is.

TOMMO No he's not ... I shot him this mornin'. The Hulk's dead as well. Have you got sweets?

GEORGE Sweets? Me? I got no sweets. Honest ...

The end

Repr. from: Alan Durband (ed.), *Wordplays 1. Six Short Plays,* Hutchinson, London 1984 ([1]1982), pp. 99–107.

Vocabulary

to pick off to shoot at – *yis* yes – *gis* give us – *nott'n* nothing – *Tarar* (=Tschüß) – *gorra* got to be

Assignments

1. What is the function of the "killing game" at the beginning of this short play?
2. Ostensibly, the children are talking about their everyday experiences; playing games, watching "telly", bargaining for sweets, keeping out of trouble. By the end of the play, do you get the impression that this is all that the play is about?
3. The appearance of Tommo at the end of the play is something of a surprise. How does the playwright build up to this?
4. To what extent is the title of the play relevant to this scene?
5. If these children were adults, which of them would you be most afraid of?
6. Do you think this is a true-to-life portrayal of the way children behave? Choose incidents from the text which support your view.
7. Which of the characteristics of the short play can be identified in *Politics and Terror*? Study the following extract:

One-Act or Short Play?

Literary critics [...] tend to drop the term *one-act play* altogether and replace it by *short play* which, in their opinion, expresses in a much better way what is characteristic of this type of play. Indeed, as regards structure and portrayal of characters, *short play* is a more appropriate word. For brevity is as much a characteristic feature of this genre as it is of the short story. Moreover the word "act" in *one-act play* is misleading in as far as it suggests that the play is only part of a more comprehensive drama.

The characteristic elements of the *short play* are:
- conciseness and brevity,
- unity of time and place,
- absence of subplots,
- emphasis on situation rather than on plot,
- concentration on critical situations,
- small number of characters,
- presentation of characters reduced to portrayal of their most striking traits,
- succinct dialogues.

In the nineteenth century a sort of short play often served the function of a *curtain-raiser*. It used to be performed before the actual full-length play started, thus catering for both "the early birds" and the late-comers in the audience. Under the influence of the repertory theatre movement (e.g. Abbey Theatre in Dublin) at the turn of this century what are short plays in our modern understanding came into being. Most of them were played as *triple bills*: three plays were staged in the course of one evening, thus presenting the audience with a kaleidoscope of characters and a wide technical variety.

A.R. Glaap (ed.), *Alan Ayckbourn, Confusions. Model Interpretations.* Klett, Stuttgart 1982, p. 7.

10 Modern Adaptations

Romanoff and Juliet

PETER USTINOV

Romanoff and Juliet *is "a comedy of Russian-American relations during the Cold War in and around their embassies in a tiny neutral state in Europe. A young Russian and an American girl fall in love and so create great embarrassment for their diplomat fathers, with at last some moderating of the feud" (From: Heinemann edition of* **Romanoff and Juliet**, *London, 1974 ([1]1957), pp. 11–15). The play invites by its title comparison with Shakespeare's* **Romeo and Juliet**.
In the following scene the lovers meet for the first time.

A pair of lovers wander into the square, too involved in each other to know where they are. They wear evening dress, and masks dangle round their necks.

GENERAL (*Softly, heartfelt.*) Oh, I hope they found each other very early in the night, for now he may notice a wrinkle under the weary, longing eye, while she may spy a trace of cruel satisfaction around his mouth. (*Sadly*). Ah, the morning after! Ah, dawn! Let us be tactful.

FIRST SOLDIER My turn to give the order.

GENERAL Sh! Dismiss, but for goodness sake don't do it as you were taught.

FIRST SOLDIER (*whispering*) Regiment. Salute the flag! Dismiss!

They march off on tiptoe with a last sentimental look at the lovers. The lovers break from a long, long kiss and look at each other in adoration.

HE Are there words which have not been used before?

SHE There are silences which have not been shared before. Why do you look at me so critically?

HE Critically?

SHE Are there bags under my eyes?

HE I would be lying if I told you you weren't tired.

SHE (*hiding her face*) Then don't look at me.

HE (*lifting her face again*) I want to guess what you will look like at seventy.

SHE It's late. We're getting silly. It's the sunlight and the weariness and the sad farewell of old champagne on the tongue. There was no edge to our thoughts when the candles and the cut-glass ornaments sent shivering milky-ways up to the ceiling, and when your eyes sparkled like mineral wealth from the rock of your face.

HE (*sadly*) You can't recapture it by language.

SHE I know.

HE Enchantment fades so quickly that after five minutes you doubt if it was ever there.

SHE Do you doubt it?

HE No. I remember it.

SHE (*desperate*) But I am still here!

HE (*holding her*) Yes, a warm, a living thing, which I desire. Last night we were as one, creatures in a dream, selflessly united in an endless waltz. From now on we are opposed, a man and a woman in love – the greatest, most exhausting struggle in the world – two moths racing for the flame, two cannibals devouring each other.

SHE Have you known many women?

HE I am a sailor by profession.

SHE Thank you for your honesty.

HE (*smiles*) You're afraid that I will compare you to the others?

SHE Inevitably.

HE And what if I say that you are better?

SHE That's not enough. I want to be alone.

HE You have never kissed a man?

SHE Only four. And Freddie.

HE Do you mean only four, and Freddie? Or do you mean five?

SHE (*surprised, she turns it over in her mind*) Five? No, I mean four, and Freddie.

HE Who's Freddie?

SHE (*enraptured*) You're jealous!

HE I'm waiting for an answer.

SHE Freddie? He's my fiancé.

HE I see.

SHE (*a little foolishly*) He's in refrigerators.

HE I don't understand.

SHE He makes refrigerators. His father made refrigerators before him.

HE A hereditary gift.

SHE Freddie believes he has a mission in refrigeration. He told me once when he was drunk that in the event of war, he has a device which can freeze the Gulf Stream, and make everyone but us very uncomfortable. Oh, Lord, I shouldn't be telling you this, should I?

HE No.

SHE You have no accent, darling. I keep forgetting who you are.

HE (*with pomp*) I serve aboard the icebreaker *Red October*. Ironic, isn't it, that it may one day be my duty to crash through Freddie's most cherished daydream.

SHE Oh, how awful. Now everything's spoiled.

HE (*kindly*) Why? Surely love recognizes no didactic frontiers?

SHE (*desperate*) But Igor! Creatures in a dream, selflessly united in an endless waltz –

HE I said that, didn't I?

SHE Yes.

HE Curious how romance tricks the otherwise logical mind into inaccuracies. Naturally, the waltz could not have been endless, otherwise it would still be going on – (*As he sees her incredulous face*) – and that is impossible since we are now here.

SHE (*in real agony*) Oh, no!

HE (*suddenly*) Does what I say sound very humourless and ... and un-Western when I talk like that? (*Silence.*) I must apologize. I can never regret a phenomenon as beautiful or as powerful as our love, but I must admit that it has created within me the most reprehensible ideological confusion. I must consult my textbooks before I can hope to interpret to you in scientific terms the exact extent of my spiritual deviation.

SHE (*hopefully*) You mean you love me more than Marx?

HE (*sharply*) Please do not speak sarcastically. It doesn't suit you.

SHE I'm sorry, but I'm jealous of the man.

HE I do not make light of your beliefs.

SHE (*tenderly*) I can't make you out.

HE (*running his hands through his hair in agony*) I can't make myself out. It's all so simple in the Arctic.

SHE Do you blame the climate, my darling?

HE No. No, it's relatively simple in the Black Sea also.

SHE You blame the dry land then?

HE Yes. It must be that. Although a great deal of good solid work has been accomplished on dry land. That is undeniable. In fact, a considerable amount of *Das Kapital* was conceived in the British Museum, which makes it all the more remarkable.

SHE Women? In general. Do they confuse you, dearest?

HE Women? I've seen women before. I served on a ship under a woman captain, although in fairness to her, you wouldn't have guessed that she was a woman. *She* did not disturb me in the least. (*Slowly, and with considerable difficulty.*) The fact is, I love you.

SHE (*ecstatic*) Oh ...

HE (*severe*) Please don't interrupt me. For my own good, for our future, I must analyse my reasons for loving you in spite of vast and irreconcilable spiritual and political divergencies. First of all, we were wearing masks. Your mask could have hidden the eager face of a freckled collective-farm girl. When we tore them off at midnight, it was already too late. I was in love.

SHE Oh, Igor, that's not true. No collective-farm girl has an American accent.

HE Yes, I was cheating. Forgive me. (*Fierce.*) I must be honest with myself. I think I know what drew me irresistibly towards you.

SHE (*coquettish*) What is it?

He (*very serious*) You couldn't possibly be the captain of a ship. You're one of the only women I've ever met who couldn't possibly be the captain of a ship.

She Dad bought me a dinghy last fall. It's moored near Cape Cod. I love the sea, angel, just the way you do.

He (*gentle*) Could you bring a six-thousand-ton cargo ship into Murmansk harbour ... without a pilot ... backwards ... in a snow storm?

She I've never tried.

He No, you couldn't. And nor could I. Glory to our women trawler-captains.

She Glory to them indeed. Kiss me.

He Not yet. I must first reach certain ethical conclusions.

She Igor, there's so little time! (*To break his mood.*) I know what I like about you.

He What?

She Your profile.

He The façade.

She I never read a book unless I like the title. Igor, I like the title. I want to read the book.

He I fail to understand.

She I like that, too. You could never understand. Kiss me.

He I forbid –

She You want to.

He No.

She Please!

He Thank you.

They embrace, and lose themselves in the silent game of love, oblivious to all around them.

Peter Ustinov, *Romanoff and Juliet,* Heinemann, London 1974 ([1]1957), pp. 11–15.

Assignments

1. In this scene Romanoff ("He") and Juliet ("She") meet for the first time. Why has their love "created within him the most reprehensible ideological confusion"?
2. Compare and contrast this scene with the following excerpt from Shakespeare's *Romeo and Juliet.*

Romeo and Juliet

Romeo (To Juliet) If I profane with my unworthiest hand
This holy shrine, the gentle sin is this,
My lips two blushing pilgrims ready stand
To smooth that rough touch with a tender kiss.
Juliet Good pilgrim, you do wrong your hand too much,
Which mannerly devotion shows in this;

For saints have hands that pilgrims' hands do touch,
And palm to palm is holy palmers' kiss.
ROMEO Have not saints lips, and holy palmers too?
JULIET Ay pilgrim lips that they must use in prayer.
ROMEO O then dear saint, let lips do what hands do.
They pray; grant thou, lest faith turn to despair.
JULIET Saints do not move, though grant for prayers' sake.
ROMEO Then move not, while my prayer's effect I take.
(*Kisses her*)
Thus from my lips, by thine, my sin is purged.
JULIET Then have my lips the sin that they have took.
ROMEO Sin from my lips? O trespass sweetly urged.
Give me my sin again.
JULIET You kiss by th' book.
NURSE Madam you mother craves a word with you.
ROMEO What is her mother?
NURSE Marry bachelor,
Her mother is the lady of the house,
And a good lady, and a wise and virtuous.
I nursed her daughter that you talked withal.
I tell you, he that can lay hold of her
Shall have the chinks.
ROMEO Is she a Capulet?
O dear account, my life is my foe's debt.
BENVOLIO Away, be gone, the sport is at the best.
ROMEO Ay, so I fear, the more is my unrest.

Repr. from: J.H. Walter (ed.), *Romeo and Juliet. The Players' Shakespeare*, Heinemann Educational Books, London 1975 ([1]1967), pp. 85–87 (excerpt).

3. Ustinov's comedy is mainly ironic. The irony is deepened by the echoes of Shakespeare. Can you find ironic contrast in this scene?
4. "I didn't give Shakespeare's play much of a thought. I want my freedom from him just as he wanted his freedom from his Italian sources" (Peter Ustinov, with reference to *Romanoff and Juliet*). What, in your opinion, is the use of writing modern adaptations of well-known plays?

11 Suggestions for Project Work

1. The so-called well-made play is skilfully put together, with a beginning, middle and ending. It revolts nobody, it brings pleasure to the audience. Read the complete text of Ayckbourn's *Absent Friends* and try to find out if this play is a "well-made play".

2. Study the following statement on the "well-made play" and make a list of the characteristic features of this type of play.

The "well-made" play [...] was perfected by Ibsen on the Continent, and exploited in England by a host of lesser dramatists from Pinero and Galsworthy to Noël Coward and J.B. Priestley. In the well-made play a conviction of reality was a prime necessity; characters must seem true and events plausible, and this illusion could be created only if the dramatist followed a firm set of rules specifically designed to capture, sustain and satisfy the spectator's interest. Suspense born of a sly control of the pregnant situation was the playwright's first concern.

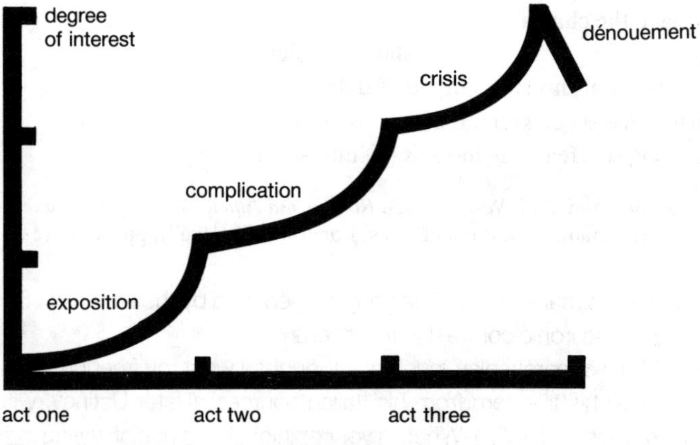

The shape of a 'well-made' play

J.L. Styan, *The Dramatic Experience. A Guide to the Reading of Plays*, Cambridge University Press, Cambridge 1980, ([1]1965), p. 72–73.

3. *Albert* is a very short play. The theme of the extract you have read is obviously lack of communication. Do you expect the rest of the play to enlarge on this theme or do you think it will develop into something quite different? Compare your ideas with the text.

4. Read *Mother Figure* or *A Talk in the Park* (in: Alan Ayckbourn's *Confusions*. Stuttgart: Klett 1982) and identify the different reasons for the communication barriers in these plays and in *Albert*.

5. Rita, in the excerpt from Russell's play, is clearly only just beginning her education. Along what lines do you think she will continue? Do you expect her to be successful or will she give up the whole idea and do something completely different? Compare your ideas with the development of *Educating Rita*.

6. Rita is taking part in an Open University course. Try to find out as much as possible about the Open University. This will help you to enjoy the play more and understand what *Educating Rita* is about.

7. Study G.B. Shaw's play *Pygmalion* or Arnold Wesker's *Roots* and compare it with *Educating Rita*.

8. What kind of play do you think Mr Turing's speech appears in? Is *Breaking a Code* a piece of science fiction with artificial intelligence taking over the earth; a Frankenstein type thriller; a comedy about an eccentric professor; a serious analysis of the effects of science on society or the individual; or ...? Read the play to find out if you are right.

9. You will have to read most of the rest of Shepard's *True West* to find out exactly what happens to the two brothers. Some of the developments might take you by surprise. Is the play "dramatic" in the sense that it "arouses certain expectations" in the audience? Discuss with reference to Dawson's comments (p. 174).

10. *True West* is embedded in American culture and attitudes. Using the scene reprinted in this book as a starting point, which aspects of American life would you expect to be mentioned in the play? Compare your ideas with the text.

11. Read the complete text of *Golden Girls*. Do the main issues in the play centre on women's rights, the rivalry between men and women or sporting ethics and morals?

12. Study *Whose Life is it Anyway?* What kind of play is this? Contrast it with a three-act play or a one-act play that you know. How do you account for the fact that many contemporary plays consist of two parts only?

13. How do you think the actress prepared herself for the role of Sarah in *Children of a Lesser God?* Would it be possible for an actress with the same disability as Sarah to play the role on stage?

14. Compare the stage directions in this play with the ones in *Politics and Terror* and account for their different functions.

15. From what you have read so far, Elsa seems to be the dominant character in Fugard's *The Road to Mecca*. Read the whole play in order to find out if the development of the plot depends on her character or on the specifically South African issues.

16. "The dramatic impact of the living moments in Fugard's plays represents a stage on a journey, when the 'external story' he has found in the lives and circumstances of those around him coincides with his own 'inner dynamic' ... For all the 'external', even documentary detail of his work, it always demonstrates a deeply personal concern for the fate of the 'ordinary', anonymous, *little* people with whom he most closely identifies" (Dennis Walder, *Athol Fugard,* Macmillan, London 1984, p. 5). Discuss this statement with reference to *The Road to Mecca*.

17. Read *'Master Harold' ... and the boys* (Oxford University Press, Oxford 1982), another of Fugard's plays in which the playwright exposes the roots of racism.

18. In *What is a play?*, Ronald Hayman comments on the difference between "script" and "performance" (p. 172). Discuss his statements with regard to Russell's *Politics and Terror.*

19. There is a great deal of paradox and satire in Ustinov's *Romanoff and Juliet*. But the general spirit of the play is also that of a light-hearted fantasy. Read the whole play and account for your own views.

20. "Making people laugh is, for me, another way of being serious ... Tragedy is always painful, and it is through Comedy that I seem to express myself, so as not to transmit even a fraction of my own sadness" (Peter Ustinov).
With reference to plays that you know, try to support or contradict Ustinov's statement.

21. There are well-known modern adaptations of Shakespearean plays. Study Edward Bond's *Lear* or Tom Stoppard's *Rosencrantz and Guildenstern are Dead* and point out similarities and differences between these plays and the respective Shakespearean plays.

22. We do not need adaptations. What is the use of reading adaptations? Go back to Shakespeare himself. – Do you agree?

Glossar

I Poetry

An explanation of most terms in the poetry section is to be found in the relevant texts and should be looked up under the respective sections "Figures of Speech".

Antithesis Contrast or opposite of words, clauses, sentences (often emphasized by parallel grammatical structure), e.g. "Man proposes, God disposes".

Apostrophe Rhetorical device in which someone (often but not always absent), some abstract quality, or a non-existant person is directly addressed as though present.

Climax Arrangement of words, phrases, or clauses in a rising order of importance. Opposite: anticlimax.

Hyperbole Exaggeration, used to produce emphasis.

Irony Contrast between what appears to be and what really is. In verbal irony the actual intent is expressed in words which carry the opposite meaning.

Metaphor Implied comparison between things essentially unlike (with word such as "like" or "as" ommitted), e.g. "he was the lion in the battle".

Metonymy Substitution of a term by means of naming part of it or an object associated with it, e.g. the *crown* for the king.

Personification Human characteristics given to something non-human.

Repetition Repeting a word or a phrase, or re-wording the same idea (in order to produce more emphasis).

Simile Stated comparison between two dissimilar things that are shown to have something in common, often introduced by "as" or "like".

Synecdoche Form of metaphor in which mentioning a part signifies the whole, or the whole signifying a part.

II Short Story / III Novel (Prose Fiction)

Acting Force Any kind of force, such as characters, abstract ideas, feelings, etc. that motivates or influences the plot.

Anticipation See "narrative order".

Atmosphere Significant details, e.g. of time and place, arousing a particular mood in the reader.

Character Person figuring in fiction.
Flat character: one-sided, easily recognizable character with predictable behaviour and little or no development.
Round character: complex, life-like and strongly individualized character who normally undergoes a development.
Type character: see "Drama".

Characterization *Direct characterization:* a person is characterized by the narrator or by another character in the story.
Indirect characterization: the character must be judged by his words or actions.

Climax The highest point of interest / tension in a story, also called "turning point" or "crisis".

Denouement see "Drama".

Description The presentation of details of time, place, character, and social setting, creating the distinct "world" of a story.

Exposition Initial situation containing all relevant detail for an understanding of the subsequent development of a story.

Flashback See "narrative order".

Frame Story A story within a narrative setting or frame, i.e. a story within a story. The frame may supply interpretative explanations or serve as comment on the story it encloses.

Hero The main character in the story, sometime referred to as the "protagonist".

Heroine Female form of "hero".

Narration As opposed to description, the telling or relating of events in a particular, not necessarily chronological, order.

Narrative Order In order to present the events of a story, the narrator may respect the chronological order, or he may break it up by anticipations (allusions to future events) or flashbacks (the presentation of events prior to the opening of the story).
The chronological order is used in stories concentrating on action and intrigue; the non-chronological order may be used for psychological reasons or for reasons of suspense.

Narrative Rhythm The rhythm of a story depends on the relation between the "narrated time" and the time needed to tell or read the story, i.e. the "narrating time". The rhythm may be slowed down by dialogue / monologue or description which suspend time; it may be accelerated by a summarizing presentation which may condense a long period of time into a few words, or by ellipsis.

Narrator Fictitious person who tells a story either explicitly, i.e. as a character of the story (explicit narrator), or implicitly, which means that he is not a character of the story (implicit narrator).

Plot The arrangement of the events / actions of a story in terms of cause and effect.

Point of View The angle / perspective from which the events of a story are related.
Omniscient-narrator point of view / third person unlimited point of view: any kind of information and comment can included in the narration since the narrator's knowledge of the events and the characters' most intimate thoughts and motives is unlimited.
Single-character point of view: everything is presented through the eyes or mind of one of the characters in the story, which means that the reader gets to know only what this particular characters experiences, hears, thinks, and feels.
Multiple-character point of view: In the course of a story the events are alternately presented through the eyes or the minds of different characters.
Narrator-observer point of view: the narrator stays outside the minds of all his characters, limiting his role to that of an eye-witness and thus reporting only what he himself can observe.
First person-protagonist point of view: the main character narrates his own story in the first person.
First person-observer point of view: a minor character in the story narrates what he observes.

Setting The background to the events of a story, e.g. of time, place, atmosphere, social conditions.

Suspense State of anxious uncertainty and expectation created in and by a story; also called "tension".

Theme Central idea or meaning of a fictional work of art.

Tone A writer's or speaker's attitude towards his subject and/or his reader or listener. The tone may be formal, informal, intimate, solemn, serious, playful, mocking, ironical, angry, etc.

IV Drama[1]

Act The main divisions of the play, usually marked by intervals in the stage performance. Five acts were common in Elizabethan drama, but three are the usual modern number. Whatever their number, an act is conceived as a substantial, unified segment of the whole play that materially advances the total action.

Action Along with *imitation*, the central element of Aristotle's theory of tragedy. A play as an "imitation of an action" means that the several events of the play together constitute one large human action. In this sense, action refers to the entire core of meaning of the events depicted on the stage. In a narrower sense, action is the physical movement of characters in the play.

Antagonist Character in opposition to the main character or protagonist of the play.

Anticlimax Period of tension after the climax, either a second climax or a lessening of the climax; also often used to denote a letdown or a ludicrous falling off from a high level.

Catastrophe In the structure of four-act and five-act plays, the final event or conclusion; generally used for the last events, often deaths, in a tragedy.

Catharsis Greek term used by Aristotle to describe the purgation of pity and fear experienced by the audience at a performance of a tragedy.

Character The word for a person in a play and the word for the qualities which constitute that person. The qualities most important in character are those of mind and spirit that, together, distinguish one person's behavior and beliefs from those of his fellow man.

Climax The highest point of audience interest in a play; sometimes loosely used as a synonym for crisis, but the two need not occur together. In the five-act play, the climax normally falls in Act IV.

Comedy In general, a drama with a happy ending. Its object is to entertain, often, to provoke laughter, and, frequently, to satirize manners. Comedy is concerned with men in their social capacities and is heavily dependent on codes of conduct, manners, and morality, which it uses to express or imply a standard against which deviations are measured.

1 Shortened and adapted version of G.B. Tennyson, *An Introduction to Drama,* Holt, Rinehart and Winston, New York 1967, pp. 112–131.

Conflict The issue around which a play revolves; often said to be the indispensable element. The rise and fall of the conflict forms the substance which the study of structure traces and reveals.

Curtain-Raiser A short play, usually a one-act farce, which comes before the main play of the evening.

Dénouement Literally, the *untying*; the moment when all the mysteries of the plot are revealed. Usually comes with, or after, the climax.

Dialogue Literally, *conversation, colloquy*; the words spoken by the characters in a play, normally in exchange with each other. Also, broadly used for all the language of a play.

Drama Literally, *a doing*, or *performing*; the word for the whole area of theatrical endeavour. Also, a synonym for a play.

Dramatic Irony The irony produced when the audience is aware of something that a character or characters in the play do not yet know. It is frequently used to heighten tension or suspense, or to increase our sympathy and understanding.

Epic Theater Term associated with Bertolt Brecht (1898–1956); denotes an anti-realistic style of play production which encourages the audience to observe, rather than to identify with, the characters. Examples are Brecht's *Mother Courage* (1938) and *The Caucasian Chalk Circle* (1944–45).

Exposition Term used, in discussing play structure, to denote that portion of the play (normally Act I) in which the playwright sets forth the information needed by the audience to understand the play and the situation. It is sometimes called the "introduction".

Falling Action Term used in discussion of play structure to indicate the period in the play after the crisis or turning point has been reached and the action is flowing to its destined end; normally comes in Act IV of the five-act play. The term applies only to the action, not to audience interest. Also called the "return".

Farce A form of comedy, the object of which is to provoke uncomplicated laughter. It usually has a highly improbable plot and a good deal of slapstick.

Genre French word for a type of literature, such as fiction, poetry, drama. In the latter, it refers to the various types of plays: tragedy, comedy, etc.

High Comedy Comedy which achieves its effect from character, plot, language, and satire rather than from physical devices. Its appeal is primarily to the intellect and it may well have an ultimately serious purpose. *Contrast* with [...] Low Comedy.

Low Comedy As opposed to high comedy, low comedy gains its effect, which is usually hearty laughter, from the use of slapstick and broad comic devices, instead of character and dialogue.

Monologue Speech delivered alone. Sometimes used to mean soliloquy. Also, the term for a short dramatic type in which one person speaks and performs all the action.

Plot The arrangement made by the playwright of the events of the story of a play, an arrangement designed to show not only sequence but also cause and effect. Plot, in its entirety, is the pattern of interlocking events that propels a story forward from conflict to resolution.

Producer The person who raises the money to put on a play and arranges the business operation of it; in England, the person who directs the play (in America, called the "director").

Prologue Literally, a *speech before*; a monologue by an actor introducing the action of the play. In Greek drama, the first passage of dialogue before the entrance of the chorus.

Protagonist Leading character in a play who is the main focus of the audience's attention. Originally in the Greek drama, the first of three who were present throughout the action of the play. The word means *first contestant*; the other characters were the *deuteragonist* and the *tritagonist* (second and third contestants).

Rising Action Term used in discussion of play structure to designate the complications of the plot leading to the crisis or turning point; normally, Acts II and III in five-act plays.

Scene 1. Physical setting of a play, or of part of a play.
2. Segment of the action smaller than an act.
Narrowly, any part of the action in a single place with an unchanging number of speakers. Broadly, a brief unified portion of the total action that has its own identity and development.

Set Any arrangement of scenery for a particular scene of a play. Plays may have a single set or several sets.

Social Problem Play Play that treats a common social issue, such as class or political antagonisms.

Soliloquy Speech made by a character who is alone on the stage, supposed to be either thinking his thoughts aloud or communicating to the audience.

Stage Directions Author's notes to a play, roughly indicating how he wants it to be acted. These notes always refer to the way the actor, not the audience, sees the stage, but sometimes they are written also with the reader in mind.

Tragedy Play dealing with a serious subject in an elevated style, frequently in poetry. It normally features a reversal of fortune from good to bad and ends in catastrophe and death for the protagonist and others. Tragedy is the genre of plays most concerned with ultimate questions of the meaning and significance of life.

Tragicomedy A play that develops tragically but ends happily, often by the use of a deus ex machina. Beaumont and Fletcher's *Philaster* (1610) is an example. Also, a term broadly used to mean any play with mixed tragic and comic elements.

Turning Point Another word for "crisis", used in discussion of play structure to mean the cresting point of the action, after which all events move in a certain direction. In five-act plays, it normally occurs in Act III.

Type Character Character drawn according to an established pattern of human behavior (for example, the jealous husband) and exhibiting little or no individual qualities.

Quellenverzeichnis

I Poetry

Text 1
Repr. by permission of Macmillan, London and Basingstoke.

Text 2
Repr. from *The World of Language*, Follett, Chicago.

Text 3
Repr. by permission of Charles Scribner's Sons, an imprint of Macmillan Publishing Company from *The Now Voices*. © 1971 by Charles Scribner's Sons.

Text 4
Repr. from *A Short Course on Poetry*, Methuen, London 1964.

Text 5–7
F. Schmidt/T. Wullen

Text 8
Repr. from *Complete Poems*, by permission of Grafton Books, a division of the Collins Publishing Group, London.

Text 9
Repr. by permission of Faber and Faber Ltd. from *Collected Poems*.

Text 10
Repr. by permission of Curtis Brown Ltd., London, on behalf of Eric Robinson. © Eric Robinson.

Text 11
Repr. by permission of Faber & Faber Ltd. from *Selected Poems 1957–1981*.

Text 12
Repr. from *A Short Course on Poetry*, Methuen, London 1964.

Text 13
Repr. by permission of Macmillan Publishing Company from *A Handbook to Literature*, 5. Edition, by C. Hugh Holman/William Harmon. © 1986 Macmillan Publishing Comp., a division of Macmillan, Inc.

Text 14
Repr. by permission of Harper Collins Publishers from *Literature: An Introduction to Fiction, Poetry, and Drama* (pp. 470–471), 4/e by X.J. Kennedy. © 1987 by X.J. Kennedy.

Text 15
Repr. by permission of Faber and Faber Ltd. from *Door into the Dark*.

Text 16
Repr. from *Poetry and Language*, McGraw Hill, Toronto/Montreal 1983.

Text 17
Repr. from *The Heath Guide to Poetry*, D. Heath & Co., Lexington/Toronto 1983.

Text 18
Repr. from *Poetry and Language*, McGraw Hill, Toronto/Montreal 1983.

Text 19
© 1941 by Theodore Roethke. From *The Collected Poems* of Theodore Roethke. Used by permission of Doubleday, a division of Bantam Doubleday Dell Publishing Group, Inc., New York.

Text 20
Repr. from *Literature: Structure, Sound, and Sense* (Seq. Num. 15657), Harcourt Brace Jovanovich, Inc., Orlando, Fla.

Text 21
Repr. from *American Literature*, Ginn/Lexington, Mass. 1981.

Text 22
F. Schmidt/T. Wullen

Text 23
Repr. from *Poetry and Language*, McGraw Hill, Toronto/Montreal 1983.

Text 24
Repr. from *With Love Somehow* by Tony Connor, O.U.P., London 1962.

Text 25
Repr. from *Poetry and Language*, McGraw Hill, Toronto/Montreal 1983.

Text 26
F. Schmidt/T. Wullen

Text 27
Repr. by permission of David Higham Ass. Ltd./Macmillan, London. From *Collected Poems*.

Text 28
Repr. from *Journeys, Delta*, Harcourt Brace, New York 1982.

Text 29
Repr. by permission of New Directions Corp. (german rights). From *Collected Poems* of W.C. Williams, 1909–1939, vol. 1. © 1938 by New Directions Publishing Corp.

Text 30
Repr. by permission of Harcourt Brace Jovanovich, Inc., Orlando, Fla. From *Chicago Poems*. © 1916 by Holt, Rinehart and Winston, Inc. and renewed 1944 by Carl Sandburg.

Text 31
© 1973/1968 by Scott, Foresman and Co., Glenview, Ill. Repr. by permission.

Text 32
Repr. from *19 New Poets of the Golden Gate*, Harcourt Brace, New York 1984.

Text 33
Repr. by permission of Random Century Group, London. Publishers Chatto & Windus.

Text 34
Repr. by permission of John Murray, London.

Text 35
Repr. by permission of Heinemann Publishers, Oxford Ltd.

Text 36
Repr. from *American Literature*, Ginn/Lexington, Mass. 1981.

Text 37
Repr. by permission of the University of Missouri Press. From *Summoned* by Diana O'Hehir. © 1976 by Diana O'Hehir.

Text 38
Repr. by permission of Rogers Coleridge & White Ltd., London. From *Collected Poems* (Allison & Busby, 1986).

Text 39
Repr. from *American Literature*, Ginn/Lexington, Mass. 1981.

Text 40
Repr. from *19 New Poets of the Golden Gate*, Harcourt Brace, New York 1984.

Text 41
Repr. from *Voices of Today*, J. Murray, London 1980.

Text 42
Repr. from *American Literature*, Ginn/ Lexington, Mass. 1981.

Text 43
Repr. from *Voices of Today*, J. Murray, London 1980.

II Short Story

Text 1
Repr. from *Tales, Poems, Essays*, Collins, London/Glasgow 1952.

Text 2
Repr. from *Short-Story-Theorien 1573–1973*, Athenäum, Kronberg 1977.

Text 3
Repr. by permission of the Estate of H.E. Bates, Laurence Pollinger Publishers Ltd., London.

Text 4
Repr. from *Modern Fiction Studies, IV*, Purduc University of English, West Lafayette, Indiana, 1958/59.

Text 5–7
Repr. from *Short-Story-Theorien 1573–1973*, Athenäum, Kronberg 1977.

Text 8
Repr. from *John Barth, Title*, 1968.

Text 9
Repr. from *Dubliners, A Bantam Classic*, New York et al. 1990.

Text 10
Repr. from *Selected Letters of James Joyce*, Faber & Faber, London 1975.

Text 11–13
Repr. from *Twentieth Century Interpretations of Dubliners*, Prentice-Hall, A Spectrum Book, Englewood Cliffs, New Jersey 1968.

Text 14
Repr. from *The Penguin Book of English Short Stories*, Harmondsworth 1978.

Text 15
Repr. from *Katherine Mansfield: Selected Stories*, O.U.P., London et al. 1969.

Text 16
Repr. from *Teaching Katherine Mansfield's "The Voyage": Metaphor Boxes, LWV XX*, Würzburg 1987.

Text 17
Repr. from *Modern Stories in English*, Copp Clark Publishing, Toronto 1977.

Text 18
Repr. from *Some Critical Considerations*, University of Kentucky Press, 1963.

Text 19
Repr. from Graham Greene, Columbia University Press, New York/London 1966.

Text 20
Repr. by permission of the Estate of Bernard Malamud, Chatto & Windus/ The Hogarth Press, London.

Text 21
Repr. from *Midnight Birds*, Anchor Press/Doubleday, New York 1980.

III Novel

Text 1
F. Schmidt/T. Wullen

Text 2
Repr. from *The Novel Today*, Fontana, London 1977.

Text 3
Repr. from *I'm the King of the Castle*, Penguin, Harmondsworth 1974. Permission granted by Hamish Hamilton, Ltd., London.

Text 4
Permission granted by David Wheldon. From *The Bodley Head*, London.

Text 5
© Times Newspapers Ltd., 1983.

Text 6
Repr. by permission of the Peters Fraser & Dunlop Group Ltd., publishers: George Weidenfeld & Nicolson Ltd., London.

Text 7
© 1986 by Max Hueber Verlag, Ismaning.

Text 8
Repr. from *Sweet Dreams*, Fontana, London 1973

Text 9
Repr. from *Ninety-Nine Novels*, Alison & Busby, London 1984.

Text 10
Repr. from *Dinner at the Homesick Restaurant*, Viking Penguin, New York 1982.

Text 11
Repr. from *Dialogue 2*, 1986

Text 12
Repr. from *Linden Hills*, Viking Penguin, New York 1986.

Text 13
Repr. by permission of Philip Roth. From Jonathan Cape, Ltd., London.

Text 14
Repr. from *The Listener*, 1985.

IV Drama

Text 1
Repr. by permission of the Peters Fraser & Dunlop Group Ltd., London.

Text 2
Repr. from *A Book of English Essays*, Penguin, Harmondsworth 1967.

Text 3
Repr. by permission of Thomas Nelson & Sons Ltd., Surrey

Text 4
Repr. from *The Critical Idiom*, Methuen, Norfolk 1970.

Text 5
Repr. from *Three Plays*, Chatto & Windus, London 1977.

Text 6
Repr. from *A Short Guide to Modern British Drama*, Heinemann Educational Books, London 1982.

Text 7
Repr. by permission of Samuel French Ltd., London, on behalf of Richard Harris.

Text 8
Repr. by permission of Methuen Drama, London.

Text 9
Repr. from *An Anatomy of Drama*, Abacus, London 1978.

Text 10
Permission granted by Amber Lane

Press Ltd., London. © 1987 by C. Hugh Whitemore.

Text 11
Repr. by permission of Faber and Faber Ltd., London.

Text 12
Repr. from *New York Theatre Review/ 21*.

Text 13
Repr. from *San Francisco Chronicle*, 1980.

Text 14
Repr. by permission of Methuen Drama, London.

Text 15
Repr. from *Brian Clark: Whose Life is it Anyway?*, Cornelsen Verlag Hirschgraben, Frankfurt/M. 1985.

Text 16
Repr. from *An Anatomy of Drama*, Abacus, London 1978.

Text 17
Permission granted by Amber Lane Press Ltd., London. © by C.M. Medoff, 1980/1982.

Text 18
© 1952 by Harcourt Brace Jovanovich, Inc., Orlando, Fla. Repr. by permission of the publishers.

Text 19
Repr. by permission of Faber and Faber Ltd., London.

Text 20
Repr. from *Drama: The Major Genres*, Doss, Mead & Co., New York/Toronto 1962.

Text 21
Repr. from *Wordplays 1. Six Short Plays*, Hutchinson, London 1982/84.

Text 22
Repr. from *Alan Ayckbourn, Confusions. Model Interpretations*, Klett, Stuttgart 1982.

Text 23
Repr. by permission of William Heinemann Ltd., London.

Text 24
Repr. from *Romeo and Juliet. The Players' Shakespeare*. Heinemann Educational Books, London 1975.

Text 25
Permission granted by Cambridge University Press.

Text 26
Repr. from *An Introduction to Drama*, Holt, Rinehart and Winston, New York 1967.

Der Verlag dankt den genannten Unternehmen und Personen – soweit sie erreicht werden konnten – für die freundliche Genehmigung zum Abdruck von Copyright-Material.
Trotz intensiver Bemühungen konnte mit den Copyright-Inhabern der Texte: **I:** 2, 4, 12, 16, 17, 18, 20, 21, 23, 25, 28, 32, 36, 39, 40, 41, 42, 43; **II:** 1, 2, 4, 5, 6, 7, 8, 9, 10, 11, 12, 13, 14, 15, 16, 17, 18, 19, 21; **III:** 2, 8, 9, 10, 11, 12, 14; **IV:** 2, 4, 5, 6, 9, 12, 13, 15, 16, 20, 21, 24, 26 kein Kontakt hergestellt werden. Für entsprechende Hinweise ist der Verlag dankbar.